The Life of the Neighborhood Playhouse on Grand Street

The Life of the
Neighborhood Playhouse
on Grand Street

John P. Harrington

Syracuse University Press

Copyright © 2007 by Syracuse University Press
Syracuse, New York 13244-5160

All Rights Reserved

First Edition 2007

07 08 09 10 11 12   6 5 4 3 2 1

Permission to reproduce all images provided by Billy Rose Theatre
Division, the New York Public Library for the Performing Arts, Astor,
Lenox and Tilden Foundations.

The paper used in this publication meets the minimum requirements
of American National Standard for Information Sciences—Permanence
of Paper for Printed Library Materials, ANSI Z39.48–1984.

For a listing of books published and distributed by Syracuse University
Press, visit our Web site at SyracuseUniversityPress.syr.edu

ISBN-13: 978-0-8156-3155-2   ISBN-10: 0-8156-3155-3

Library of Congress Cataloging-in-Publication Data

Harrington, John P.
The life of the Neighborhood Playhouse on Grand Street / John P.
Harrington. — 1st ed.   p. cm.
Includes bibliographical references and index.
ISBN-13: 978-0-8156-3155-2 (cloth : alk. paper)
1. Neighborhood Playhouse (New York, N.Y.) 2. Theater—New York
(State)—New York—History—20th century. I. Title.
PN2277.N52N454 2007
792.09747—dc22
2007031388

Manufactured in the United States of America

Contents

Illustrations

Acknowledgments

As will be obvious to any reader of the citations to this book, this history could not have been told without the very large archive that constituted the "Neighborhood Playhouse Gift" to the New York Public Library, where it currently resides in the Billy Rose Theatre Collection. Given to the library by Alice Lewisohn Crowley in 1947, the archive is omnivorous: scripts, correspondence, meeting minutes, fan mail, hate mail, costume fabric swatches, blocking diagrams, diaries, billing accounts, photos, posters, memorabilia, and ephemera. It is an exciting and chaotic record of an exciting and chaotic company and a treasure for theater historians. The citations of this work are those of the New York Public Library. In addition to archival resources, the Billy Rose Theatre Collection has, in its librarians and other professional staff, provided me with expert and tireless collaborators for this project.

Other than Alice Lewisohn Crowley's memoir, *The Neighborhood Playhouse: Leaves from a Theatre Scrapbook,* which was published in 1959, there is no single published volume devoted to the history of the company. Two impressive doctoral dissertations, however, have been extremely helpful. Doris Fox Benardete completed her dissertation, "The Neighborhood Playhouse in Grand Street," at New York University in 1949. A worker at the Neighborhood Playhouse who later turned to scholarship, she recorded a highly personalized and invaluable history that could not have been reconstructed by anyone not an actual member of the company. In 1994, Melanie Nelda Blood completed her dissertation, "The Neighborhood Playhouse 1915–1927: A History and Analysis," at Northwestern University. In addition to her own account and analysis, in the bibliography of "Appendix 2" she put some order on the Neighborhood Playhouse Gift and some of the other relevant material at the New York Public Library. I am indebted to both works throughout this one.

In the course of my research, I was also given considerable help by the Neighborhood Playhouse School of the Theatre and the Museum of the City of New York. Part of this project, particularly work on the Lillian Wald Papers at Columbia University, was supported by a fellowship from the Gilder Lehrman Institute of American History. All of this project was supported in visible and invisible ways by the two institutions where I worked during completion of it: the Cooper Union for the Advancement of Science and Art and Rensselaer Polytechnic Institute.

The Life of the Neighborhood Playhouse on Grand Street

Introduction

The Life of the Neighborhood Playhouse

On the evening of May 19, 1927, *The Grand Street Follies* opened at the Neighborhood Playhouse at 466 Grand Street on the Lower East Side of Manhattan. This was the "Fifth Edition" of the follies and one of the major end-of-season dates for the artists, producers, critics, and fans of theater in New York. Joseph Wood Krutch, by mid-century one of the city's most eminent men of letters but at that time a young critic for the *Nation*, contributed a program note that declared the Neighborhood Playhouse unquestionably superior to its leading contemporaries in the ambitious, noncommercial theater context of the time, the Provincetown Players and the Washington Square Players. Brooks Atkinson, senior critic for the *New York Times,* filed not one review but three stories about events on Grand Street. Both of the critics, like most of their colleagues, noted that while experimental and bohemian companies like Provincetown and Washington Square had become increasingly "uptown" in institutional organization, location, and audience, the Neighborhood Playhouse had willfully disregarded all marketplace sense and remained even further downtown than Greenwich Village in a sprawling slum area. Krutch, evidently not a neighbor, called the location "a peculiar quarter."[1]

It was not high art that brought both intelligentsia and mainstream critics so far downtown in May 1927; it was a cutting send-up of the pieties of the intelligentsia and the mainstream critics. There had been predecessors to the first *Grand Street Follies:* the Greenwich Village follies began in 1919 and the Neighborhood Playhouse editions in 1922. And there had been successors, such as the Theatre Guild's fund-raiser in 1925

1

to which Rodgers and Hart contributed that memorable song, "The Gar-rick Gaieties." But only the *Grand Street Follies* narrowed its focus from all the possibilities for revue sketches to parody the vanities, excesses, and absurdities of theater alone.

In 1927 Krutch and Atkinson, arbiters of taste in drama, watched Al-bert Carroll, a long-time member of the Neighborhood Playhouse com-pany who made a specialty of such things, impersonate the renowned doyenne of the American stage Mrs. Fiske, who had recently appeared in a highly praised modern-dress production of Ibsen's *Ghosts,* in a sketch called "A Fiord Joke" that included an onstage argument between the actress and the critic Alexander Woollcott. In the same program, in "School for Rivals," Carroll returned as Ethel Barrymore playing a maid in a collision of the Sheridan restoration comedies then enjoying a new vogue for celebrity and even benefactor star turns. *The Grand Street Follies* also included a satire of the theater world's perennial debates over propri-ety and censorship by casting company member Aline Bernstein, the great theater designer and the first woman to gain entry into the United Scenic Artists Union, along with the company's well-known actors Doro-thy Sands and Marc Loebell, as artists doing hard time in prison for crimes against propriety: "Stars with Stripes."

One great uptown success of the season had been Sidney Howard's *The Silver Cord,* a Freud-literate parlor drama of a son's oppressive rela-tion with his mother; *The Grand Street Follies* responded with "A Bedtime Story," in which Carroll, now "Mother's Boy," sings lyrics written by Agnes Morgan, director of most Neighborhood Playhouse productions and instigator, with her companion Helen Arthur, of the follies:

Mammy won't you love your baby?
Mammy won't you cuddle me some more?
Roll your eyes across me
Then pick me up and toss me
And let me sleep beside you on the floor.

To which Dorothy Sands, impersonating the mother as played by her up-town counterpart Laura Hope Crewes, returns:

Baby won't you kiss your mammy?
In your little nighty
Hold your mammy tighty
Just like the flower draws the honey bee.
Ah but now we know
Things should not be so
To such love they now insist a meaning clings.
And my passion mad
Means I'm longing for your dad, so
Untie those silver strings.[2]

The long program of nineteen numbers included a "posthumous" work of Gilbert and Sullivan ridiculing Calvin Coolidge's isolationism ("Hurray for Us!"), a transformation of Dorothy Parker and Elmer Rice's *Close Harmony* about the homogeneity of middle-class life into an extraordinarily diverse minstrel show called "Close Harmony in Detroit," and, as finale, Albert Carroll returning in his annual burlesque of John Barrymore playing Hamlet in the celebrated 1922 production designed by Robert Edmond Jones.

The energy and frivolity of the 1927 follies is in retrospect all the more striking because five weeks earlier the Neighborhood Playhouse, producing plays on Grand Street since 1915, had announced that it would close. The story was newsworthy enough to be placed on the front page of the *New York Times*. "In announcing the decision to close the present theatre," it reported, "the Misses Irene and Alice Lewisohn, who have sponsored the enterprise from the beginning, said that it was a step dictated not by the failure of the theatre, but by its success and the necessity for expansion."[3] The Lewisohns, unmarried at the time and often paired as "Misses," were members of one of New York's most distinguished philanthropic families. Since 1903 they had been involved in many of the educational and artistic activities of the Henry Street Settlement, the Neighborhood Playhouse's inspiration, sponsoring institution, and source of nonprofit status. In 1915, Alice and Irene had built and opened the Neighborhood Playhouse building at 466 Grand Street, near the Henry Street Settlement. For thirteen years they remained virtually the sole benefactors of a theater enterprise that had evolved from an instrument of social betterment into, at the time of closing, one of only two (the other was the Theatre Guild) theatrical producing institutions in New York City both noncommercial and independent of the Shubert organization. The value of their support was cited by the *Times* as $540,000 as an annual endowment of $45,000. That total, provided by the Lewisohns, was generally accepted; the annual commitment, however, had escalated from an original pledge of $10,000 per year, and in order to reach an average of $45,000 would have to be considerably higher in 1927. The funding was an annual contribution annually negotiated and not the standing restricted capital fund usually considered "endowment." It was softer funding, increasingly strained, and not at all secure.

No one at the 1927 follies seemed to accept the Lewisohns' public claim that the closing was only a pause before expansion. Krutch's piece in the follies program mourned that "it will leave an absolute blank in its place." Atkinson's notice, "Last of the Neighborhood Frolics," announced that "this was the last Neighborhood production . . . the delights offered on the exotic East Side have now come to an end." Atkinson's follow-up feature a week later on the front page of the Sunday entertainment section eulogized the company and memorialized its end: "when the curtain descends the most inspiring acting organization in this city will conclude a noble little career among the pushcarts and gents' furnishing shops of the east side."[4] The full impact of the closing had special urgency in less mandarin spheres of the theatrical world. Leon Whipple, writing that summer in the *Survey Graphic,* a journal of the social settlement movement, asked his readers: "Does America want a theatre with a soul? Can we provide the environment for an institution that combines intellect, sincerity, and esthetic culture with an open-minded quest for the new, the charming, and the historic? The challenge is not to them [the Lewisohns], but to us. To give up what the Neighborhood Playhouse stands for will mean a defeat to our whole culture."[5]

The Neighborhood Playhouse was launched in the same month—February 1915—as the Provincetown Players and the Washington Square Players. When it closed, the Neighborhood Playhouse had outlasted in original form the first, by then in a more commercial reincarnation as the

Provincetown Playhouse, and the second, which, reorganized uptown as the Theatre Guild, was at that moment in 1927 expanding operations for an additional Chicago season. The closing was to the public unexpected because the Neighborhood Playhouse, on the basis of two remarkable productions, was coming off its most successful seasons. The 1925–26 season had opened with an acclaimed original staging of a well-known Yiddish folk tale of transmigration of souls called *The Dybbuk*. After angry and divisive board meetings in January 1926, the final decision was against moving the production uptown to a mainstream theater and larger grosses. Other credibly bohemian and artistic productions were doing just that: one week after *The Dybbuk* move was vetoed, Eugene O'Neill, Kenneth Macgowan, and Robert Edmond Jones, having revised Provincetown Players into Provincetown Playhouse, then abandoned that entity and produced *The Great God Brown* as the Greenwich Village Theatre and moved it uptown to larger audiences for a substantial additional run of 278 performances. In the season before, 1924–25, the Neighborhood Playhouse season had opened with *The Little Clay Cart*, a dance-drama adaptation of a Hindu tale that, again, despite critical and popular acclaim, and against theater business trends of the time, was not transferred uptown. In earlier years, the company had with considerable success transferred uptown productions of the works of Shaw, Lord Dunsany, and Harley Granville Barker. Bitter organizational disagreements on the Neighborhood Playhouse board, the many artistic and commercial motives to move or not to move, and the complex issues of mission in conflict with opportunity are part of the record of what Brooks Atkinson called "the most inspiring acting organization" in New York in one of its greatest decades of theater.

Unlike its nomadic contemporaries, the Neighborhood Playhouse was rooted in locale, and transformation of that place into an asset would be a greater challenge than working with Cape Cod or Greenwich Village. Atkinson, like Krutch and all others, repeatedly drew attention to the setting of the theater, to the "neighborhood," that remote and, to most, genuinely frightening location to which the company only provided independent transportation in the last month of its existence. The theater built by the Misses Lewisohn still stands on Grand Street, but the rest of the block has been radically transformed by modern "urban renewal" and housing development. The first urban design for the area, beginning in the 1830s, was based on some of the first tenement housing in New York City. That infrastructure soon decayed into a vast, dense, and fractious Irish slum (with Irish theater, as popularized later by local product Ned Harrigan), and then, from the 1880s, into a vast, dense, fractious Jewish slum (with Yiddish theater, as popularized later by local products the Marx brothers). The program for the opening of the theater at 466 Grand Street in 1915 announced its intention "to be a community playhouse, where the traditions of the neighborhood can find artistic expression, where anyone with special gifts can contribute his talent, and where interesting productions of serious plays and comedies as well as the lighter forms of entertainment may be found."[6] The program gave directions to the theater by subway, elevated, and streetcar; the theater's old-numeration telephone number, resonant of pushcart commerce, was 1365 Orchard. The press consistently drew on the image of limousines among pushcarts and tuxedos amid Hassidic dress to highlight contrasts between the theater and the neighborhood. The formula of community playhouse from the opening program was a mission and an agenda that would require constant reexamination and renegotiation over the life of the company. In search of an integration of broad, quantitative participation and high performance quality, the enterprise on many occasions could have been described as "the neighborhood versus the playhouse," and though priorities shifted, the conception never completely lacked either of its polarized identities. On closing, and in this context and time frame, both the neighborhood and the playhouse retired undefeated.

This theater was one of many attempts, and ultimately one of the most successful, to intervene in urban blight compounded by stupendous numbers of new immigrants. In 1893, Lillian Wald, who had forsaken finishing school for nursing school, moved into the neighborhood to address slum conditions from the standpoint of disease prevention. She secured support from the philanthropist Jacob Schiff, who, like the Lewisohns, was an assimilated and established German Jew and so as much an outsider on the Lower East Side as Wald herself among the new waves of Eastern European immigrants then not called "Jews" but "Russians." Wald's nursing organization became one of the most prominent models in the contemporary settlement movement. In 1913, on the twentieth anniversary of the founding of the Henry Street Settlement, the Lewisohns staged a weekend-long festival, and in the process attracted some of the long-standing directors of the company, such as Aline Bernstein, Helen Arthur, and Rita Morgenthau, as well as a large number of less managerial volunteers. The city agreed to repave the street and install the new electric street lighting, and the board of education loaned school space to dress a cast of 500, mostly children and mostly from the neighborhood. They acted out in song and dance the evolution of the neighborhood from the Dutch period of New York to the present for an outdoor audience of 10,000, mostly new immigrants. By coincidence, the festival occurred on the same weekend in 1913 as the far more radical Paterson Strike Pageant at Madison Square in support of striking workers in New Jersey. Newspaper editorials quickly drew the contrast between the exemplary Henry Street festival and the dangerous Madison Square riot.

After 1913, the Lewisohns staged as many as five festivals outdoors, then produced plays in rentable space at Clinton Hall on Nassau Street, and then, in 1915, under tax-exempt status by virtue of its affiliation with the Henry Street Settlement, opened at 466 Grand Street the rather opulent theater building based on European designs that they named the Neighborhood Playhouse. In Wald's first autobiography, *The House on Henry Street*, which was published in the opening year of the theater, she expressed hope "that the playhouse, identified with the neighborhood, may recapture and hold something of the poetry and idealism that belong to its people and open the door of opportunity." In her second autobiography, *Windows on Henry Street*, published in 1934, she recalled only that "when it was realized that the pressure of the expedient would gradually compel a departure from the more informal point of view, the closing of the Neighborhood Playhouse was inevitable."⁷ Wald was capable of very powerful prose, alternately vehement and hilarious in speech and written word. This cryptic dismissal—even so long after the fact—suggests some of the tensions inherent in the link of the leading institution of the settlement movement with the leading institution of the little theater movement. The same change in tone can be traced in the arc over time of a voluminous correspondence between "Miss Lillian" and the sisters, addressed together as "Alirene," that changed from personalized enthusiasm to frosty business notes. Wald was no enemy to serious theater: she particularly admired the Neighborhood Playhouse production of John Galsworthy's *The Mob,* an antiwar statement, in 1920, against a wave of American isolationism and Red baiting that could find enemies at will on the Lower East Side. Wald, however, was also skeptical of the financial extravagance and artistic egoism necessary to take a successful production from the neighborhood audience to an uptown, larger, and more profitable one, and she saw production transfer uptown in terms of departure and loss rather than destination and opportunity. As the history of the company progressed, Wald remained unswayed from founding principles, Helen Arthur and her partner Agnes Morgan developed professional credentials and ambitions, and Alice and Irene, both benefactors and ambitious performance directors, attempted to resolve another polarization as foundational to the company as that between theater and community.

To this place, the Lower East Side, and to this institution, the Henry Street Settlement, the Lewisohns brought Charles Frohman, the producer; the real Ethel Barrymore; the leading British actresses Ellen Terry and Gertrude Kingston; the monologist Ruth Draper; Sarah Cowell Le Moyne, senior stateswoman of the American stage and mentor to Alice; and a new company led by Whitford Kane known as the Irish Players. All this was produced at the Neighborhood Playhouse in the first five months of its existence in early 1915. In the same period, the "producing staff" of the Lewisohns, Agnes Morgan, and Helen Arthur staged three original productions: a dance drama, *Jephtha's Daughter,* directed by the Lewisohns; a realist drama called *The Waldies* codirected by Morgan and Alice; and a bill of one-act plays including the Irish playwright Lord Dunsany's *The Glittering Gate,* Shaw's *Captain Brassbound's Conversion,* and Wilfred Wilson Gibson's *Womenkind.* The season ended with a ten-day outdoor festival, "The Greek Games." The drafts, typescripts, and filed memoranda from this period and later constitute the enormous "Neighborhood Playhouse Gift" archive left to the Billy Rose Theater Collection of the New York Public Library by Alice, in 1947, after Irene died. The archive includes pages and pages of notes and carbon copies of memos from Alice to others about the playhouse frenzy of activity including productions by the Neighborhood Players, productions by the Festival Dancers, visits by guest artists, motion picture offerings on weeknights, script readings, musical offerings, entertainments for children on weekends, exhibitions in the theater foyer, meetings of the producing staff, meetings of the advisory board, meetings of Henry Street Settlement clubs, business meetings, publications and programs meetings, and so on and so forth.

The Neighborhood Playhouse at 466 Grand Street would operate as originally constituted by the Lewisohns for thirteen seasons, including one roughly midpoint "sabbatical season." The most prominent productions in a great volume of activity in the first years included a staging of Stravinsky's *Petrouchka* days before its official New York opening at the Metropolitan Opera, American premieres of works by Dunsany, Shaw, and W. B. Yeats, productions with designs by Robert Edmond Jones, and dance performances by Michio Ito. All this was accomplished by a company of amateurs and volunteers. Because of its successes, the company gradually "matured" and became professionalized in actors, office staff, and backstage crew. In this middle phase of its evolution, the Neighborhood Playhouse produced works by Harley Granville Barker, staged the English-language premiere of James Joyce's play *Exiles,* the first production of Eugene O'Neill's *The First Man,* and an original "lyric drama" based on the works of Walt Whitman called *Salut au Monde.* For a tenth anniversary celebration on February 11, 1925, the celebrated George Pierce Baker, leader of the "47 Workshop" that produced many American theater professionals including O'Neill and Agnes Morgan, came to Grand Street to express thanks for the Neighborhood Playhouse. From its own stage, he thanked the company on behalf of "a whole group of experimenting little theatres that has always looked to the Neighborhood Playhouse for inspiration and guidance—to the direction, the acting, the costumes, the settings, and to the spirit of its workers."[8] Even at this moment of celebration, however, economic concerns were challenging artistic ones. Wald was a prolific writer of thank-you notes and a great keeper of her own records, most of which are now housed in the Lillian Wald Papers at Columbia University. Having read Baker's speech, she wrote to him two days after the anniversary to thank him for his words and to apologize for being absent at another event. She added, "The Misses Lewisohn have been most generous, but the cost of the Playhouse is greater than they can carry, and we may have to give it up at no distant date if we do not find understanding help."[9]

At this point, in 1925, the Neighborhood Playhouse had already invented sales of theater subscriptions and developed a list of 10,000. It had gradually increased ticket prices, and it had professionalized publicity efforts. At New Year in this eleventh season, it also decided against moving its immensely popular production of *The Little Clay Cart* uptown. Both George Pierce Baker and Lillian Wald, from very different perspectives on theater, recognized the Neighborhood Playhouse as an "experiment," and the paradox of the experiment is that its greatest degree of success coincided with its sudden demise. A little later, in the summer of 1925, the novelist Thomas Wolfe, then aged twenty-five and another recent graduate of Baker's "47 Workshop," was composing fiction based on the Neighborhood Playhouse during a torrid affair with Aline Bernstein, then forty-four years old. What he composed later appeared in *The Web and the Rock:*

> The theatre, one of those little theatres that had their inception as a kind of work of charity, as a sort of adjunct to "settlement work" among "the poor classes," was supported largely by the endowments of wealthy females, and had grown quite celebrated in recent years. In the beginning, no doubt, its purposes had been largely humanitarian. That is to say, certain yearning sensitivenesses had banded together in a kind of cultural federation whose motto might very well have been: "They've *got* to eat cake." At the inception, there was probably a good deal of nonsense about "bringing beauty into their lives," ennobling the swarming masses of the East Side through the ballet, "the arts of the dance," "the theatre of ideas," and all the rest of the pure old neurotic aestheticism that tainted the theatre of the period.[10]

But the Neighborhood Playhouse had many commitments to separate itself from "the tainted theatre of the period," and chief among them was settlement work, which as practiced by the Lewisohns and others, and as monitored by Lillian Wald, was much more than the passing amusement of wealthy women. Their experiment existed to bring theater of ideas and dance to the slums of the Lower East Side, and at this they succeeded extraordinarily. In Wolfe's fictionalized version of the "Community Guild," activist aspirations from the inception of the theater deteriorate as an uptown audience comes downtown, bringing "neurotic aestheticism" with it. But bringing greater New York to the Lower East Side was the among the aspirations of the Neighborhood Playhouse; this it achieved far beyond expectations, and this it accomplished without succumbing to any corrupting influences of commerce. In its last years, while producing some programs that would qualify as "high" art in any neighborhood, this theater had its most exhilarating moments with original works like *The Little Clay Cart* and *The Dybbuk* that were less "cultural federation" than what in a more recent vocabulary would be called "cultural diversity." Even the young Thomas Wolfe saw this. His cynical young narrator grows beyond the smug expectations quoted above when he comes to the Lower East Side to meet the luminous, maternal stage designer "Mrs. Jack" at a comic revue including an actor impersonating John Barrymore playing Hamlet.

Nor were the principals of the Neighborhood Playhouse the passive kind of administrators of the "endowments of wealthy females" imagined by Wolfe's narrator. The producing staff from the founding in 1915 was Alice and Irene Lewisohn, Agnes Morgan, and Helen Arthur. By closing in 1927 Aline Bernstein and Alice Beer had joined them on the masthead listing. Lillian Wald, Rita Morgenthau, and others watched from an administrative remove as an "Advisory Committee." But the same four —in her letters to Wolfe, Bernstein called them "the N.P.H. Women"[11]— continued to debate all decisions at great length, to vote on them at business meetings for which Beer kept copious minutes, and then, however reluctantly, to speak with one voice about the course of the Neighborhood Playhouse. One valuable witness to this process was Doris Fox Benardete, who, as Doris Fox, worked in the theater office, where she met Mr. Benardete. Twenty years after the theater's closing, she wrote a narrative of her experience as a dissertation at New York University. The entire dynamic of the organization, in her account, was a matter of "pretty intense personalities": "Helen Arthur and Agnes Morgan lived together as friends, but they had chosen each other as adults; their affection was a matter of choice. The Lewisohns, on the other hand, lived together as sisters, not from choice as adults but largely from habit and the force of circumstances. Some say they lived together too long."[12]

The N.P.H. Women had been brought together by the Henry Street Settlement. Arthur had been a volunteer at the settlement and briefly Wald's lover. The Lewisohns' involvement in the settlement brought in Morgan when they sought professionals through theater acquaintances for the early dramatic productions in Clinton Hall. Arthur dressed in men's clothing, Morgan was an aspiring playwright who discovered herself as a director, Alice was famously ethereal, and Irene, the youngest, was sensitive to perceived slights and consequently aggressive. The Lewisohns, providers of the subsidy, wanted to reign autocratic; the codirecting couple known as "the Morgan-Arthurs" provided professionalism and patronized the patrons, and so management and governance became, over time, a third polarization within an idealistic enterprise, the Neighborhood Playhouse.

These intense personalities working in complex organizational relationships found a outlet in the self-parodic and anarchic *The Grand Street Follies* satirizing both themselves and their work. The enterprise had begun even before the Neighborhood Playhouse opened when, after an early Clinton Hall season in which Alice played a maid in Galsworthy's *The Silver Box*, Morgan, for a staff party, staged a burlesque of the heiress bravely trying to play a maid. The Grand Street Follies became public at the end of the 1921–22 season when, lacking the promised final June production, the directors invited the subscribers to their annual party. Since they had succeeded so well that season with Harley Granville Barker's *The Madras House*, which had moved uptown, they parodied their success in "The Mattress House," in which the business empire of the play became a brothel, Agnes Morgan every man's "Oriental Dream," and Helen Arthur "Turkish Delight." Irene Lewisohn's greatest labor of the previous season had been a ballet, *Royal Fandango,* in which she danced the lead, and this returned in the Follies as "The Royal Damn

Fango," with Irene as the male lead and Albert Carroll dancing Irene. The opening skit of the first follies presented "the first dramatic critic," Adam, attributing great mischief to theaters like the Neighborhood Playhouse, and the last skit, in the lobby of the building, presented David Belasco, Laurette Taylor, Alla Nazimova, and others damning the whole little theater movement and the Neighborhood Playhouse in particular. Though the book credit was given to "Everybody," Alice's name does not appear on the program. One week later she chaired a "vital meeting" of the staff, and two days after that the Neighborhood Playhouse, at the moment of greatest success yet, announced that it would remain closed in 1922–23 as a "sabbatical season."

It did reopen in 1923 after the sabbatical, but it did not reopen after the announcement of closing in 1927. That 1927 follies, in which neither Alice nor Irene appeared, later moved uptown under the auspices of a new entity, the Actor-Managers Company that included Arthur, Morgan, and Bernstein. It continued for several years, offered opportunities to young actors such as James Cagney, and toured widely, but it never achieved the kind of New York recognition given to the Grand Street versions by critics like Joseph Wood Krutch and Brooks Atkinson. The Lewisohns also produced uptown and also failed to achieve the kind of influential successes they had already achieved downtown. Irene and Aline Berstein collaborated on the creation of an archive of productions that became the Museum of Costume Art and later the costume collection of the Metropolitan Museum of Art. Thanks to the energies of Rita Morgenthau after 1927, the name of the original company survives today in the Neighborhood Playhouse School of Theater located on the Upper East Side of New York. In 1928 the building built on Grand Street was sold by the Lewisohns to the Henry Street Settlement, which operates it today as part of the Abrons Arts Center with local performances for the new Lower East Side neighborhood and school programs reaching into the New York City public school system.

All these projects are very different from that well-defined, successful, and instructive life of the Neighborhood Playhouse on Grand Street from 1915 to 1927. The verses from the Rodgers and Hart "Garrick Gaieties" bring out in comic fashion the extraordinary ambition of this experiment to bring uptown downtown, high culture to broad audiences, Eurocentrism to globalism, and by art to cause social change:

> Neighborhood Playhouse may shine below the Macy Gimbel line,
> It was built to make a ride for people on Fifth Avenue.
> To Yeats and Synge and Shaw and such we add an oriental touch,
> We bring out the aesthetic soul you didn't know you have in you!
>
> We like to serve a mild dish of folklore quaintly childish,
> Or something Oscar Wildish, in pantomime or dance.
> Grand Street Folk we never see 'em, they think the place is a museum.
> And we know just what we do, because we always take a chance.[13]

Gaieties being gaieties, Hart was free to parody the effort. But the Neighborhood Playhouse had succeeded with art, with audiences, and with activism. And it closed abruptly. In front-page coverage of the announcement, the *Times* followed the Lewisohns' logic that it was closing because of success. However, in the Neighborhood Playhouse archives left by the Lewisohns to the New York Public Library, there is an undated, unsigned typescript with edits in the hand of Irene Lewisohn that reads rather differently:

> In 1927 when we closed the doors of the building in Grand Street we announced that having completed a certain phase in the development of our idea we felt it necessary to pause and contemplate the next step. To many that gesture indicated a finality—a sudden cessation of an activity just growing into an institution—a cutting off in its coming of age of a child ready to achieve its heritage. Constantly we are met with the question: "Why did the Neighborhood Playhouse stop?"[14]

At that point, certainly in the early 1930s, she understood the damage done: the failure to establish institutionality and so perpetuation of an ideal beyond oneself. But she still could not answer that question: "Why did the Neighborhood Playhouse stop?"

When the Neighborhood Playhouse closed in 1927, Joseph Wood Krutch wrote of it, "Though it has never made any pretense of calling itself a national or civic theater, it has, nevertheless, come nearer to being that than have any other more ambitiously named enterprises."[15] The singular qualities of the company were that it was civic, that it was a noncommercial business endeavor, and that it was managed as such, as an "enterprise," as Krutch put it. The archive of the "Neighborhood Playhouse Gift" in the New York Public Library makes it possible to write its history as the life of an organization with a beginning, an end, and copious documentation of all actions in between. The life of the organization is recorded there not only in the work of playwrights but the work of the business meetings, publicity materials, production bills, box office receipts, and payroll accounts that make theater companies function. There were four chief managers from beginning to end: Alice Lewisohn, Irene Lewisohn, Agnes Morgan, and Helen Arthur. The life of the organization is also the story of their interaction, their evolving goals, and at different times their attempts to discover, to revise, to recover, and to sustain the company that they all considered the principal work of their lives.

The accomplishments of the Neighborhood Playhouse at the beginning of the twentieth century, celebrated by Krutch and many others in its time, seem less evident at the beginning of the twenty-first century. Earlier, this company was a primary subject of theater criticism and cultural history. When Kenneth Macgowran in 1929 published *Footlights Across America: Toward a National Theater,* for example, he wrote that "a very remarkable fact about the Neighborhood Playhouse is that its external history is the history of the whole little theater movement."[16] By "little theater" he meant the whole of noncommercial theater on a national scope, and he, like many others, thought that the Neighborhood Playhouse was the most salient example of this dimension of performing arts in America. Though usually mentioned in standard new reference books today, the Neighborhood Playhouse is generally eclipsed in the recent histories of American theater by its contemporaries the Provincetown Players, later the Provincetown Playhouse, or the Washington Square

Players, later the Theatre Guild. This is true, for example, of reference books such as the *Cambridge History of American Theatre*, of theater histories such as Ronald H. Wainscott's *The Emergence of Modern Ameican Theatre 1914–1929*, or cultural histories such as Christine Stansell's *American Moderns: Bohemian New York and the Creation of a New Century*. These excellent works reflect what has come to be valued most in the history of theaters: the playwrights, plays, and related artists. On those criteria, the four managers of the Neighborhood Playhouse might not seem of primary significance. However, what is lost by considering those criteria only are the many and complex civic dimensions of theater that were distinguishing qualities of the Neighborhood Playhouse and evidently not much valued later in the twentieth century when its reputation faded.

The Neighborhood Playhouse name was chosen well because the company was unique in its link to a locality on the Lower East Side of Manhattan at one of the least glamorous periods in a generally dismal history. This was not an easy relationship to maintain, and the company history frequently appears to be about the neighborhood versus the playhouse or the playhouse versus the neighborhood. The interest of its history is precisely in the many organizational strategies devised to advance the role of the theater in the neighborhood and its capacity to link art to activism in the service of assimilation. The Neighborhood Playhouse was also unique in New York in its institutional relationship with the Henry Street Settlement, and that relationship is recorded in the interactions of "the N.P.H. Women" and the Henry Street Settlement founder and director, Lillian Wald. Part of the history of noncommercial theater that Macgowran thought written so well in the Neighborhood Playhouse is the larger context of philanthropy that linked playhouse to settlement and bound it to a social mission. This was the role that tempted Krutch to call the Neighborhood Playhouse a "national or civic theater."

The history of the Neighborhood Playhouse compliments the many histories of its contemporaries, the Provincetown Players and the Washington Square Players, by adding to comparable artistic accomplishments a social dynamic specific to it alone. Although those contemporaries had place names in their titles, only the Neighborhood Playhouse built a theater with high artistic ambitions in a slum, set itself the task of changing the neighborhood, and remained rooted there for the life of the company. Its history has interest for feminist, urban, and economic studies. It also has the remarkable quality of representing American theater in organizational design. Many companies represented distinctly American issues concerning immigration and assimilation in the plays they produced. The Neighborhood Playhouse, by building an organization of assimilated and unassimilated immigrants, by housing under one roof the work of students, volunteers, professionals, and benefactors, by setting the highest artistic expectations, by doing so in an unpromising locale, and by doing so in the difficult times of "Red scare" isolationism, as a whole represented the dynamic of social integration characteristic—in its successes and in its failures—of America in the early twentieth century.

1

The Henry Street Settlement and Its Playhouse

Why did the Neighborhood Playhouse begin?

On January 24, 1902, Leonard Lewisohn, father to Alice and Irene and a recent widower, wrote, on office letterhead and in elegant, formal penmanship, to Lillian Wald:

> Dear Miss Wald
>
> Please do not forget to let me know regarding the house 299 Henry Street. It will be sold at auction febry 4. Also kindly inform my daughter Alice about the class you are forming. If you will invite my daughter and myself to visit your settlement at some time again we shall be pleased.
>
> With the utmost respect and regards
>
> Leonard Lewisohn

He had been in correspondence with Wald earlier that month about 299 Henry Street, and eventually the building was acquired for the Henry Street Settlement. Alice was invited to the class, presumably one for children that she would teach, but never attended it, because, as Leonard wrote a week later, "she must remain in the house for the present and be very careful until she gets somewhat stronger again."[1] Leonard had previously visited the settlement with Alice, who was then eighteen years old, and he had taken a great interest in the kind of financial support he could provide. He would not visit again, because he died suddenly one month later during a business trip to London.

Leonard Lewisohn and his younger brother Adolph were at that point the greatest copper magnates in America. Leonard was born in Hamburg in 1847, worked for his father in pig bristle, ostrich feather, horse hair, and related merchandise from the age of fifteen, and came to New York in 1865 to extend the trading reach of the family business. In three years Adolph arrived in New York, the business shifted to lead exports, and Lewisohn Brothers was born. They purchased their first copper mine in 1879 and built that into a corporation that was continental in reach, owning copper mines in the east, in Montana, and in Arizona, and representing most major copper operations that it did not own. By the time of Leonard's death, the Lewisohns were on a corporate level high enough to team with William G. Rockefeller and Henry H. Rogers to create the United Metals Selling Corporation that, at the turn of the century, controlled more than half of all copper produced in the United States and exported from it. They had also gotten the worst of a deal in another corporate merger with the Guggenheim brothers. Adolph was conspicuous with his wealth, buying the Harriman Mansion on Fifth Avenue, building palaces in the country, and donating enough money to have the stadium at City College named for him. Leonard was more beneficent to specifically Jewish charitable institutions: the Hebrew Sheltering and Guardian Society, Jewish Theological Seminary, Mount Sinai and Montefiore hospitals. He also sought direct involvement in social programs, including the Henry Street Settlement, and wrote to Wald, for example, to find boarding for six individual boys he was sponsoring through college. By contrast, in the years after Leonard's death, Adolph's typical interaction with Henry Street Settlement consisted of sending a staff-typed letter to Wald that misspelled her name and promised to "tell my head gardner [sic], Mr. Canning, to stop in some time and see in what way he can be of any help."[2]

The Lewisohn brothers' styles represented only two of many possible responses to the extraordinary issues surrounding philanthropy in the 1890s. The end of the century was both the Gilded Age and the Progressive Era, and in this conflict between extravagance and reform, in this period of growing urban and labor violence, many new strategies were devised to address glaring social inequities. In a study of philanthropy in Chicago, Kathleen D. McCarthy has described the cultural tensions common at the time that Leonard Lewisohn first became involved with the Henry Street Settlement:

> The excesses of the Gilded Age brought the very notion of noblesse oblige, and the elitism it embodied, into question. Even as Carnegie was formulating his Gospel of Wealth, social critics were beginning to reassess the meaning of charity and benevolence in a democratic state. In the process, a new definition of civic stewardship was posited, stressing decentralization, research rather than impulse, flexibility, a working partnership between donors and professionals, and deinstitutionalization. In effect, the progressive reassessment represented a thoroughgoing rejection of the institutional ideal of the Gilded Age elite.[3]

This is the kind of close partnership of benefactor and professionals devised in New York by Leonard Lewisohn and Wald, subsequently passed on to the daughters Alice and Irene, and by them exercised in the form of the Neighborhood Playhouse.

Issues surrounding philanthropy and social reform were especially complex for New York Jews. The German Jews of an earlier immigration, like the Lewisohns, had, by the 1890s, become the cultural elite and benefactor class. The Eastern European Jews arriving in large numbers in a later wave of immigration were the indigent and needy. The first group had been greeted in America by an earlier, robust economy, and in the course of their success they reformed in religious practices and became acculturated in social ones. The second group had been driven by pogroms from homelands in the Ukraine, Poland, and Austria-Hungary in enormous numbers (1.4 million from Eastern Europe arrived in New York City between 1880 and 1910 and stayed there) with religious beliefs and revolutionary passions intact and conspicuous. As Stephen Birmingham has memorably described the resulting clash in his popular history *Our Gang:*

> To the older-established Germans, who had acquired the patina of manners and respectability, this vast mass of gruff-voiced, "uncouth, unwashed" Russians who had the temerity to call themselves fellow Jews and therefore brothers was a distinct embarrassment. Newspaper stories

of "horrible conditions in the Jewish quarter" on the Lower East side—with reports of overcrowding in tenements, vermin, garbage, marital disorders, violence, starvation, and crime—were a grievous thorn in the German Jewish side. . . . In blaming the Russians for the anti-Semitism that existed in New York, the Germans themselves began to display anti-Semitic attitudes.

In addition, Birmingham continues, given the gross economic inequity between the two groups, "it was worker versus boss, mass versus class, vulgar versus genteel, 'foreigner' versus 'American,' Russian versus German, Jew versus Jew."[4] This was the context into which Leonard and then Alice and Irene Lewisohn traveled downtown to the Lower East Side to do good. In this context, it is not hard to understand some of the consistent skepticism and occasional hostility of the neighborhood to the Neighborhood Playhouse, and specifically to Alice, who was dismissed by the Yiddish press as "Miss Neighborhood Playhouse." It is harder to understand her extraordinary determination and tenacity.

In 1959, or more than thirty years after the closing of the theater, Alice, under the name Alice Lewisohn Crowley in deference to her brief marriage in 1924 to the designer Herbert E. Crowley, published a memoir, *The Neighborhood Playhouse: Leaves from a Theatre Scrapbook.* She prefaced her account by asserting that "these memories of the Neighborhood Playhouse are in no way thought of as an historical record; dates, definitions, personalities, or even reference to the legion that contributed time and personal service to a cultural enterprise have been sadly neglected." Instead, she wrote, she would attempt to "recapture values." The disclaimer should not be disregarded. The first sentence of the text proper states that "the original image of the Neighborhood Playhouse entered the secret door of our nursery when my sister Irene and I were three and six years of age." In fact, the sisters were nine years apart in age. By the time she composed her memoir, Alice had been for many years residing in Zurich as a member of the Carl Jung circle, and the retrospective influence of dream analysis and the archetype of the child informs her account of a first conception of the Neighborhood Playhouse, ostensibly in about 1895, when Irene would have been three years of age and Alice twelve:

It came as a sudden vision vividly contrasting with the drab life of city children, so startling that it was guarded as a secret never to be divulged. But later it emerged out of hidden depths of memory as an expansive hillside on whose treeless crest a temple stands severe in form, of sparkling stone which appears white in the brilliant sunshine. Children are seen coming toward the temple from all directions, some leaping, some dancing down more distant slopes. Approaching it they form in procession, carrying garlands which they place upon an altar in the portico of the temple as they sing.[5]

In retrospect, she intentionally located the impulse in the notion of festivals, which occupied the early years, and not in increasingly professional stage productions, which filled the years after the theater was built. Whether drawing on collective unconscious or shared visions, Alice seems to have rediscovered a lot of the imagery from her contemporary Susan Glaspell's account of the Provincetown Players, *The Road to the Temple*, which was first published in same year the Neighborhood Playhouse closed.

Alice's memoir describes first meeting Lillian Wald a year before Leonard Lewisohn's death, or in 1901, when she accompanied her father to dinner at 265 Henry Street. "To my mind," Alice wrote, "she conjured a being who, with a wave of her hand, could convert arid wastes into happy playgrounds, cramped homes into surroundings of dignity and beauty." What she met at the settlement was not much different than what she imagined. She met "the lady of miracles," in her blue Visiting Nurse uniform, "as she mixed the crisp green leaves in the salad bowl, while she clarified some problem about unions, interlarding her conversation with whimsical stories." She returned with her father on visits to "the Leading Lady," and states that she began an association with the settlement in the year of his death, 1902. On that moment of first commitment to the settlement, her recollection of values, if not of the historical record, is quite clear. "The choice was not without conflict," she wrote more than a half century later. "For at one end of the spectrum of my values was a passion for acting and the desire for study, at the other end, a social conscience, more correctly the memory of those hopeless eyes of pushcart vendors that greeted me on my first visit to Henry Street."[6] The same conflict across the spectrum of values from artistic to activist would face the Neighborhood Playhouse throughout its existence.

The Lady of Miracles had absolute confidence that conflicts could be resolved. Wald had been born to German Jewish parents who were established in midwestern America, in Cincinnati, and her early education occurred there and in Rochester, New York. On failing to gain admission to Vassar College, she instead entered a New York Hospital training program for nurses when that profession was scarcely professionalized. She was involved in various medical volunteer activities in the Lower East Side when, by her account, she was fetched by a young girl to help her mother, visited the mother, was horrified by tenement living conditions, and had a clarifying vision about the need for home health care as a way to preempt many illnesses, including tuberculosis, that had advanced beyond possible cure by the time undereducated and insecure recent immigrants approached overcrowded hospitals. She saw the need for local residence of trained professionals, for a welcoming hospice, and for home intervention. These were accomplished by recruitment of Visiting Nurses, many volunteer, but all professionally trained: from the original duo of Wald and Mary Brewster in 1893, the number of Visiting Nurses grew to 92 in 1913, the twentieth anniversary and occasion for the Lewisohns' anniversary pageant, and to 250 in 1927, the year the Neighborhood Playhouse closed. As a representative example of Henry Street Settlement work, the *Handbook of Settlements* of 1911 cited the nurses' efforts to prevent the spread of tuberculosis:

> The pioneer nurses in 1893, realizing the danger to the community from the ignorance of persons suffering from tuberculosis, secured the names of such persons applying for admission to hospitals. These, and others discovered by the staff, were visited; sputum cups and disinfectants were supplied; and instruction in hygiene provided. In March, 1905, the department of health took up the work systematically, and the city nurses now carry on the plan of visitation and education.[7]

Many of Wald's most effective strategies—school nurses, public playgrounds, regular sanitation—followed this pattern: begun as intervention by the Henry Street Settlement, they were eventually institutionalized by municipal government as policy. Across that vast, conflicting spectrum of values, from individual activism to governmental structure, Wald found resolution.

The autobiography Wald published in 1915, or the year of the opening of the Neighborhood Playhouse, is considerably more analytical than the one Alice Lewisohn Crowley would publish forty years later. *The House on Henry Street*, in place of Alice's vision of a temple, opens with Wald's confession of ignorance. Given the volunteer nurse's working hours, she wrote, it is not strange "that I should have been ignorant of the various movements which reflected the awakening of the social conscience at the time, or the birth of the 'settlement,' which twenty-five years ago was giving form to social protest in England and America." Not only had she known little about social protest, she also, "like the rest of the world," knew little about the Lower East Side of New York City, and in that "inexperience," she wrote, she became part of "the dumb acceptance of these conditions." In addition to preventive and emergency health care, the Henry Street Settlement, more than most contemporaries, had a broad educational mission and philosophy. First, it would educate residents about their neighborhood and its history and architecture: "the settlement, through its preservation of several of the fine old houses of the neighborhood, maintains a curious link with what, in this city of rapid changes, is already a shadowy past." The settlement houses and the theater were and are on Henry Street, Pitt Street, and Grand Street, and the surrounding present-day housing project exercises in "1960s brutalism" of towers on cleared acreage confirm her sense of the positive value of a visible past to inspire reform and progress. Wald's second tenet held that the settlement would educate about the present: "a characteristic service of the settlement to the public grows out of its opportunities for creating and informing public opinion." In this effort—educating the public about current conditions in the least desirable and least visible neighborhoods—all forms of exposure, especially when uptown came downtown, and public relaions, especially as generated by newspapers eager to cover theatrical events, were instrumental. Third, and last, she wrote more than once in *The House on Henry Street* about personal potential best stimulated by the arts. "Drama is taken seriously in our neighborhood," she wrote in a chapter devoted not to the arts but to "Social Forces." Describing the clash there between "American" and Yiddish drama, she displaced her opinions to others but plainly indicated that the agenda for the future was assimilation and the means was theater. Noting that Yiddish drama often received a cool reception because of that "contempt that Americans not infrequently feel for the alien," she further noted that there was "also a fear, on the part of members of the older Jewish communities, that the Yiddish theater might retard the Americanization of the immigrant."[8] For this conflict, the Neighborhood Playhouse, and the Misses Lewisohn, suited Wald's strategies extraordinarily well.

Alice Lewisohn's image of Wald as the Lady of Miracles in the blue uniform was a very selective one. The social critic Christopher Lasch has written well about Wald's great contemporary and colleague Jane Addams, and the great damage done to her work by a myth of saintliness: "Praising her goodness, her saintliness, was a way to avoid answering her questions. The myth of Jane Addams served to render her harmless. The process by which Jane Addams, the social critic, became Saint Jane is an excellent example of the way in which American society manages to incorporate its critics into itself, thereby blunting the edge of their criticism."[9] Something of the same can be said about the myth of Lillian Wald, visiting nurse, and in this hagiography Alice was collaborator.

The anti-myth side of New York's best-known advocate for assimilation and Americanization was Lillian Wald, anti-American. One year before the Neighborhood Playhouse opened, she sponsored at the Henry Street Settlement the inaugural meeting National Association for the Advancement of Colored People. The open meeting of that first conference was held in The Great Hall of The Cooper Union, located a short distance further north on the Bowery. There, on the stage where Abraham Lincoln debated Stephen Douglas, Wald delivered a blistering attack on the Woodrow Wilson administration, from which she had every reason to seek financial support, and its complacency on race issues: "This question of segregation looms up in my mind as of mountainous significance. I see in it an invidious and subtle poison that is being instilled into our national ideals. It is not because it is a political question, or not so much because it is a personal matter to those involved, though this is of grave importance, and should not be minimized, but it is a moral question that we should not dodge." Wald once said that "I just hate like thunder to speak." In fact, she spoke like thunder.

In 1915, she returned to The Cooper Union to angrily denounce World War I with tales of atrocities and cited the current production at the Neighborhood Playhouse, an Old Testament dramatization called *Jephthah's Daughter*, about the sacrifice of a young woman, as an "analogy of the barbarity of the sacrifices that are now being made in the name of a god of war."[10] A year later, Wald created the American Union Against Militarism, which organized and demonstrated for peace as the United States prepared for World War I. All this led to denunciations of her "anti-Americanism" from such official voices as the Overman Committee in 1919 and the Lusk Report in 1921. During and after the "Red scare," the Neighborhood Playhouse was producing, along with rather elevated classics, "foreign" fables, such as *The Dybbuk* and *The Little Clay Cart*, that were easily denounced, along with the settlement, as "socialist" and anti-American. No dispute fazed Wald, who expected and studied resistance to her very clear vision. Instead of the image of saintliness, there is the cool and calculating Lillian Wald best described by Irving Howe in his general history of the East European Jews in America: "As her work succeeded, Miss Wald's power grew, and she used it shrewdly and to keen effect."[11]

The same cannot be said of the Lewisohns, who, in their close contact and long years of work with Wald, were always a striking contrast to her in personality. In *Windows on Henry Street*, Wald wrote that "none of our activities in the arts is to be compared with the contributions made by Alice and Irene Lewisohn through their inspired leadership in the festivals, in music, the dance, and in the many arts of the theatre." But in another of those cryptic passages concerning the Lewisohns in the second, later of her autobiographies, after the personal and professional relations had ceased, she continued: "Their achievement displays never a moral, but always a purpose."[12] Perhaps Wald's expectation was that the two should always be contiguous.

After Leonard's death, Alice continued to visit the Henry Street Settlement, to give small gifts to the children there, to purchase items such as pianos, and eventually to serve as benefactor in the settlement's acquisition of a neighboring building. Wald was the better keeper of files, and so the Lewisohn end of their correspondence survives in fuller form in the Lillian Wald archives. Most of the early letters are undated, but they begin in about 1904, two years after Leonard's death, when Alice was twenty-one, Irene twelve, and Wald thirty-seven. For example:

Dear Miss Wald:

The day after I saw you, I went up about those packages. The family was getting ready to move, and in the hall was a lot of bundles containing red winter things—which they expected the settlement to call for. I don't think the matter is worth troubling about—do you? So I'm afraid your two pianos have dwindled into worthlessness. It has been so careless of me, not to have let you know about this sooner. I promise to be more responsible next time, so do let me know if there is anything else I can do. Miss Wald, last week Irene and I came down to you so full of thought and wanting help and support so much—but somehow, I don't know why, I couldn't talk—in fact I don't know when I felt more stupid. It is impossible to write all, but you must know my feeling for the settlement. It's not for its own sake that I love it, for what it stands for or what you are accomplishing but also for what you are working toward and helping bring about—"Socialism" and that is what Irene and I are living for. We are leaving for the country the end of this week, but in any case I shall see you before we go up to "Grand View." It was just lovely yesterday notwithstanding the rain.

With love

From affectionately

Alice Lewisohn[13]

Alice's salutations quickly progressed from "Miss Wald" to "Dear, dear loved Lady," and her closes to "Ever and always" and "Dearest blessing of foresight." "The Family" referred to above in her reference to donated clothing seems to have consisted of Alice and Irene alone. In fact, there were seven older brothers and sisters, and one brother between Alice and Irene in age, but those never enter into any of the correspondence with Wald or appear in the various memoirs and retrospective notes left in the Neighborhood Playhouse archives. Nor did any of those brothers and sisters leave any accomplishment approaching the Neighborhood Playhouse and its legacies. Doris Fox Benardete, whose Ph.D. dissertation relishes gossip more than most dissertations, reports that Alice and Irene had an aversion to "fanfaronade." Perhaps, she offered, this was "the result of disagreeable early impressions when their brothers, who were grown men when the sisters were born, had achieved notoriety in the yellow journals of New York."[14]

However embarrassed by her brothers, Alice was neither shy nor invisible. She was a contrast to the shrewd, efficient, and supremely capable Lillian Wald, and, in the role of patron and benefactor, she was a contrast to her father's style as well. In his history of "The Guggenheim-Lewisohn Battle" over corporate control of American Smelting and Refining, Stephen Birmingham describes how "inconspicuousness" had become a key concept in German Jewish life: "It was to be inconspicuous that Meyer and Barbara Guggenheim, and so many others, had abandoned the orthodoxy of their parents and become Reformed (or less noticeably Jewish) Jews, and had joined the German Jewish Temple Emanu-El. To be inconspicuous, many Guggenheims had scattered themselves in large, but anonymous, brownstones on the less fashionable West Side. Inconspicuousness was synonymous with decorum."[15]

When Leonard died, the family lived on the West Side at 46 West Fifty-second Street. Two years later, in 1904, Alice was overseeing a major renovation of far grander quarters at 43 Fifth Avenue, on the lower avenue at Eleventh Street, to remove the "faithful nymphs" of an older decorative style for cleaner space and light in a more contemporary design. In the renovation, she wrote to Wald, "it's quite respectable for foundlings to be homeless" in reference to both nouveau decorative images and herself and her sister. With a characteristic rapid chain of associations, the letter continued, "The apartment on the contrary is furnished in excellent taste but to these shockingly fastidious children it seems congested. Is there anything I can do for scholarship matters?"[16] Inconspicuousness was not Alice Lewisohn's style, and her long involvement in "Asiatic" dramas from *Jephtha's Daughter* to *The Dybbuk* was the inverse of an effort to appear "less Jewish" or to be synonymous with decorum.

Alice actually tested the limits of visibility appropriate for an heiress. By 1906, as her involvement with the Henry Street Settlement was growing, she had begun training for the stage under the guidance of Sarah Cowell Le Moyne, a distinguished actress whose specialty was poetic dramas, especially dramatizations of texts from Robert Browning. In November 1906, Alice, under the stage name "Eleanora Leigh," appeared in a Le Moyne production as a young bride. "Broadway heard with interest the news that the young woman, who has a large fortune in her own right, is interested in things histrionic," reported the *New York Herald.* "Disappointment was keen when Miss Lewisohn made it plain that she had only used some of her pin money for pin feathers and that she had absolutely no intention of sprouting full grown wings."[17] The production was *Pippa Passes,* which Alice would stage at the Neighborhood Playhouse with herself in the Le Moyne role eleven years later. In 1906, it was staged by Henry Miller at the distinctly upscale Majestic Theatre as a matinee production (three times per week at 2:30 P.M.), making it about as "proper" as any stage appearance by an heiress could possibly be. But she was unhappy when she was discovered by the press. She told the *Daily Tribune* that "I have no intention of remaining on the stage or even of appearing in any other play," and that the only reason she appeared as Eleanora Leigh was "to gain experience for my dramatic work at the Henry Street Settlement." On that work, she said:

> So much philanthropic work is of a utilitarian character. We give the poor lectures and classes and other useful things, and forget that they want pleasure and some means of artistic expression. These foreigners that are coming to us are so artistic and they find so little of the beautiful side of life in New York! My sister and I have been working chiefly among the Russians, and have found it a great pleasure. We have been trying to revive the old song and dance festivals, and they enjoy it so much, particularly the children.[18]

Alice and Irene did sometimes appear in Neighborhood Playhouse productions, though they more often worked in director roles. Doris Fox Benardete, on the basis of a "personal interview," reports that "had they
not associated round themselves a committee of codirectors, they would
have appeared more frequently than they did."[19] The interview was probably with one of the codirectors, because when Benardete wrote Alice
was in Europe and Irene was deceased. An onstage role by a benefactor
would have raised the issue of the benefactor benefitting from philanthropy more than the object of it; the final *Grand Street Follies* performed at
Grand Street, in 1927, satirized patrons casting themselves in sponsored
productions. Even the director's role, of course, could confuse vanity with
charity. The codirectors, Agnes Morgan and Helen Arthur, were, to Benardete's mind at least, a control on that, which implies a compensating
control by the Lewisohns on the Morgan-Arthurs' greater appetite for
professional theatrical success than for settlement success.

In November 1906, Irene, included by Alice as collaborator in "our
work" in her remarks for the *Tribune,* was barely fourteen years old. However much her stage prospects may have been limited by propriety or
codirectors, she became and remained as focused on dance as Alice was
on drama. Irene was a self-styled student of dance, developing a style of
modern movement that was distant from classical dance, intensely musical, international in idiom, and without either models or imitators.
Among the many influences on her was a trip to Asia with Lillian Wald
in 1910 that included extended study in Japan with Noh dancers and
Michio Ito, who would visit the Neighborhood Playhouse and perform
there in its fourth season. Alice's devotion to a poetic drama like Le
Moyne's, which was far in style from both "artistic" saloon realism and
"popular" parlor drama, in conjunction with Irene's devotion to stage
movement and "lyrical" dance, insured that their contributions to the
Neighborhood Playhouse production record would be unlike what was
happening on stage elsewhere in New York whether uptown or downtown. The grounding of the playhouse in contemporary theater practice
would be provided by Agnes Morgan and Helen Arthur. The sisters codirected a poetic spectacular based on the poems of Walt Whitman called
Salut au Monde. They also worked independently: of the two most signifi-

cant productions late in the life of the Neighborhood Playhouse, Irene codirected *The Little Clay Cart* (with Agnes Morgan) and Alice codirected *The Dybbuk* (with David Vardi). But their partnership was quite intense. Irene died of cancer in 1944, or twelve years before Alice wrote her memoir. In it, Alice wrote that "the partnership between my sister Irene Lewisohn and myself which began with the children's festival productions continued uninterruptedly over the years" and that by this partnership they hoped to succeed in creating stage spectacles in which "the mood outweighed the structure" and "a lyric quality was intrinsic."

Lillian Wald, in image and in fact, virtually embodies the ethic of the settlement movement. The Lewisohns did not. It is clear that funding, performing, and directing a personal fantasy of theater was not a priority of the settlement movement. It is also clear that settlements existed only because of benefactors, and in these tensions lie some of the drama of the Neighborhood Playhouse and the issues embedded in the settlement ideal itself. Taking its impulse from British Christian Socialism and its reaction to industrialism, the settlement movement tried to correct practices of charity and to create a system of reform that would address causes of poverty and not just symptoms of it. From Ruskin it took the ideal of a holistic, organic continuum of environment and culture that would repair the damage done by industrial urbanism. From Carlyle it took a lesson in the power of alms to create the dependence known as "pauperism." In organized form, the settlement movement first became visible in 1884, when students from Oxford created the Universities Settlement organization in East London in a house called Toynbee Hall. The effort took its inspiration from ideas at Oxford, especially those of the historian Arnold Toynbee, who had died a year before, and so was born with some of the tensions between poverty and privilege that will become evident in the Lewisohns' experience. Toynbee Hall was followed almost immediately by Oxford Hall, and in the next twenty years another twenty settlements would open and survive in other industrial centers such as Glasgow, Manchester, and Birmingham.

The London settlements attracted visitors from many university groups as well as religious ones. One American visitor, Samuel Coit, returned to New York and in 1886 on Forsyth Street opened the Neighborhood Guild (gesturing toward beneficiaries); in 1891 he renamed it the University Settlement (gesturing instead toward benefactors). It was joined on the Lower East Side in 1887 by the College Settlement on Rivington Street, whose founders were the college women who introduced Lillian Wald to her first settlement experiences. In Chicago, Jane Addams opened Hull House in 1889, and, in Boston, Robert A. Woods opened Andover House in 1891. In the 1890s the movement was thoroughly international, with adaptations of the Toynbee Hall model opening in Canada, Finland, Amsterdam, Japan, and elsewhere. But the American movement soon became distinct because it more than any other had to address the unique conditions bred by distinctive immigration patterns into city settings. In the Lower East Side, in particular, there was soon a Grand Street Settlement, a Christie Street Settlement, and many others. By 1919, when the United Neighborhood Houses was founded, the organization could list 37 member settlements in New York City and 400 elsewhere in America.

Robert A. Woods became a principal spokesperson for settlements in the 1920s, when, coincident the highest profile years of the Neighborhood Playhouse, the settlement movement had its greatest and also its most turbulent era. He stated the principle of settlements quite clearly: "Philanthropy, however well devised, is not their final end and aim. Their real use in the world is to reestablish on a natural basis those social relations which modern city life has thrown into confusion, and to develop such new forms of cooperative and public action as the changed situation may demand."[20] In this statement one finds the two fundamental goals of the movement. First, it would offset the dehumanizing effects of urbanism by restoring "natural" relations, especially those of family life, against the divisive forces of exploitive labor and oppressive housing. Second, it would bring about public and political reform to prevent the recurrence of those conditions. The first effort addressed poverty as environmental rather than moral in origin and prescribed delivering and sustaining on a local level services such as education, counseling, or, in the case of the Henry Street Settlement, nursing. Hence the emphasis on the names "neighborhood" and "settlement." The second effort required ardent and also quite calculated political activism including labor reform that was not always welcome by benefactors.

The movement had its critics. When Lillian Wald published *The House on Henry Street* in 1915, the reviewer for the *New Republic* dismissed the movement as "young ladies with weak eyes and young gentlemen with weak chins fluttering confusedly among heterogenous foreigners, offering cocoa and sponge cake as a sort of dessert to the factory system they deplore."[21] The proliferation of settlements, their long survival, and the lasting commitment to them of so many volunteers and residents doesn't suggest ineffectuality and confusion at all, and a much longer record of settlement work that extends into and through the present refutes this kind of personalized criticism. But the criticism persisted, as when Sinclair Lewis, in 1933, "exposed" the whole movement in his novel *Ann Vickers* with specific reference to the Lower East Side. In the novel, Ann Vickers serves as a resident at a settlement that has a Dramatic Association known for its productions of Broadway revues. After Ann endures an abortion, and after a suicide by a lesbian colleague, Lewis's heroine concludes:

> It was too parochial. It touched only a tiny neighborhood, and left all the adjoining neighborhoods that did not have their own settlements, which was most of them, without provision for such recreations, education, emergency relief, and advice as the settlement could give. . . . It taught, but it did not teach well. The professional teachers of the city schools were better, and considerably more enduring, than the earnest volunteers (so like the Sunday school teachers of Ann's childhood) who, out of a wealth of ignorance and good intentions, for a year or so instructed the poor Jews and Italians and Greeks concerning George Washington and double-entry book-keeping and the brushing of teeth. The night schools did it better. The ambitious youngsters—the only ones who were worth the trouble—did it better by themselves.

Lewis's animosities are evident, but the settlement movement could then and especially now, after a more than a century of work, persuasively point to evidence that it reached people, especially new residents, who were not reached by the schools or who were prevented by working conditions from reaching them. In both of these examples, from the *New Republic* and *Ann Vickers*, on occasions more than fifteen years apart, the authors were quick to exempt Lillian Wald from their sweeping generalizations. But the issue remained: that whatever the intentions of the movement, for Lewis, the entire enterprise "smelled like the sour smell of charity"[22] and so had failed to reverse patterns of pauperism and dependence.

A more penetrating criticism, one that was recognized early on by the movement itself, was the issue of relations between benefactors and beneficiaries. Lewis did not ignore this potential conflict. Ann Vickers understands the mission of the settlement movement to be bringing "together the well-to-do and the unfortunate," but in her disillusionment she wonders if the actual outcome is not instead "that the prosperous may broaden and deepen their sympathies by first-hand contact with the poor."[23] The issue had been cast much earlier by Arthur C. Holden, who was as much a national spokesperson for the movement as Robert A. Woods. In his early book *The Settlement Idea: A Vision of Social Justice*, Holden listed as a fundamental condition of settlements the mix in which "the residents and the volunteers are representative of a class of people who have enjoyed peculiar advantages of education and position in society, while in general the people of the neighborhood represent those whose opportunities in life have been far more limited." But, for Holden, the outcome clearly was recognition that "the first purpose of the settlement is to give to the people of the neighborhood some of the advantages which unfortunately have been denied them."[24] The whole matter had been cast in higher style even earlier by Thorstein Veblen, who, in 1899 in *The Theory of the Leisure Class*, recognized "the invidious motive" by which benefactors, especially those providing "large and conspicuous expenditures," create civic organizations that "keep them in mind of their superior status by pointing [out] the contrast between themselves and the lower-lying humanity in whom the work of amelioration is to be wrought; as, for example the university settlement, which now has some vogue."[25] For Holden, Veblen, and even Lewis, at issue is the question of outcome: will the primary beneficiaries be the donors or the recipients?

For Lewis, in the case of the settlement movement, at least in its later stages or beyond the watchful eyes of Lillian Wald, the net gain was to the donors, whose philanthropy was designed for self-gratification: "Let them watch themselves being superior to the unfortunate!"[26] The founding and operation of Neighborhood Playhouse, with its close contact of "humanity" and "conspicuous" patrons further complicated by conflicting Jewishness, and with its dynamic of politics and performing arts, provides a superb test case for this continuing issue in philanthropy. Who gained by the Neighborhood Playhouse: the neighborhood or the Lewisohns?

One of the objects of scorn among some critics of the settlement movement and one that continues into the present, was the conviction that assimilation, and in this case Americanization, was a benefit to the poor. The alternative view holds that the consequent loss of cultural identity dehumanized "humanity" and that the sole benefit was the pleasure of the benefactors in seeing their cultural identity, often only recently achieved, replicated by the needy. In this debate, the work of the Lewisohns, when their contributions to the Henry Street Settlement became organized and continuing, confronts the issue directly. The first extensive contributions that they made to the Henry Street Settlement that were not monetary were the series of festivals begun at the settlement by 1906. These earliest dramatic works created by organization of the various children's clubs at the settlement, were, in Alice's recollection, "the germ which animated a decade of intensive experiment in various aspects of the theatre. Quite apart from their naive form these festivals stimulated an indefinable mood for the audiences as well as for the children taking part."[27] They were not in any way the kind of profane and anarchic festival associated in folklore practices with carnival and expression of repressed revolutionary impulses. These were, instead, the kind of public pageant provided by the establishment in celebration of tradition. But in the series launched in the settlement gymnasium, Alice and Irene seemed to alternate regularly between old world and new world traditions, between festivals with Jewish themes and those with American ones. The "Three Impressions of Spring" in 1906 was followed by "Miriam: A Passover Festival" in 1907, then by "Hiawatha" in 1908, then by "Chanukkah:

A Midwinter Festival of Lights" in 1909, and so forth.[28] The result was, as Alice claimed, engagement of the past of the audience, presumably parents of the settlement children, and the future of the children. The series may have been naive in roduction style, but it was not in its conception of assimilation, which was addressed as a desirable condition and neither an irrefutable imperative nor a distinctively American peril.

Staging the festivals with children required long rehearsals of song and dance and many volunteers for work in design, construction, coaching, and costuming. It was in this role as volunteer that Helen Arthur first met the Lewisohns and began the association that led to her long tenure as business manager of the Neighborhood Playhouse. She was born in Wisconsin in 1879, graduated from Northwestern University, and in 1900 was at New York University to study law. Her work as an attorney eventually brought her into contact with Lillian Wald, and by 1906 she was living as a volunteer at the settlement. That summer she vacationed outside New York City with Wald, and a collection of intimate letters from the "Judge" (Arthur) to the "Court of Appeals" (Wald) survives from their love affair and immediately following it. As Clare Coss has written of the letters and the relationship in *Lillian D. Wald: Progressive Activist*, "Wald, who delighted in the happiness of her friends, apparently never wanted for herself or encouraged an exclusive or permanent partnership. . . . She preferred personal independence, which allowed her to move quickly, travel freely, and act boldly."[29] Arthur continued to volunteer at the settlement, although her role shifted from legal advisor to festival volunteer. She was an avid theatergoer, and by 1907, in theater circles, she met Agnes Morgan, who would become her lifelong companion. Theater finally drew her entirely away from law, and, after serving as manager for a series of professional actors and companies, she became an executive secretary in the Shubert organization. Arthur had enormous energy, an outsized personality, and a talent for fictionalizing experience. By her account, she staged a satire of Shubert organizational behavior and was summarily dismissed for it. By another, she was traveling for the Shuberts when the first Henry Street publicity managers, Grace Griswold and Grace Halsey Mills, vacated a salaried position, and Morgan seized the opportunity to put Arthur on the permanent payroll. Arthur's influence was great even before she officially became business manager of the Neighborhood Playhouse in 1917. Doris Fox Benardete, who worked in the theater office, observed that, "for some reason," the names of Grace Griswold and Grace Halsey Mills "were scarcely ever listed in the early printed circulars when the list of directors appeared. Perhaps those early circulars were composed by Miss Arthur."[30]

The festivals continued in the settlement gymnasium in a series that never disavowed "Asiatic" identity: after "The Discontented Daffodil," direct address to audience history was increased in "The Revolt of the Flowers" and further in an "Evening of Russian Music and Slavic Dancing." In her memoir, Alice claims that at this time, 1912, "the senior clubs at the Henry Street Settlement had been urging me for some time to form a dramatic group."[31] At their urging or her own, the result was a staging of *The Shepherd* by Olive Tilford Dargan in Clinton Hall, a trade unions assembly hall. The production of Dargan's play is a good example of the pressures of internationalism bearing on the Lewisohns, their pupils, the settlement, and the neighborhood. The play was an adaptation of a Tolsoy story about serfs treated unfairly; the author, born in Kentucky, graduate of Radcliffe, former New Yorker who was then living in England, later retired to North Carolina and became well known for "mountain poetry" and stories about rural, Appalachian life. Both of the Lewisohns were in the cast: Irene as a revolutionary and Alice as a princess. The director, Sarah Cowell Le Moyne, perhaps dismayed by the rest of the amateur cast, brought in Agnes Morgan, on Helen Arthur's recommendation, to drill the ranks. All the volunteers spent six weeks in rehearsal and performed in uniform tunics variously dyed on a temporary platform and dried on fire escapes that doubled as routes from dressing room to stage. When it was performed in February 1912, the mostly settlement audience was appreciative, although Alice remembered being disappointed: "It was a play of ideas, but the ideas never really emanated from the characters, which served merely as voices for the author's thesis. The lesson of all those weeks of dealing with starving peasants was that a play lives only through its power of characterization. We had also learned that an audience does not necessarily agree with this conclusion, judging by the excitement that the play aroused."[32] The performance had been planned for a single weekend. Because of the "excitement," it was repeated the next weekend, and then in the following June performed at a number of other settlements. By the end of its run, the club of volunteers had adopted the name "The Neighborhood Players."

Alice's comments on *The Shepherd* reflect a continuing issue in the entire life of the Neighborhood Playhouse: the performing arts required a high quality of production values that could divorce it from settlement functions and Lower East Side audiences. Over the years, as artistic aspirations rose, the company would become professionalized, the performances would gain greater recognition, and the key figures would debate whether that direction served or undermined founding principles and settlement ideals. The issue began to develop one year after *The Shepherd* when, in 1913, only months before its summer pageant in celebration of the twentieth anniversary of the Henry Street Settlement, the Neighborhood Players produced John Galsworthy's *The Silver Box* at Clinton Hall. Though apparently directed by a committee of the Lewisohns, Helen Arthur, and Sarah Cowell Le Moyne, *The Silver Box* production plainly indicated the emergence of Agnes Morgan as leader of the production staff. She was older than either Alice or Irene, and she was a graduate of Radcliffe and George Pierce Baker's "47 Workshop" in which play scripts served as the dissertation. Her work had been produced in Cambridge, Massachusetts, and in Chicago, and she was working in New York in the publicity department of the Shubert organization when she met Helen Arthur, who would refer her to Le Moyne for *The Shepherd*. Morgan had much more practical experience in theater than the others and added some common sense to the Le Moyne glamour, the Lewisohn ideas, and the Arthur animation. After the Neighborhood Playhouse, and after its successor the Actor-Managers Company failed in the 1930s, Morgan's pragmatism would support elaborate traveling productions for the Federal Theatre Project.

The choice of *The Silver Box* in 1913 initiated an ongoing debate about whether the production of, by Lower East Side standards, patrician British playwrights such as Galsworthy, Lord Dunsany, or Shaw best served the interests of the audience or the producers. Alice was plainly disappointed that the audience identified so closely with Tolstoy's "starving peasants," and *The Silver Box* would not offer them that simple "excitement" again. In 1913, Galsworthy was not yet the Nobelist associated with *The Forsyte Saga*, but he was already much more recognized and established than Olive Tilford Dargan. The play had opened in London in 1906 as part of the matinee series produced at the Court Theatre by John Vedrenne and Harley Granville Barker as a way of bringing new "realist" work to potential producers in a London theatrical world still dominated by melodrama. *The Silver Box* was acclaimed, moved to evening performances, and then produced internationally, including a New York production with Ethel Barrymore. In the play, a wealthy playboy and a drunken laborer are both accused of theft, the latter of the cigarette box of the title; the matter goes to court, and wealth prevails over justice. Alice took the Barrymore role of the charwoman and abused wife Mrs. Jones, who enters explaining how her husband, the accused laborer, "made me get up, and he knocked me about. . . . He's such a violent man when he's not himself." Irene played the fabulously wealthy Mrs. Barthwick, mother of the accused playboy, who regularly comments on how "Education is simply ruining the lower classes. It unsettles them, and that's the worst thing for us all. I see an enormous difference in the manner of servants."[33]

It certainly was a great distance from the Lower East Side to the Barthwick residence. In her memoir, Alice described how the young student playing the playboy had never seen, let alone worn, evening dress until his opening night. In order to stage the dinner at the Barthwick's, Alice had dinners for the cast at her own home, by now 43 Fifth Avenue, to drill them in formal table manners. Alice also ate bacon stew daily and practiced peeling potatoes to prepare for the role of Mrs. Jones. But however distant in setting from the lives of its audience, the production of *The Silver Box* stirred its own excitement. It was not an apology for class difference but a dramatization of it played before an audience that may have been ignorant about evening dress and British table manners but understood impoverished living quarters, wife abuse, hard labor, and hostile legal systems quite well. In the final scene, as the innocent laborer is hauled off to prison for the crime of the aristocrat, a stage chorus of the London poor moan in grief. The contrast of classes was evidently very vivid. *The Settlement Journal* reprinted a review from the *Boston Globe* that praised Alice for "a touching picture as the crushed, cringing char-woman" and the scene in her flat as "squalid . . . with damning reality."[34] Far from being a narcissistic exercise in superiority by clueless benefac-tors, the Neighborhood Players production of *The Silver Box* was a shrewd and self-aware experiment with social commentary in dramatic form for a new audience. The degree of self-awareness is documented by the fact that the production inspired the first of those exercises in self-critique that would evolve into *The Grand Street Follies*. Planned for a single weekend, the play was repeated in March in a performance that was attended by former president of the United States Theodore Roosevelt. Between those performances, on Alice's thirtieth birthday, April 17, the cast and support-ing staff staged satiric skits including "The Silver Hoax: A Classy, Up-town Drama."[35]

Classy uptown drama would always remain a part of the Neighbor-hood Playhouse repertory, but it would never be the whole of it. Before, during, and after the production of *The Silver Box*, even more energy was being directed to the June 7, 1913, street pageant in celebration of the twentieth anniversary of the Henry Street Settlement. This project first brought Aline Bernstein into the group. She volunteered with her sister Ethel Frankau and from January through June created costumes for 500 children on a budget of fifty cents per suit. It was a defining experience at the settlement for Rita Morgenthau, who wrote an internal history of the first twenty years that culminated in the pageant as apotheosis of settlement ideals. She was a member of one of New York City's great wealthy families, she created acting clubs for girls, she served on the exec-utive committee of the Neighborhood Playhouse, and, after 1927, she di-rected its subsequent entity as the Neighborhood Playhouse School of Theater. A Henry Street Settlement committee including Morgenthau was formed to organize the 1913 pageant, and their authorization of the Lew-isohns to create the anniversary festival, as well as its ultimate success, led directly to the building of the theater at 466 Grand Street.

Such pageants were not unknown at the time. There was then an American Pageant Association whose dictum was "As the community pageant must be about its people, it should be done by its people for the education and betterment of its people."[36] Alice and Irene's script (they initialed notes "A.I.L.") followed this dictum directly. "The plan of the pageant," the script explains, "presents characteristic social gatherings in Henry Street during the various periods of its history . . . the incidents suggested in each episode are based on real traditions of the neighborhood." In its performance of the area history from precolonial to present conditions, the Henry Street pageant of 1913 suggested future assimilation into mutual, collective traditions that extended rather than obliterated or replaced immigrant traditions and identities, and so integrated identity and assimilation. In song and dance, it communicated a social message. The script emphasized that "the main desire is to recreate an atmosphere of old New York by reviving the types of olden days in the social life of the street."[37]

The form of communication they chose was a spectacle too large to ever rehearse in entirety. The city contributed street improvements, bleachers, lighting, and a large police force. Wald sat in reserved seating with the Warburgs, the Schiffs, Adolph Ochs, Borough President George McAneny, and 350 others. The most desirable seating for the remaining 10,000 spectators were in the windows facing the street, which required special logistics. Among the notes archived are the directions to "House Chiefs" such as "number 303 [i.e., 303 Henry Street] will be filled first beginning at top, five to each window except toilet room on second floor. When house is full notify Mr. Morgenthau at the 299 door by means of messenger. Do not leave your posts." While preliminary acts performed songs and dances, the main procession formed along Scammel Street in impressive numbers. The Dutch alone included children dressed as sixteen windmills, sixteen morris dancers, six mothers, six children, fourteen linen girls, eight wooden shoes, and six tulips. The procession began at darkness, to exploit fully the effect of the new outdoor electric lighting. The first to enter Henry Street in episode 1 represented the Indians. Their script directions were:

> 3 squaws carrying tom-toms center, circle fire and sit down in background—beating tom-toms as signal for council. 8 braves enter; they circle fire and sit in semi-circle after spreading their fur robes on

ground—their bows and arrows beside them. Chief enters followed by Dutch traders and Indian Squaws and papooses. They all sit around fire. The Squaws sing.

And so it went through the history of the neighborhood. By episode 4 they were up to "The Coming of the Foreigners" in the form of groups of "Irish" boys and girls playing on harps and singing "Kathleen Mavoureen." The "Irish" were played by boys with names like Moses Brodsky, Moses Leventhal, Moses Goldberg, and Solomon Siebowitz; the "Irish" girls included Rose Bacarsky, Tessie Becker, Ertie Tennenbaum, Ella Friedman, and Laura Glickstein. By episode 6 all waves of immigrants were on the street stage at once, with the script direction that they would come on twice, go off twice, and in between dance "the Irish Jig, the Highland fling, a German hopping dance, the tarantella, a Russian folk dance, a Yiddish song, and a Russian Kasatchek, followed by the Settlement Song and an exit march." The final marching group, in a more direct reference to the settlement, was a company of visiting nurses in blue uniforms saluting Lillian Wald.

The event certainly pleased everyone involved, both performers and audience. Newspapers gave it major coverage. The *Tribune* called it "one of the most remarkable spectacles a New York Street ever saw," and the *Herald Journal* described the celebrities present and "the thousands of tenement residents of the street [watching from above] as if in imitation of prehistoric cliff dwellers." The *New York Times* devoted an editorial to a comparison of the Henry Street pageant, which its publisher Adolph Ochs attended, and the Paterson Strike pageant staged at Madison Square Garden the same night by John Reed and organized labor, which Ochs did not. At Henry Street, according to the *Times*, "Russian immigrants and their children, who have profited by the educational advantages offered to them, have acquired knowledge of the history of this country and the meaning of its institutions, and are on the way to overcome the obstacles of poverty and become good and thrifty citizens." By contrast, at Madison Square Garden, "a series of pictures in action were shown with the design of stimulating mad passion against law and order and promulgating a gospel of discontent." Only a few years later, in the Red scare, the Henry

Street Settlement and Lillian Wald would be accused of anti-American activities, but on this evening in 1913, for the *Times*, "in the Henry Street celebration the motive was to exalt progress, intellectual development, and the triumph of civilization. In the other the motive was to inspire hatred, to induce violence which may lead to the tearing down of the civil state and the institution of anarchy."[38]

In a report prepared for the Henry Street Settlement committee, Alice Lewisohn put the effect in less reactionary and less incendiary terms. "Forever Henry Street will be glorified by the memory of that night," she wrote in an unsigned draft of the report. "Instead of the bare sordidness that clings to our congested city streets, instead of the clutter of the ash cart or the frieze of garbage along the sidewalks, thousands of faces appear illumined against the sky-line; fire escapes, dull and heavy become animated with life and color."[39] This was the effect that she hoped to enlarge in dramatic presentations staged within the Neighborhood Playhouse. The effect rather than the self-gratification was the incentive. It provided the basis for a relationship of a playhouse with a settlement and a settlement with theater professionals. The relationship would be tested many times, but the effect would have influence beyond the neighborhood and so exceed the expectations of the settlement movement critics.

2

1915–1916

Opening the Little Theater of Art and Activism

Alice wanted congested streets to be animated with life and color, and the Neighborhood Playhouse at 466 Grand Street began to animate the Henry Street area on February 12, 1915, when it opened the new building with *Jephtha's Daughter,* an original dance adaptation of an Old Testament story. The building opened in the context of the European war and three months before the sinking of the *Lusitania.* As Alice wrote of the building, "Each nail hammered, each brick laid, now became a challenge to liberate values of the spirit, in opposition to negative and destructive forces elsewhere in command, forces directed to crush the impulse of life."[1] It opened as an architectural statement compatible with the principle of the Henry Street Settlement to evoke history and so to inspire transformation. Doris Fox Benardete described the Georgian style on the Lower East Side as reminiscent of "when New York was young" and getting to it as "an adventure."[2] In its first two seasons, conflicting interests and competing priorities immediately tested whether the neighborhood and the playhouse were friends or foes.

The theater opened at a particularly dynamic moment in the history of theater in New York. In that spring season, Harley Granville Barker was in New York with a repertory of new plays and Shakespeare revivals staged at the old, crumbling Wallack's Theatre on Union Square just before its demolition. Among Barker's designers was Robert Edmond Jones, who simultaneously was involved with Eugene O'Neill and the Provincetown Players organizing on Cape Cod in early 1915 before they came to New York. All would become associated with the Neighborhood Playhouse. One week after the opening of *Jephtha's Daughter*, the Washington Square Players, forerunner of the Theatre Guild, opened its first production. Despite their name, that opening was uptown at the Bandbox Theatre on Fifty-seventh Street.

By virtue of its location and remaining in it, the Neighborhood Playhouse maintained a unique dynamic: it never could, and it never would, remove itself from crucial tensions within the relations of art and politics or of artists and audience. The location aligned these opposing priorities in conflict and so made resolution of them a visible agenda. From the beginning, evaluations from different perspectives helped define the task. For example, when Susan Glaspell and Jig Cook, original members of the Washington Square Players and founders of the Provincetown Players, attended *Jephtha's Daughter*, they had an inspirational revelation. They believed that they saw a ritual "full of feeling immeasurably old" and so they had discovered "why the things we had been seeing uptown found no feeling in us." The neighborhood audience, however, or at least its Yiddish newspaper, *Der Tag*, thought that what they saw was considerably less than inspirational. *Der Tag* believed that "the human interest and life feeling of the legend is practically unexpressed." Another Yiddish newspaper, *Die Wahrheit*, was blunter: "the heiresses of the Jewish copper kings have wasted their money and their energy."[3]

The Neighborhood Playhouse plan was more than energetic. In the first of many statements of purpose printed as pamphlets, the playhouse announced its blizzard of activities for the first season. Following eight seasons of festivals and dramatic productions by the Neighborhood Players, the plan stated, the new "experimental theatre" had been built because "the development of the players, the interest of the audience, and the response of the neighborhood seemed to demand erection of this playhouse." The playhouse planned to operate multiple programs and so "to appeal to a public of diverse tastes, interests, and ages, and in this way to share in the life of the neighborhood." The promised variety included both festival productions like *Jephtha's Daughter* and dramas of British origin. In the first spring season the dramas were self-produced, including a bill of three one-act plays less than one month after *Jephtha's Daughter* and a full-length drama at the end of the first season in June.

Dramatic performances also included visiting companies, and in its first spring these included Whitford Kane and the Irish Players and Gertrude Kingston and the London Little Theatre. These productions filled the theater on Saturday and Sunday evenings, with admissions of twenty-five and fifty cents. In a policy that would be challenged later, the playhouse opened on Sundays, when licensed theaters remained closed, because its connection with the Henry Street Settlement made it a uniquely nonprofit theater classified as an educational organization.

In addition, Saturday and Sunday afternoons were reserved for children's programs such as pantomime ballets and fairy tale presentations, including ones by the settlement clubs. On weeknights, with lower admissions of five and ten cents, the theater opened for programs advertised in advance as "moving pictures, playlets, camera talks, folk songs and dances, illustrated fairy tales, marionettes and music, running continuously from half-past one until eleven o'clock," with late-afternoon programs "adapted to the interest of school children." Monday evenings were reserved for rehearsals. Further, the plan promised to offer classes and workshops in costuming, set construction, and "arts and trades connected with stage production." The prospectus listed as sole directors of all these activities the two heiresses of the Jewish copper king, with an advisory committee of Lillian Wald and Rita Morgenthau and a producing staff of the Lewisohns, Helen Arthur, and Agnes Morgan.[4]

The gift of the Neighborhood Playhouse to the Henry Street Settlement was extraordinarily large, but not necessarily as vain as, for example, Adolph Lewisohn's named stadium. The original lot, roughly 50 feet wide and 100 feet deep, and the theater constructed on it cost $150,000; that alone, in 1916, equaled the annual budget for the settlement.[5] However, to Lillian Wald, recalling the opening in her autobiography *Windows on Henry Street*, construction was a necessary extension of settlement activities. After reviewing the long and growing list of club and class functions, she wrote that "when all this activity encroached too far on the Settlement House, the Neighborhood Playhouse was built."[6] Alice, too, recalled the building years later as a necessary settlement hub and not as an exclusive venue for Irene's dance programs and her dramatic ones. In her autobiography, she described settlement clubs rehearsing in borrowed gymnasiums and performing outdoors or in rented halls. "Although the idea of a new building was to carry further the work of the festivals and plays," she wrote, "its possible scope and value extended beyond our own productions."[7] On the day before *Jephtha's Daughter* opened on February 12, 1915, the Lewisohns conveyed the deed of the building to the Henry Street Settlement; transfer was recorded by the city on February 20, and the new title was conveyed to Lillian Wald on March 2. The gift of 1915 was a capital improvement that did not distract the host institution from its mission or drain its resources. By 1920, while the Neighborhood Playhouse was subsidized by Lewisohn annual contributions rising from $10,000 per year, the total Henry Street Settlement annual budget had more than doubled to $300,000. In its first five years and annual budgets, the Neighborhood Playhouse dimension of the settlement was a shrinking portion of overhead in relation to the whole and could scarcely be challenged as a diversion from settlement goals. However, the enterprise did need a plan for institutionalization within the Henry Street Settlement that would make it independent of annual Lewisohn contributions.

In the context of the miscellaneous buildings of the settlement, the new building at 466 Grand Street was a premiere part of the whole and architecture with signature, emblematic value. Although designed to be integrated into ongoing functions of the settlement, it was in quality extraordinary on the Lower East Side. The brick, Georgian facade of the original building was, according to Alice, "modestly in keeping with the character of the neighborhood's early nineteenth-century architecture." But to Doris Fox Benardete, the red brick, marble trim, and green window boxes and shutters were a contrast to "the most unspeakable squalor" of the area around Pitt, Henry, and Grand Streets: "to visitors from afar, it sprang out of its milieu, 'an orchid in a cabbage patch.'"[8] The effect was not from any extravagance in design, but from the contrast of its substantial investment and new construction to a desolate and deteriorating area. The facade closely resembled those of the distinguished Henry Miller Theatre and Winthrop Ames's Little Theatre uptown, both of which were also designed by the Neighborhood Playhouse's architects, Harry Creighton Ingalls and Francis Burall Hoffman Jr. Uptown, the design may have been contextualized and compatible with neighboring buildings, but downtown the same design stood in dramatic contrast to a decrepit and vulgarized setting. "No flaring posters, no glaring lights advertise a theatre that consciously strives for modesty and refinement," stated an approving review of the Neighborhood Playhouse in the *Architectural Record*. "The designers' aim has been to be distinguished, rather than vociferous."[9] The *Record*'s sense of the theater's neighbors is evident.

The interior was at the time of opening extraordinary anywhere in New York. Like the apartment the Lewisohns renovated on lower Fifth Avenue, the theater building attempted the then novel design of establishing form without decoration. Writing long after opening the building and leaving it behind her, Alice's greatest pride was that "decorative values were indicated merely through architectural proportions, the use of materials, and the play of light and shade produced by a special system of indirect lighting. Not only were hangings and upholstery eliminated but the same frugality was observed in relation to the stage lighting equipment, and so forth, so that ingenuity and imagination might be the directing forces in all departments."[10] There was a dark proscenium arch over a stage fifty feet wide, but its embellishments were minimal and elsewhere inside the theater off-white shades prevailed. The original seating was for 300 in the orchestra and 99 in the balcony, all in the form of unupholstered, wooden chairs. When the Neighborhood Playhouse opened in 1915, it was one of the most expensive theaters in New York and also the third smallest.

The theatrical function of the interior was the result of two separate trips by Alice and Irene to Europe, where, in the summer of 1914 and during the onset of World War I, they particularly studied German models such as those of the Reinhardt Theatre in Berlin and the Dalcroze School in Hellerau. The design principle they adapted was the replacement of elaborate stage machinery with new electrical lighting systems. Hence the stage was wide and deep, but without extensive fly spaces above or wing spaces on sides. Instead of bare, raw space to be hidden by a set, the back wall of the stage was constructed as a concave plaster surface, or "cyclorama," for lighting effects. A complex, for its time, electric switchboard was visible to the left of the stage, and so its physical

1. Interior of the main house of the Neighborhood Playhouse, 1915.

operation was part of the effect of lighting changes in the course of performance. One of the first spectacular applications of the lighting system would be the climactic burning of Jephtha's daughter. In later years, the Neighborhood Playhouse would continue to upgrade this new electrical technology, stage whole programs around its effects, and introduce electrical lighting to the theatrical arts taught in its classes and workshops.

Uptown came downtown to the Neighborhood Playhouse with the aid of another pamphlet devoted to directions for strangers to the Lower East Side. In 1915 there were three elevated train lines with stops on Grand Street, but they were all far to the west of 466. There were no buses, and the best transportation east was the Grand Street Ferry tramcar. Taxis were reluctant to travel where they could not expect a return fare, and the drivers of private cars were unlikely to know the area. Only in its last year did the Neighborhood Playhouse introduce its own bus to the theater from Times Square. When audience members arrived, they found a

2. Lobby of the Neighborhood Playhouse at 466 Grand Street, 1915.

theater without a marquee. Instead, in that fashion of modesty and refinement admired by the *Architectural Record,* the theater announced its
presence with a white signboard that reminded Alice of old bucolic inns.
Beside the "old inn" on Grand Street there were blaring billboards for
the adjoining shops of Ulm's Boots and Cherey's Trusses. The effect of
the facades was one of contrast rather than harmony, but the tension and
the dissonance was intended, at least, to be proactive rather than disre-
spectful and an invitation through design to civic engagement.

If traveling to the site was an adventure for the uptown audience,
entering its foyer was an equal culture shock for the downtown neighbors. The lobby included a gallery space with exhibits related to any current stage production, such as costuming, stage design, art work, or cast
photographs. Unlike any popular theater, this lobby also included in the
foyer a bookstall selling plays and books on ballet and the little theater
movement. Alexander Woollcott thought that this feature distinguished

the Neighborhood Playhouse from others including the temporary quarters occupied by the Washington Square Players. He praised this "mark of intellectualism" on Grand Street as equaled only by one that "Granville Barker used to maintain so temptingly and so profitably in the lobby of the Kingsway when he ruled the destinies of that charming London playhouse."[11] Like many things in the Neighborhood Playhouse, the bookstall could please uptown connoisseurs and local patrons. For Doris Fox Benardete, it didn't smack of a London playhouse so much as "a lodestar for friends" and "the homelike warmth of a hearth fire."[12]

A distinctive quality of the new enterprise on opening was this ability to attract if not always to appease equally multiple constituencies who might disparage each other as "elitist" and "needy." As much as the Neighborhood Playhouse took its form in relation to the Henry Street Settlement, it also, as launched, had great resonance with contemporary events in New York theater. For Wald, exposure of the Lower East Side to new audiences was part of her campaign for visibility. In the fall of 1914, the New York Stage Society created the first New York exhibition of stage designs, especially American ones. One major attraction of the exhibit was a demonstration model of a cyclorama like the one in construction in the Neighborhood Playhouse, and so when the theater opened some of its audience was versed in its design innovations. Another attraction of the exhibit was Robert Edmond Jones's design for a production of Anatole France's one-act play *The Man Who Married a Dumb Wife*. Like the Lewisohns, Jones had researched his theater projects in Europe and returned with an aesthetic that valued design over decoration. Jones's project immediately attracted Harley Granville Barker, then in America at the invitation of the New York Stage Society and on a personal, continuing campaign against illusionist, or "realist," stage settings. When Granville Barker's play opened on January 27, 1915, or about three weeks before *Jephtha's Daughter*, *The Man Who Married a Dumb Wife*, planned only as a curtain-raiser for Shaw's *Androcles and the Lion*, created a precedent for "modern" design on an American stage and for visual design as a theatrical dimension equal to star billing or sensational stage machinery. These priorities were equally evident in the production of *A Midsummer Night's Dream* that Granville Barker opened in repertory with the other plays on

February 15, 1915, three evenings after the opening of *Jephtha's Daughter*. Barker's production, which had been seen in London, dispensed with "realist" forest settings for suggestive design. Like the interior of the Neighborhood Playhouse, Barker's production in the skeletal Wallack's Theatre also dispensed with footlight illumination for newer electric projections of color. The Neighborhood Playhouse would in its early years mount productions of Barker's plays and also bring in Robert Edmond Jones to design their production of Eugene O'Neill's *The Last Man*.

At the moment of the Neighborhood Playhouse's birth, "Modern Stagecraft" was a novel sphere of dramatic thought and experiment and not a mere adjustment of familiar theater practice. Another new movement of which the Neighborhood Playhouse was both cause and part of the phenomenon was the "little theater" movement sweeping America in the years leading to 1915. Taking its inspiration from European models, especially that of the Abbey Theatre of Dublin after it began to tour America in 1911, little theater would propagate the staging of artistic plays, frequently programs of one-act plays, in intimate settings and at levels of cost within the modest means of new, nonprofessional producing groups and new, "popular" audiences. Thus, little theater was seen by many as antidote to the commercialization of theater as entertainment and to the depersonalized character of increasingly dense urban centers. In the years before 1915, small theater groups flourished nationally. "Little Theater" was taken as title by groups started in Chicago and in New York in 1912, in Philadelphia in 1913, in Duluth in 1914, and in Indianapolis in 1915. The New York flagship, housed in the building that was the prototype for the Neighborhood Playhouse, was the influential model created by Winthrop Ames as an alternative to mainstream theater around Broadway before that district had even taken shape; on opening in 1912, Ames's Little Theatre seated 299, or less than the Neighborhood Playhouse, but the capacity was quickly doubled. At the same time, variations on the title Little Theater were fashioned by the Toy Theatre of Boston in 1912, by Little Country Theatre of Fargo in 1914, and by the Arts and Crafts Theatre of Detroit in 1915. By 1916, or soon after the opening of the Neighborhood Playhouse, there was a Little Arts Theater in Los Angeles, and by 1917 there were two popular and influential histories of the movement: Constance D'Arcy Mackay's *The Little Theatre in the United States* and Thomas H. Dickinson's *The Insurgent Theatre*. The first of these listed sixty-three American companies that could be called little theaters. The second listed the repertories of many, and its author, Dickinson, would later become advisor to the Neighborhood Playhouse.

All little theaters, including the Neighborhood Playhouse, were prone to conflicts between amateurism and professionalism, between the needs of audiences and the needs of producers, and between art and commerce. At its most idealistic, by virtue of its emphasis on art and accessibility to enthusiastic amateurs, the movement was part of the contemporary democratization of leisure and of technology, a counterbalance to consumerism, and so a matter of general civic import. Percy MacKaye, the son of a hugely popular stage melodramatist, or theatrical professional of the old kind, and himself a leading theorist of alternative little theater, formulated that focus on civic value in one of the earliest statements of the purpose of the little theater movement. "The vital problems which confront the drama in America to-day are not primarily questions of dramatic art," he said in a popular lecture from about 1909 on "Theatre and Democracy in America." "They are questions which concern the opportunities for dramatic art properly to exist and to mature. Primarily, therefore, they are not aesthetic questions; they are civic questions."[13] Just so, the questions concerning the Neighborhood Playhouse and its fortunes on opening are more than aesthetic, and the "opportunities" specific to it include the offstage social forces such as location and audience.

Immediately, there was considerable ridicule of the little theater movement, and the vehemence of its detractors certainly cannot be explained on aesthetic rationales alone. Perhaps the most negative critique was made by the impresario David Belasco, whose self-interest in large-scale, high-profit, and titillating productions was well known. Later, in the 1920s, ever opportunistic, he would reverse himself and find little theater admirable when it had become marketable and profitable. But earlier, in the second season of the Neighborhood Playhouse, Belasco repeatedly denounced the deprofessionalized presentation of "the diseased output of diseased minds":

> As cubism became the asylum of those pretenders in Art who could not draw and had no conception of composition in painting, so "new art of the theater" is the haven of those who lack experience and knowledge of the drama and of the theater, and whose mental conception is so dull that only the grossly exaggerated and perverted forms of life and its expression in the written and spoken word can appeal and be grasped. The whole thing merely shows an ignorance and a diseased and depraved understanding and no appreciation of any art at all.

There were rebuttals to Belasco, and many, such as the *New York Globe*, cited the Neighborhood Playhouse as counterexample to the charges of depravity and perversion.[14] But the "experimental" quality of little theater and its new leader, the Neighborhood Playhouse, was confirmed by the vocal opposition.

Perhaps the most acute charges against the new theatrical counterculture were those based on skepticism about the real commitment of little theater producers to an amateur, nonprofessional, and non-narcissistic agenda. This issue was later raised most wittily by Lorenz Hart in the *Garrick Gaieties* song that celebrated the Neighborhood Playhouse by name in its verse:

> We bring drama to your great metropolis,
> We are the little theatre group.
> Each of us has built a small acropolis
> To hold our little theatre troupe.
>
> We'd be very glad to meet you,
> And greet you, and seat you, and treat you just great.
> For all commercial art is hollow,
> So follow Apollo and swallow our bait.[15]

However great the civic idealism of the Neighborhood Playhouse project, and however convincing its support from the Henry Street Settlement, both the uptown audience, which had limits to how far it would go for Apollo, and the downtown audience, which awaited the new acropolis on their Grand Street with evident skepticism, could well wonder about the commitment not just to beginning as a noncommercial enterprise but to remaining so. The "amateur model" would not remain the foundation of the Neighborhood Playhouse activities, and to different audiences the reorganization toward professionalism was either pursuit of higher art, as in Apollo, or corruption and deception, as in switching the bait.

The date of opening night, February 12, 1915, had been chosen for the idealism of Abraham Lincoln's birthday and the pragmatism of there being only a single other holiday premiere that night in New York theaters. The date may have also been optimistic because both the production, including choruses that made the cast more than seventy, and the building, still under construction, were not entirely ready. Alice Lewisohn recalled the evening as a "nightmare": "As last, the dreaded moment of opening the doors. The audience assembled terribly on time. Irene and I, both playing in this dance drama, were in the dressing room 'making up' when the manager reported in dismay that the seats were still being fastened in and that the setting was unfinished."[16] Consequently, while a full-house audience waited, Helen Arthur was sent out on stage to soothe them with comic stories about the creation of the theater.

Then, before the program proper, Lillian Wald took the stage and addressed the audience without any humor, to rouse them and not to sooth them, and with the usual personal charisma. She described the long commitment to the Henry Street Settlement by Alice and Irene. She praised the production about to be staged but described it as essentially an effect of the long effort to create a "belief that a people, even a local neighborhood community, has an art expression to contribute." Then, in the context of World War I suspicion of foreigners, she described that community not as grateful impenitents but as gift-bearing newcomers laden with assets for the United States: "It pleases me to think that what will seem best to-night has been woven out of the traditions of our neighborhood, and that the music and the dance and the color are part of the dower brought to New York by the stranger." In closing, she rang a hopeful note on the project of little theater: "Above the din of industrialism and the roar of machinery of the city, there rises the hope that a community playhouse, identified with its neighborhood, may recapture and hold something of the poetry and the idealism that belong to its people."[17] This was a criterion that she would evoke again: the question, for Wald, was not whether the neighborhood was worthy of the theater, but whether the theater was worthy of its neighborhood.

What the producing directors of the Neighborhood Playhouse had woven out of the Jephtha story of Old Testament *Judges* was a revisionist, self-assertive account of the sacrificial virgin story, and they presented it in vivid, dynamic, modern dance performance. The original script had as title "Jephtha's Daughter: A Biblical Ballad Dance Drama in Three Scenes," until the softening word "ballad" was dropped. When the curtains opened, the first scene revealed a high altar surrounded by choruses and backed by the curved rear cyclorama wall lit in blue. The effect, according to the reviewer of the *Times,* was that of a "wrinkleless sky far superior to scores of skies professional stages of Broadway have shown."[18] Before the blue field, choruses of men and women chanted to original music by Lilia Mackay-Cantell the rather tortured lyrics by Alice Lewisohn:

> Oh God, keep not thou silence
> Help us to overcome our foe.
> The Ammonites take crafty counsel against us,
> To slay thy people Israel do they seek.[19]

In the opening act, Jephtha is recruited to lead Israel into battle. In the Neighborhood Playhouse staging, Jephtha, played by David Solomon, the first male lead to emerge from the Neighborhood Players, entered with a company of warriors and his daughter, played by Alice. Before the altar, Jephtha, in this version as an act of arrogance rather than reverence, pledges that if victorious he will sacrifice the first person he meets on return from battle to Mispah (the script spelling). The second act revealed a new set for the city gates:

> The gates of the city and back center the wall extending either side. Beyond the wall is the open country. To the right adjoining the wall is a flight of steps leading to Jephtha's house, the loggia of which is open to view.

The maidens of Mispah rejoiced at the news of Jephtha's victory and danced to choreography by Irene Lewisohn. Jephtha approached the city to horn fanfares, his daughter entered to welcome him, the gates were swung open, and thus the daughter becomes the first person seen by Jephtha and so the sacrifice he has promised.

The third act returned to the set of the first, with a foreground altar and background of an early-morning sky. On the morning of her sacrifice, Alice as Jephtha's daughter prayed:

> I cry unto thee O Lord
> My spirit is overwhelmed within me.
> Deliver me from this sacrifice or give me strength to do thy will.
> My heart within me is desolate.
> Be merciful oh God. Be merciful.

She was answered by God in the form of the voice of Sarah Cowell Le Moyne, who told her that the outcome will be sacrifice, not deliverance. Surrounded by a chorus of wailing women and children, Jephtha's daughter danced before her own funeral pyre. In the words of the script, probably written by Alice for her own role, "J. D. steps forward, seizes the torch and dances in wild ecstasy whirling with the torch till she reaches the altar, lights it, then flings herself upon it."

Jephtha's Daughter certainly succeeded by most theatrical standards, though not necessarily most cultural or settlement ones. All performances over two weekends were sold out in advance. The *New York Times* believed that the show proved that "interesting things are to be done in this little theatre on the East Side."[20] Rachel Crothers, American playwright of the moment on the subject of sexual equality, provided a public letter on its success and promise. Susan Glaspell took *Jephtha's Daughter* as exemplum for her work with Jig Cook and the Provincetown Players. George Foster Platt, then a leading "art" director moving from stage to screen, also provided a public letter, one that presumed that "the 'Neighborhood' no doubt feels grateful for its Playhouse." "It should stand to them," he wrote in a testimonial published in *Settlement Journal*, "for rather more than a shelter for entertainment and be recognized as a monument of the

3. Alice Lewisohn approaches the sacrificial bier in *Jephtha's Daughter,* 1915.

time wherein the interests of all classes are becoming more closely linked."[21] However, the universality and timelessness of the artistic vision was precisely what "the Neighborhood" objected to in the Lewisohns' playhouse and in little theater generally. As Platt wrote about "them," so the Yiddish weekly *Der Tag* in its review of *Jephtha's Daughter* wrote about its opposite: "The wealthy men and women certainly do not need to come to Grand Street, near Pitt and Willett, to satisfy their esthetic desires. For them there are much prettier, finer theatres in more gorgeous surroundings." As Platt was pleased because he thought his interests were exemplified in the production, so *Der Tag* was displeased because its were not. "When one thinks of the little theatre with such an artistic and refined atmosphere," *Der Tag* wrote in the week the Neighborhood Playhouse opened, "it is really disappointing that the donors did not think of creating a really Jewish Theatre of art which the Jewish public needs so badly."[22]

In fact, considerable thought and no small amount of energy had been given to the question of a really Jewish Theatre of art by donors and others. Lillian Wald's account of the Henry Street Settlement published in the year *Jephtha's Daughter* opened, 1915, placed under the heading "Social Forces" the fact that "drama is taken seriously in our neighborhood, particularly among people whose taste has not been affected by familiarity with plays or theaters classed as typically 'American.'" Wald pointed to the example of Jacob Gordin, a great playwright of Yiddish theater who had died in 1909. Gordin was known for going beyond the native, folkloric traditions and sentimental vehicles already well-established in Yiddish theater in New York. Wald chose *The Jewish King Lear* as typical of his best and most popular work, and she also described how she brought English high culture to the drama of the people in New York by escorting the Ibsen translator and promoter William Archer to Gordin's *The Jewish Nora*. The issues at play when one took drama "seriously" in her neighborhood, she thought, were American contempt for "the alien" and Jewish suspicion of "Americanization of the immigrant."[23] For her, characteristically, the project was a resolution of the conflict rather than a choice, a compromise solution, or pacification of either extreme. For her, the neighborhood in the theater, as performers and as audiences, synthesized identity and future. For Wald, at least at the time of the building opening, the neighborhood and the playhouse did not rival each other so much as they complemented and completed each other.

Alice, who was much less analytic and programmatic, was both offended and delighted by the negative reactions of the Jewish audience. "Our orthodox neighbors were scandalized at the free interpretation of the Bible text," she wrote in her memoir. "Caricatures of us appeared in the Yiddish press showing 'Miss Neighborhood Playhouse' slamming the door in the face of the Yiddish playwright."[24] There were other criticisms from the local audience: that the performance was insufficiently radical because the text was Biblical instead of taken from such sources as Gorky or Andreyev, and, from other segments, that it was grossly improper because the chorus of girls danced barefoot. But playhouse time for Yiddish playwrights became the primary ongoing issue, especially as the first season continued with performances by luminaries of the New York and London stage such as Ellen Terry and Gertrude Kingston and subsequent seasons gave prime stage time to Bernard Shaw playlets or Robert Browning vehicles, all of which could suggest, to some on Grand Street, an inflexible agenda of high culture and assimilation, along with implicit class insults. Criticism of stifling the local voice continued even after the Lewisohns loaned the theater in its first months to Jacob Ben-Ami, a younger and similarly cosmopolitan force in Yiddish theater as Jacob Gordin, for a production of three one-act plays in Yiddish.

The matter of neighborhood time on the playhouse stage crystallized in the fall of 1915 around the participation of the *Freie Yiddishe Volksbuhne.* The dispute is absent from Alice's retrospect, but it was preserved very well in an oral history of Jacob Fishman, secretary of the *Volksbuhne,* which was later translated and recorded in Doris Fox Benardete's account of the theater. The "Free Yiddish Theater" was tied to more radical agitators in the Workmen's Circle, and these, according to Fishman, reacted angrily to what they perceived as "the stubbornness of an iron will, the wall of assimilation of American Jewish daughters." Members of the Workman's Circle felt that the Lewisohns' offer of an audition rather than a direct grant of theater time proved their hostility to "Yiddish in their temple." In Jacob Fishman's account, the problem was how to "convince the *Yiddishe Shickses* who didn't understand a Jewish word?" So, he said, "one fine day," audition of a folk play by the *Volksbuhne* was staged with an English-speaking prompter: "The prompter wanted to do his best, and he started to prompt on the highest octaves not only in words but also in intonation; and the result was that the prompter started to play theatre by himself, shouting, louder than all the actors combined. Of course this made everybody nervous, and Irene Lewisohn decided that we should have another tryout of the very same play with a little quieter prompter."[25] The subsequent audition was more successful, and the theatre was given over to the *Freie Yiddishe Volksbuhne* for four weekends beginning in January 1916.

The opening prospectus of the Neighborhood Playhouse had advertised its intention "to share in the life of the neighborhood." Its first test did not come from artistic mandarins but from local organizations like *Volksbuhne* that were scarcely older but believed in a prior right to own the life of the neighborhood. In ways that were not fully appreciated by Percy MacKaye or other theorists of the democratic benefits of the little theater movement, creating opportunities for dramatic art to exist and to mature was indeed a matter of participatory civics. However much Lillian Wald may have transcended or appeared to transcend the problem, there was great tension between the neighborhood and the playhouse in the Neighborhood Playhouse.

The new enterprise at 466 Grand Street was not entirely alone in its time, and comparison with contemporary little theater companies helps define its niche. Walter Prichard Eaton was an early historian of the movement, which he claims was sometimes derided by critics as "the Uplift." In his history of the Theatre Guild, Eaton describes its birth as the Washington Square Players in the same week as the Neighborhood Playhouse. The Washington Square Players was created by theatrically minded members of the Liberal Club including Susan Glaspell, Jig Cook, Robert Edmond Jones, and Lee Simonson. Their enterprise crystallized during a reading next door to the club in the Boni Brothers bookshop, a center of Greenwich Village intellectualism. The text for the reading was *The Glittering Gate,* by the Irish playwright Lord Dunsany, whose works later became a staple of Neighborhood Playhouse productions. However, although the Liberal Club was notably activist, and although its theater arm took its name from a locality, its first statement of mission and plans lacked all the emphasis on class and social context integral to the plans of the Neighborhood Playhouse. "We have only one policy in regard to the plays which we will produce," said the opening manifesto of the Washington Square Players, as quoted by Eaton: "they must have artistic merit."[26]

Artistic merit in the opening production of the club, which was staged out of the neighborhood on East Fifty-seventh Street at the Band Box Theatre, was found mostly among members: its program on February 19, 1915, was *Licensed,* a slightly leering exposition on birth control written by member Lawrence Langner under a pseudonym; member Edward Goodman's *Eugenically Speaking,* a more leering extension of Bernard Shaw's enthusiasm for human geneticism; and Maeterlinck's verse drama *Interior* as staged by Robert Edmond Jones. The program closed with a comical pantomime, *Another Interior,* of human digestion with a liquor cordial, played by Philip Moeller, entering the stomach and prompting theatrical representation of gastric upset. In the little theater "Uplift" playoff of February 1915, the degree of engagement, of testing the priorities of art and audience, of challenging commercial wisdom and local traditions, was certainly greater downtown on Grand Street than uptown in the Band Box. Not everyone at the time saw that engagement as an intrinsically good thing. In another early history, published while the Neighborhood Playhouse was open, Sheldon Cheney, like Eaton a greater fan of the Theatre Guild, reported with evident dismay that the Neighborhood Playhouse, while "fulfilling its destiny more flourishingly than any other of our institutional theaters," nevertheless is "likely to be an art theater only second, and a social-experiment theater first through all its life."[27] In fact, the demise of the theater would come when art usurped social engagement.

The subsequent productions of the Washington Square Players continued to feature new work by members and quickly shifted casting from amateur to professional players. Having begun as small and "local," it quickly became big and national in its identity as the Theatre Guild and defined the health of the company in terms of growth. The subsequent season of the Neighborhood Playhouse, however, continued to pursue original artistic mission and educational function on the original scale. In advance publicity for its second opening, a group of one-act plays that followed *Jephtha's Daughter*, Irene Lewisohn was quoted in the New York *World Magazine* on her belief "that every one should have a share in the world's treasures of imagination and poetry, and in return contribute something to the interpretation of human experiences." Organizing a collective contribution, she said, is "the social expression [that] we feel is the really significant purpose of the neighborhood festival and drama." *Jephtha's Daughter* was considered a dance drama, with company corps prepared specifically for its demands. The next production, which opened on March 20, 1915, was considered the first dramatic production, and so the debut in their home theater of the Neighborhood Players.

The program, codirected by Alice and Agnes Morgan, consisted of Lord Dunsany's *The Glittering Gate*, a humorous playlet about petitioners at the pearly gates of heaven which had attracted founders of Washington Square Players and many other little theater groups; *Tethered Sheep*, a comedy by Robert Gilbert Welsh about moonshine in American Appalachia; and *The Maker of Dreams* by Oliphant Down, like Dunsany's work a stage fantasy popular with little theater groups. From the Lewisohn point of view, the goal was more than artistic merit alone. The same magazine article that quoted Irene on goals also quoted Alice on method. "Putting aside for a moment the higher and artistic development which such work must bring," she said, "there is the craftsman side, too, which has practical value. The young men will become familiar with all the handiwork of the theater." For that reason the Dunsany, Welsh, and Down productions were not solely about playwrights or about players: "the community playhouse," Alice told the *World Magazine,* "is really a college of instruction."[28]

In the second dramatic production that inaugural spring, the limits of community and the elasticity of goals were tested. On April 3, with both the dance and the dramatic corps having spent most of their available time in the previous two months performing rather than rehearsing, the Neighborhood Playhouse "college of instruction" was opened for the first time to visitors, Whitford Kane and his Irish Players. Kane was a veteran of the British stage who, like many others, found while on tour that America was also a land of theater opportunity, especially for ethnic vehicles, and supremely so for exoticisms like Irishness that were sufficiently nonthreatening. As he recalled much later in his memoir, in 1915 Kane and his theater colleagues in New York "were both piqued by the fact that New York contained no Irish Theatre, while other nationalities, the Italians and the Jews in particular, were liberally represented by their own playhouses. We were confident that there would be a demand for our product, as we had seen so-called Irish plays done so badly that we could not believe the public would unresistingly swallow such travesties of Irish life for ever." He found his first opportunity in the Neighborhood Playhouse when, invited to do a celebrity turn by the Lewisohns, he lost the leading lady of his customary melodramatic vehicle and instead presented a working-class English playlet by Harold Brighouse, *Lonesome-Like,* and a violent inversion of quaint Irish comedies called *Red Turf* by the Ulster playwright Rutherford Mayne. The program opened with a revival of an earlier Henry Street production in Clinton Hall, *Womenkind,* but its greatest interest lay in the last play, which dramatized murder in a land dispute in the west of Ireland.

The issues surrounding the "real" Ireland on stage had been argued ardently in New York since the visit of the Abbey Theatre of Dublin company in 1911: should the home and heritage of Irish immigrants be idealized to aid their American assimilation? According to Kane, in *Red Turf* "a realistic scene went down hard with the audience":

> One man, unable to contain himself, burst out in the middle of the play, shouting, "Libel! Libel! It's all libel! You're in the pay of the British Government." Before we had a chance to defend ourselves against this attack, our critic added, "If you want to see a real Irish play, why don't you go over to the Lexington Opera House and see *Hearts of Erin*? There," we were informed, "we would see a play about the real Ireland everybody loved, not a sordid story of bickering farmers." We promised our excited playgoer we would do as he wished.[29]

Like the Yiddish press reviewers of *Jephtha's Daughter*, the Irish witnesses to *Red Turf* felt that the "realistic" portrayal was in fact the "travesty" because it did not serve the immediate needs of the group it represented. The Irish constituency had vacated the neighborhood, as the 1913 pageant had recorded, and so complaints about their representation on the Neighborhood Playhouse stage had less immediate impact than complaints about "really Jewish" theater. There were obvious parallels between the Irish and Jewish disputes over the social import of art and the prerogatives of artists and audiences. In the coming years, largely due to the Lewisohns' insistence and sense of cultural parallels, audiences at the playhouse would have regular productions of Irish exoticism in the works of Lord Dunsany, Bernard Shaw, and William Butler Yeats.

Whitford Kane was a great admirer of Helen Arthur and Agnes Morgan, and in the chemistry of the Neighborhood Playhouse he, like them, represented theater professionalism more than the theater idealism that was certainly sought if not always achieved by Alice and Irene. Though the revival of *Womenkind* on this third production slightly covered the program's departure from stated goals—the community playhouse as a college of instruction—the conflict between internal and external productions was evident at this early stage and joined both art priorities and audience priorities as tensions especially evident in the experiment that was the Neighborhood Playhouse. Kane would remain associated with the Neighborhood Playhouse, notably as the lead in its production of Granville Barker's *The Madras House* in 1921. He would be most prominent when the balance of power of the frequent codirectors Agnes Morgan and Alice Lewisohn tilted toward the former. But Kane's personal investment in the Neighborhood Playhouse was limited: this early program of the Irish Players soon relocated to the Band Box Theatre where it would draw on the audience and emulate the plan established there by the Washington Square Players. Later, Kane would portray the "real" Ireland in Belasco spectaculars such as *Dark Rosaleen.*

The goals of the playhouse and the nature of its relation to the settlement were further tested in the inaugural spring season of 1915 by a series of celebrity turns on the Neighborhood Playhouse stage: Ethel Barrymore, Ellen Terry, Gertrude Kingston, and Alice's mentor Sarah Cowell Le Moyne. Barrymore's visit, in April 1915, was a single performance of her current vehicle, *The Shadow,* which she had been playing uptown, and the patron of the downtown performance was her regular New York producer, Charles Frohman. Only one week later, Ellen Terry, then sixty-seven, visited to perform a reading on Shakespeare's birthday. For the occasion, J. P. Morgan loaned a copy of the First Folio and a portrait of Shakespeare for display in the Neighborhood Playhouse lobby. Only a week after that, Gertrude Kingston made her New York debut on Grand Street with her touring London Little Theatre production of Shaw's *Captain Brassbound's Conversion.* And the week after that, Le Moyne performed her Robert Browning adaptation. The last was a timely gift to the playhouse and to Alice, because Le Moyne would die two months later. Interwoven into the schedule of visitors were several productions more in keeping with the settlement aims of the theater, including an in-house production of G. J. Hamlen's *The Waldies,* a festival of games on the rooftop, and a program by the Yiddish Folk Song Singers. But the celebrity visits certainly highlighted the tension within the playhouse between the limousine crowd and the pushcart crowd. In a privately printed commemorative program of the Ellen Terry evening, the unsigned but likely Lewisohn author stated that "the people who make up the audience of The Neighborhood Playhouse, far from the glittering lights of the theatre district uptown, are those who love the theatre and the best things for which it stands."[30] Among the issues developing around this and future Neighborhood Playhouse seasons was exactly what "best" stood for and how far Grand Street was or should be from glittery theater. Lillian Wald was enthusiastic about the visitors. She was as delighted to provide a post-performance dinner for Ellen Terry in the Henry Street Settlement as she had always been to entertain philanthropists like Otto Kahn or even Alice and Irene's father. But the celebrity evenings were not benefits: the gifts from the actresses had been to perform for the regular admissions of twenty-five and fifty cents. They certainly brought the theater credibility, but it was not a credibility that directly lent itself to settlement goals.

The inaugural season of 1915 ended with the kind of burlesque that was already evolving into a ritual. As they had since their first private satire of their own production of *The Silver Box* in 1913, the Neighborhood Players acted out their conflicts in the precursors of *The Grand Street Follies*, now, in June 1915, for the first time performed in the Neighborhood Playhouse. Whitford Kane recalled it as a "a private frolic" in which he and Le Moyne parodied Shakespearean pretensions and, presumably, their recent guest Ethel Barrymore. Agnes Morgan and Helen Arthur, creators of the regular parodies, caricatured Dunsany's *The Glittering Gate* by deflating the aesthetic fantasy with topical references. The play had been Alice's enthusiasm, and Kane recorded that "their burlesque was entirely too pointed in its clever remarks."[31]

The need to counterbalance the celebrity turns and exercises in high art with more evidently local and political ballast was clearly on the minds of the Lewisohns when the new theater season began in fall 1916. The tension between these aims continued to be not just an effect but also the intention of their programming. The opening production of the season was a "Thanksgiving Festival" that returned to the staging of large choruses of children from the settlement as in the pageant of 1913. This new festival was revived for several months and performed on the first anniversary of the building on February 12, 1916. Opening publicity for the new season stressed the scheduled performances by the *Freie Yiddish Volksbuhne,* the Festival Dancers, and the Neighborhood Players. The season included both folk plays, such as *Wild Birds* by Violet Pearn, and working-class playlets, such as *The Price of Coal* by Harold Brighouse, that were performable by children and accessible to young audiences. But it also included one of the first performances at 466 of Ruth Draper's new monologues and an evening of songs by Yvette Guilbert, the "diseuse" then in great vogue for saucy versions of Parisian songs. Among the season's most ambitious performances was the American debut of Stravinsky's *Petrouchka* as scored for two pianos and danced by the Louis Chalif Dancers. It was performed while the Ballet Russes company was in New York, and it shared in the crest of its popularity among uptown audiences. One of the pianists was Charles T. Griffes, whose compositions would be featured prominently after his death in the last seasons of the Neighborhood Playhouse. Griffes's work, like that of the Lewisohns, attempted to bridge high and low culture: at the time of the *Petrouchka* performance, he was also composing musical settings for both Oscar Wilde poems and Rumanian folk songs. The difficulty of actually managing that leap in performance is suggested by Griffes's own comment, on being paid $150 for eight performancs of *Petrouchka,* that the amateur or nearly amateur commitment was "long and tiresome"[32] in comparison with high and higher paid art.

The Lewisohn intention to manage the resolution of conflicting forces was at this early point in the evolution of their theater quite clear and quite determined. Alice used similar language in other publicity pieces, but the most visible at the outset of the second season was a *New York Times* Sunday feature on "The Neighborhood's Year." After recounting the internal productions and the guest performances planned for 1915–16, the *Times* gave Alice several paragraphs to restate the mission of the organization. She repeated her practiced phrases on the imagination of the neighborhood, the benefits to children of exposure to art, and the contributions that can be made in the settlement context. To these she added an articulation of the dual vision of new and old and future and past that produced her programming. First, there was "the desire to widen the vision of the children and to broaden their horizon by giving them an opportunity to glance into other lands and learn to understand other customs and other peoples." The counterpart to that desire was "the wish to revitalize and interpret for them their own traditions and symbols . . . so we set ourselves the task of re-reading the old legends and ritual ceremonies, so full of poetic fancy, that are associated with the Hebrew Festivals."[33] The various criticisms of the first season had not lessened her ambitions. In fact, there was some encouragement: *East and West*, a magazine published in English for a Jewish readership, complimented the Neighborhood Playhouse's "success": "the appreciation of artistic effort cannot be confined to any one locality and although the patrons of the Playhouse have more often come from the West End and the Heights, they have also included those from the East Side who have been sufficiently awake and alive as to what is what."[34] Rather than be content with the mix of a divided audience, Alice would by the end of the second season sharpen a conception of performance that linked drama and dance as resolution of conflicts between high and low art. By this she hoped to combine the internal, stabilizing interests of the neighborhood with the broader, more progressive ones of "artistic effort." *East and West* plainly thought that the neighborhood audience, or at least those who knew "what is what," would be improved by attendance beside the patrons from the West End, and Alice had a similar confidence that they would be improved by exposure to Barrymore, Draper, and others who were especially effective models for young women.

Something of the conflicts they faced, including the great gap between artistic ambition and the minutiae of operating a theater, can be seen in the Neighborhood Playhouse Committee meetings that began in December 1915 and would continue through the last days of the organization and its final debates over moving successful productions uptown. In 1915, one important task was creating a sufficiently democratic process that would prevent repetitions of the episode in which the Yiddish press detected a Neighborhood Playhouse policy of excluding the unfashionable and "really Jewish." Meeting at the playhouse without Alice, who was in London, or Irene, who was evidently outside the city for holidays, Lillian Wald, Rita Morgenthau, Agnes Morgan, other staff members or volunteers, and Grace Mills, who kept notes, began to address matters large and small as a committee on December 20. They were facing a large number of petitions for use of the stage, preferably for free. Their first action was to rent the playhouse to a local orchestra group for fifteen dollars instead of their usual fee of twenty-five. Educational films were also given an encouraging discount as a matter of considerable pride because these differed dramatically from the very popular commercial films educators and social activists deplored. At the first committee meeting, a proposal from Public School 188 that it provide all film programming was declined but left open for discussion. A Festival Dancers production called *The Gifts of the Fairies* was very popular and scheduled for extended performances. A local group wished to send a child to petition its audience during intermissions for donations to the Lady's Auxiliary for War Sufferers; the idea was rejected for the festival performance, but permission was given to show a relevant slide during a break in a film projection. Grace Mills's notes detail low-level management issues at the first meetings, possibly because major ones were deferred until the return of the Lewisohns. But in the midst of her lengthy notes on the cost of a piece of glass for the box office or "Bender the reel winding boy's" request to borrow a piece of equipment for his school presentation, there are suggestions of higher-level issues. Lillian Wald advised against a repeat performance by Ruth Draper, and all present seemed uninterested in trying to schedule the dancer Ruth St. Denis. Individuals were given fundraising assignments such as contacting the Guggenheims about sponsoring *The Gifts of the Fairies* for extended performances. Alice, in London, had written to suggest booking Ben Greet's dramatic company for a New York appearance, but the degree of committee enthusiasm was underwhelming. Whether outsiders were welcome to Grand Street, whether a nonprofit enterprise could balance mission and budget, and the nature of the influence of principal benefactors emerged immediately as issues in these first meetings of "The Committee."[35]

While in London in the winter of 1915–16, Alice missed another series of meetings that suggests something of the context in which a theater made programming decisions at this time. Lillian Wald, New York feminist Crystal Eastman, settlements organizer Paul Kellogg, and others, including Alice, had created an organization to counter the American war industry, or, as one newspaper put it, to "put the fist in pacifist."[36] Originally called the Anti-Preparedness Committee to reflect their sense that American "preparedness" was a misnomer for xenophobia, the founders eventually, after great debate in that winter, renamed the organization the American Union Against Militarism. With Wald as president and Eastman as executive director, AUAM set out to offset a growing military patriotism directed not only at Germany in the years of debate about American entry into World War I but also at American intervention in Mexico. In its first year of existence, 1915, the organization developed a membership of 6,000 and organized public lectures, produced educational material, and lobbied in Congress effectively enough to attract government raids on its offices and post office censorship of its publications by mail. By February 1916, Alice, who was on the executive committee, had returned from Europe and resumed attendance at its meetings, some of which convened in her home on Fifth Avenue. She was evidently a benefactor board member rather than an expert, political, or celebrity board member, and was present but passive at meetings. The affiliation, however, was a significant commitment on volatile issues of the time.

On April 6, 1916, AUAM staged a massive rally at Carnegie Hall in which Wald, as opening speaker, declared that "fear has dethroned reason, and people are seeing things at night." The in-house crowd was a self-selected, positive one, and the external audience was not sympathetic to the position: even Wald's staunch supporter the *New York Times* ran its account under the headline, "See America's Hope in Unpreparedness." On the Carnegie Hall stage, Wald directly addressed President Wilson and ex-President Roosevelt, both of whom she had already met to make this case. In the *Times* account, she denounced the invasion of education systems by military "preparedness" in these terms: "Extraordinary and unprecedented measures have been taken to promote a public demand for military and naval expansion, and these have brought in their train of hysteria the camp followers of self-interest."[37] In a draft of the speech, in words she may or may not have delivered, she directed particular scorn at her friend Roosevelt's enthusiasm for military training in schools as a means to develop health and stamina: "All the available evidence from the days of Athens to our own times, from the age of Alexander of Macedonia to that of Theodore Roosevelt of Oyster Bay, points to the opposite conclusion. . . . Military training in schools tends to produce an unhealthy youth, with distorted views of morality."[38]

Later in 1916, the American Union Against Militarism could claim considerable credit for the change of American policy in Mexico from invasion to restraint. After that, it turned its attention to conscription and World War I. The first meeting of the executive committee after the Carnegie Hall rally was held at Alice's apartment, and she remained on the executive committee until late 1917 when Wald, too, resigned over an internal dispute over priorities and relations with other activist groups. But at this moment, spring 1916, the oddity of Alice, no political agitator, participating in a self-declared subversive union, is best explained as how far she would at least try to advance forms of educational alternatives and cultural intervention over the artistic culture she understood best.

The American Union Against Militarism is a useful reminder of the number of contrary forces Alice Lewisohn was attempting to balance in the first seasons of the Neighborhood Playhouse and of the strength of her conviction that an art theater in a settlement context was ideal resolution for them. The settlement ideals set out by Robert A. Woods of the South End House in Boston, also secretary of the National Federation of Settlements since 1914, set the high agenda of creating for individuals a promising future and of creating social change by organized action. The arts—visual, musical, and theatrical—had been an element of settlement activities since Jane Addams created the Hull House Players in Chicago in 1901, and Hull House had served as a model for Henry Street in the eyes both of the Lewisohns and Lillian Wald. In time, leadership of the settlement movement passed from Woods to his longtime assistant at South End Albert Kennedy, who officially succeeded Woods as secretary in 1922 but had taken a leading role in the Federation of Settlements much earlier. Of Woods's two prongs of individual empowerment and collective action, Kennedy put priority on the first: for Clarke Chambers, historian of the settlement movement, Kennedy was "of all settlement leaders the one most explicitly concerned with the arts, declar[ing] their ultimate intent 'to enrich impoverished personalities, to open the doors of self-expression to thwarted and repressed people of all classes.'"[39] In comparison with Woods, Kennedy put much greater emphasis on the personal dimension of corrective intervention. Their manual of sorts, *Settlement Horizon* of 1922, coauthored but plainly more Kennedy than Woods, found in theater "the pre-eminent settlement pursuit to which the average neighborhood young people come in a state of readiness for discipline and drill. . . . Some who can achieve it in no other way reach personal distinction in acting."

This intervention into education seems rather like Roosevelt's plan, at least as Wald saw it: the end remains personal discipline and strength although the means is art rather than militarism. But the issue in the shift of settlement orientation from Woods to Kennedy, and the issues facing Wald as host and the Lewisohns as creators of theater in a settlement, was whether art could lead beyond personal improvement to public action and social reform. *Settlement Horizon,* even if written as useful strategies for volunteers, suggests an effort to depoliticize the movement. In their chapter on the arts, Woods and Kennedy present "the beautiful" as an unquestioned ideal and direct that "every neighborhood should have one room set apart to show beautiful things."[40] This direction would shift again in the later 1920s, when Paul Kellogg's prominence and political priorities replaced those of Kennedy. In the opening seasons, the Neighborhood Playhouse faced this dilemma of politics and art, of the American Union Against Militarism and "beautiful things," and attempted to resolve them on the stage. The later shift in official settlement orientation, and Paul Kellogg's succession to Albert Kennedy, would coincide with the closing of the Neighborhood Playhouse in 1927. The great years of the Neighborhood Playhouse coincided with the years when official settlement policy defined beauty as empowerment, and that cultural view meshed well with Alice's predisposition to the work of a Draper or Ruth St. Denis over that of a Harold Brighouse or a Violet Pern. But the settlement perspectives would evolve into a political stance where "beauty," or in Alice's preferred term "poetic fancy," was perceived as self-evidently the opposite of empowerment, and that evolution coincided with the decline of the Neighborhood Playhouse.

In spring 1916, the company concluded its second season with a program that best represented its attempt to synthesize politics and art, and its reception was an extraordinary critical and artistic success that vindicated decisions to date and influenced all subsequent ones. The program caused *Vanity Fair* to celebrate the Lewisohns, Helen Arthur, and Agnes Morgan by name, along with the "group of sincere, gifted amateurs skilled in various arts, music and painting included." The *New York Times* called the final of the program's four one-act plays "as fascinating and stirring a play as New York has seen since the season began." Both commented on the great distance—geographical, cultural, and conceptual—between Broadway and the playhouse on Grand Street.[41] There were significant cultural differences between the parts of the program as well. The opening was the English-language premiere of *Mitn Shtrom* by the Yiddish playwright and novelist Sholom Asch as *With the Current*. It was followed by a revival of *The Price of Coal* by the Midlands English playwright Harold Brighouse. The second half began with Chekhov's farce *The Marriage Proposal* (elsewhere frequently translated as "The Proposal"). The conclusion of the program was Lord Dunsany's *A Night at an Inn*, which attracted the most attention, not just of the program but evidently of the New York theater season.

The program was given no collective title, and the individual plays would be revived as parts of different programs. But the sequence as presented on premiere night, April 22, 1916, presented provocative opening and closing images separated by two comical and more innocuous skits on marriage proposals. The Brighouse production was the first American one of this work and followed an English import of his much more popular comedy *Hobson's Choice* the previous fall uptown at the Princess Theatre. *The Price of Coal*, which would be popular with little theater companies because of its small cast and minimal set requirements, presents Jack, a coal miner, waiting for a decision from Mary on his marriage proposal. Jack goes to the mine, his mother enters to report on her night of dark dreams of pit accidents, the mine alarms sound, and after comic business between the women Jack reappears only slightly harmed and his proposal is accepted. The sentiment, delivered by the mother—and to judge from the Neighborhood Playhouse script, very much in full Midlands accent—is that "There's women keepin' house in the places the coal goes, that pay for their coal with money. We pay a sight heavier fer it

here. We pay wi' the lives o'men.'"[42] The Chekhov piece, one of his original stage farces rather than a stage adaptation of a story, presented the
quarrels of an engaged couple with amusing commentary by the girl's
father. Like the Brighouse, it was a slight piece that lent itself to minimalist production. Also like the Brighouse, the Chekhov was an early representation of that playwright on the American stage. Chekhov had been
produced in New York before but mainly by Russian émigrés. A month
after the Neighborhood Playhouse produced *The Marriage Proposal*, the
Washington Square Players staged *The Sea Gull*, but widespread productions of Chekhov in the United States still awaited inspiration from the
Moscow Art Theater's touring visit in 1923.

The lighter fare in the middle of the program may have been intended
to control the potential for pretentiousness in the very new and striking
one-act plays that opened and closed it. Sholom Asch's work was known
in Europe and had been produced in Germany by Max Reinhardt, whom
Alice Lewisohn admired and visited. At the time of the production of
With the Current, Asch had not yet become, as he would, the prominent
Yiddish writer determined to open orthodox Jewish ways of life to gentile
audiences. Later, in New York in 1923, his *God of Vengence*, about a brothel
owner who buys a Holy Scroll, was picketed by offended Jews. Even later,
in the 1940s, his novels in Yiddish on Christian themes (*The Nazarene*,
The Apostle, and *Mary*), were angrily denounced by Jews and even some
progressive journals such as *Forward*, which had published earlier Asch
works. But in 1916, in New York at least, Asch was a new and unfamiliar
source for dramatizations of lives most like the lives of the neighbors of
the Neighborhood Playhouse. *With the Current*, and the program as a
whole, opened with the curtain rising to reveal a full set of a bookish
apartment. In the opening dialogue, the wife of a rabbi, Hindel, consoles
her daughter, Rachel, who is distraught over her husband's restlessness.
Later, while offstage sounds mix murmuring prayers with the crackling
ice of a frozen river, the husband, David, laments his tradition-bound
life: "Our long, dead winter stretches from generation to generation. The
Father passes it to his son, and the small child as soon as it opens its eyes
is taught to be old." In words that must have been resonant on Grand
Street, David vows that "I don't want my boy to be a dried-up ghetto

child." The rabbi, Reb Zorah, enters, delivers Biblical prophecies, and tells David that "We need no Jews like you." David leaves, the rabbi cuts his and his daughter's clothing, and chants, "Our inheritance is turned to strangers, our houses to aliens, our children to the stranger."[43] Jews in the audience, if not the theater press, could closely identify with the conflict between tradition and individualism in characters visibly and culturally like themselves and recreated onstage by friends and relatives in the settlement dramatic club.

Lord Dunsany was already well known for fantastic playlets and stories, but on this program his *Night at an Inn* gained from the emphasis on aliens and strangers established by *With the Current*. The Neighborhood Playhouse had produced his *Glittering Gate* the previous year, and Dunsany, or Edward Moreton Plunkett, had been so delighted by what he had heard and by what he had seen in set designs that he gave Alice *A Night* for its world premiere. Done with a full, constructed set, and so without the cyclorama, the play presented three merchant sailors and one newly destitute aristocrat ("the Toff") in a roadhouse admiring a ruby they have stolen in the east from a Buddha statue. They soon learn that they have not completely shaken the Priests of Klesh who guarded the statue, and most of the play's action is a slow and suspenseful pantomime in which the Toff lures individual priests from outdoors into the roadhouse, where they are captured and stabbed to death by the sailors. After the third priest has been killed, the sailors are congratulating themselves, when, with elaborate light effects and sounds, the statue itself appears and reclaims the ruby. The statue then exits and offstage calls the individual sailors by name to come to their deaths, which they do. In the final stage image of the evening, the offstage, heavily accented voice calls to the Toff ("Meestaire Arnold Everett Scott-Fortescue, late Esquire") to come to his death.

The script for *A Night at an Inn* did not soften Dunsany's language about "niggers" and "black devils,"[44] and although the production was most often praised for its sustained suspense, any audience, whether from Grand Street or only visiting Grand Street, would recognize in the play presentation of East and West, of empire and colonials, and the violence acted on the stage as a paradigm of dispossession and a belated vindication of the oppressed. It was the work of a British baron, but it could not be considered propaganda for assimilation and Americanization. The casting aided provocation because David in *With the Current,* the blasphemer of tradition, and the Toff in *A Night,* the thief of holy relics, were played by the same actor, David Solomon.

Although derived from the clubs and the amateurs of the Neighborhood Players and situated as far from the theater epicenter as the island of Manhattan would allow, the production values and even the location of the program were universally praised—somewhat incredulously—by the press. The *Times* celebrated in perfectly usable blurbs the location ("not in the Strand nor on Broadway but in Grand Street at the little Neighborhood Playhouse") and advertised that the program ("half-hysterical with excitement" and "stirring beyond belief") "richly rewards a journey." The real rewards, though, from the *Times* account, were to be found in *A Night at an Inn.* It was also *A Night* that most mesmerized Clayton Hamilton when he covered the opening for *The Bookman* and even when, twenty years later, he reflected on his forty years as a drama critic: "I now realize that the most thrilling single hour in that long experience [the forty years] was furnished by the Neighborhood Playhouse, at 466 Grand Street, in the midst of that vast and somewhat East-of-Suez region which is generally labeled the Lower East Side." In retrospect, he recalled his own sense of the audience in the theater, with "audible gasps of irrepressible excitement," including his seatmate Alexander Woollcott, who "gripped the arms of his seat so tightly that I could clearly hear the nervous scratching of his fingers on the wood."[45]

The program was a striking success as measured by the criteria set by Alice at the outset of the first season. By subject and by means of production, it shared in the life of the neighborhood and satisfied settlement ideals. In its gushing reception by the mainstream press, it satisfied artistic standards as well. The fully realized performance integrated local participation and high artistic values. In the coming seasons, the Neighborhood Playhouse could pursue its mission with real credibility and consider new options from the advantageous position of already having a role in both the life of the neighborhood and in the theater world of New York City. Immediately, however, a tension between new terms of praise and previously formulated goals began to test the mission of the theater. The press had given *With the Current* the same praise but not the same space as *A Night at an Inn*. In a series of summer benefits for organizations such as the Women's Trade Union League and the United Neighborhood Houses, *With the Current* was dropped from the program and replaced by lyric dances and excerpts from *Petrouchka*. Introduction of the dances helped to better balance stage time and exposure between the Festival Dancers and the Neighborhood Players, both of which were clubs formed from the neighborhood. However, dropping *With the Current* had the effect of removing Jewish subject matter, and with it another dimension of the life of the neighborhood, from the theater repertory. While clubs continued to perform folk dramas of Jewish and other origin, the most dramatic return of Jewish drama to the main stage and major productions would not come until 1925, with *The Dybbuk*. That return would represent the highest artistic and popular success of the company. But in the summer of 1916, the Asch play *With the Current* went without revivals, unlike the Brighouse, the Chekhov, and the Dunsany. In the years between it and *The Dybbuk*, the theater when weakest featured less threatening exoticisms, especially Irishness, in the years when, as Wald proclaimed in Carnegie Hall, "fear has dethroned reason, and people are seeing things in the night."

3

1916-1920

Art, Militarism, Movies, and Mission

In early August 1916, after the great success at the end of the second season and anticipating the options that would open for the theater, Alice Lewisohn drafted and redrafted a new declaration of goals that she labeled "Statement Aug. 1916." The opening read, "Before developing more intensively for another season the activities of the Playhouse, we want to consider very carefully our trend, so that we may be quite sure that we are carrying out our obligations." In her first draft, the "obligations" were "to the children." In the typescript that finally emerged, the "obligations" were "to those who come under our direction." The hardening of the language represents very well the gap opening between the "trend" and the "obligations" of the playhouse as soon as its second season concluded. This distance between opportunities and mission would be managed but never completely resolved by extensive administrative effort over ten years. As early as August 1916, or eighteen months after the opening of its theater building, the Neighborhood Playhouse, to use Alice Lewisohn's favorite metaphor, faced temptations to stray from its chosen path.

Alice's drafting and redrafting of a mission statement reflects the changed relation of the playhouse to the neighborhood that would prevail from 1916 though 1920 and the new producing agenda that would prevail from the third through the sixth seasons of the Neighborhood Playhouse. Following its early years of settlement activities and its two debut seasons, these next four seasons represent the first fully formed, operative, public identity of the company. In a paragraph of "Statement Aug. 1916" later deleted completely, Alice stated her sense of accomplishments to date:

> From the first festival in the settlement gymnasium which crudely attempted to weld ancient ritual and ceremonial into an art form, through the production at Clinton Hall of the first play, a poetic drama dealing with the Russian Revolution [Dargan's *The Shepherd*], to the final production of last season, the audiences have always been considered an integral part of the performance. Whether the theme has been an interpretation of the orthodox Hebrew ritual or the imaginative flights of Dunsany, these audiences have exemplified the cosmopolitan interest that drama inspires.

The later drafts dropped this paragraph and all other characterization of the theater as an audience-driven enterprise. That sense of relationship was replaced by a new "standard of aesthetic appreciation." In one draft Alice called the new standard a "lighter" one, and in another she called it a "higher" one. Her new conception of the playhouse role was to improve the neighborhood by bringing into it a higher form of cultivation as exemplum, and not, as she had said in earlier years, to better the neighborhood by creating that model within it.

In one heavily revised sentence that emerged, the new standard would be "a more cultivated use of leisure, a more socialized art, and therefore social contribution should be along those lines." In the rewriting process, "cultivated use of leisure" was inserted in front of "socialized art." In March 1915, Alice had told *World Magazine* that her community playhouse was "really a college of instruction" with crafts and practical value. In August 1916, in a declaration of intentions that would never circulate in public, she wrote that:

> Sensitiveness to aesthetic emotion is necessarily the characteristic of a comparatively small group. In order to meet this real and vital need it is important to intensify the training along art lines. Temporarily it may be necessary to exclude other opportunities and even social meetings of the club group just as a college career may postpone entrance into the social world of activities. This does not mean that we need to create a profes-

sional group or concern ourselves only with genius, but it does mean that we feel that a certain number of those adapted tempermentally to this experience should have their leisure freed to dedicate themselves to the pursuit of an art expression.

In fact, in 1920, after pursuing this new expression for four seasons, the Neighborhood Playhouse would indeed create a professional group. But at this moment, in the summer of 1916, Alice was confident that the higher standard of art expression could be accomplished within the amateur and club forms of settlement structure, even if they needed to be amended to allow a more leisurely pursuit of art freed from "the social world of activities." Her sense of obligation had not lessened, but her focus had shifted from playhouse participation to playhouse product. "We believe that the real obligation of the P.," she wrote in closing the "Statement Aug. 1916," "is to create an atmosphere for those who desire to forget themselves in the pursuit of an art expression."[1] This atmosphere, constructed and subsequently revised, would include both a new foundation in professionalism and ultimately allow enterprise into the noncommercial theater in the form of uptown transfers from Grand Street to mainstream theaters.

Alice raised the curtain on what she had brought to the neighborhood on November 14, 1916. The *Times* gave it the slightly qualified praise as "the dramatic event of the week," one that, even though located on the Lower East Side, would "shift for a while the center of things theatrical" because it brought to New York "the foremost Irish dramatists—George Bernard Shaw and Lord Dunsany."[2] Alice referred to the plays as "The Two Queens," meaning Dunsany's *The Queen's Enemies* and Shaw's *Great Catherine,* and by that obscured from her memory the opener, Shaw's *Inca of Perusalem,* which featured a princess if not a queen. The program featured three strong female characters; exoticism in Incan, ancient Egyptian, and Russian royalty; and both direct and indirect allusions to the war in Europe. But the nature of the works certainly dulled the female edge of works like *Jephtha's Daughter* or the ethnic one of *With the Current.* The program represented two potential administrative paths for the playhouse. The first, in the new Dunsany, was to capitalize on critical success, in this case by bringing back the playwright of *A Night at an Inn*. In this Alice was encouraged by Dunsany, who continued to be delighted with reports of his productions in the United States and so offered the unpublished script of *The Queen's Enemies* for a world premiere at the Neighborhood Playhouse. The second, evidently promoted by Helen Arthur, was to build audiences with celebrity appearances, in this case to engage Gertrude Kingston, who, as earlier with *Captain Brasshound*, was on American tour with vehicles written for her by Shaw. Both directions pragmatically mixed artistic with commercial incentives. But the activist edge of performance and direct address to the local audience, alternatives best promoted by Lillian Wald, were absent from this program and diminished over the four seasons of the first playhouse identity from 1916 to 1920.

Alice certainly had her own interest in Kingston, and in her memoir she later described how at that moment "everything about Miss Kingston . . . savored of the theatre of sophistication and intellectuality."[3] Kingston had been a starring ingenue of the London stage, working with large late-Victorian theater conventions like those of Beerbohm Tree. In 1910, almost at the age of forty-five, she revised her repertory and her stage persona, and established her Little Theatre of London, one of several models for the Neighborhood Playhouse. Then she found in Shaw, with his relish for reversing stereotypes, an ample source of witty and frivolous playlets in which, in these examples, the empress of Russia throws a British officer into a dungeon and tickles him, or a quite capable woman seeking an inheritance outwits a caricature of the kaiser, played by an actress who had already transformed herself. Shaw had been well known in the United States for many years: his first substantial royalties had come from American productions by Richard Mansfield and Arnold Daly of works such as *Arms and the Man* and *Candida*, in which antimilitarism and feminism were evident. But Kingston brought to the United States the later works of Shaw, who himself characterized *Great Catherine* as "boyish rubbish . . . a music-hall sketch and utter slosh at that."[4]

The opener of the premiere of the 1916–17 season, *The Inca of Perusalem*, had the novelty of being both a new play and an American premiere. It had been first performed only a month earlier, in Birmingham, with a cast that Kingston left in England when she sailed on tour. It features the very capable Ermyntrude Roosenhonkers-Pipstein, played by Kingston, in extended argument with an "Incan" dressed and moustachioed like the kaiser and evidently not directly portrayed in London as such for fear of offending the lord chamberlain with his censorship powers. The play suited the little theater model in that it had minimal production requirements, only six characters performing before a curtain backdrop, and intellectual ambitions. But it may have failed for too much intellectual ambition: *Theatre Magazine* of New York, predisposed to defend little theater, described how "the Kaiser, nobility, democracy, the United States, war, nationalism, and humanity are among the targets at which Bernard Shaw fires his broadsides."[5] None of the notices commented on the neighbors of the Neighborhood Playhouse as members of the audience; if present, they must have been conspicuous by their difference from most of Gertrude Kingston's loyal audience. The overall program was successful, and that success was based in large part on the attraction to the Lower East Side of an audience unlikely to be there without an uptown lure.

Great Catherine was more familiar, and it had already been published and produced to excellent notices in London and in Boston. In it, the empress, in a throne room, a bedchamber, and a torture chamber, all represented minimally by individual furniture props, is revealed in witty repartee to have ordinary, bourgeois yearnings for company and love. Her visitor, an English officer in full Light Dragoons uniform, is wooed by the empress but remains faithful to his fiancée and to English values. Catherine bravely consoles herself with her project, the Hermitage. The highest praise that the *New York Times* could muster for the event of the week was that it was "gay and competent."[6] Perhaps precisely those values limited its welcome on the Lower East Side and enhanced it uptown.

In January, *Great Catherine* transferred to the Maxine Elliott Theatre (by February *Inca* was replaced on the program by another Shaw playlet in Kingston's repertory, *Overruled*) and so became the first Neighborhood Playhouse production to move uptown to a larger house and away from the Lower East Side. Alice claimed that the reason for the transfer was *Catherine*'s popularity and the impossibility of extension at 466 because of another production in rehearsal. But the reception was not overwhelming, and the other production, C. B. Fernald's *The Married Woman* by the

Neighborhood Players, was in fact postponed. In her memoir, Alice did concede that at least one factor was Kingston's fee, which, as a percentage of box office, was minimal at 466, where admissions were still fifty and twenty-five cents for less than 400 seats. Kingston did much better at the Maxine Elliott, and in the program there Helen Arthur, who still had ties to the Shubert organization and understood theater as commerce at least as well as theater as art, was listed as her manager. In the memoir, Alice noted that Kingston's fee for *Catherine* was "nominal," but reasoned that "all the professionals in the Playhouse productions received their slender weekly envelopes in the spirit of an honorarium, proving again and again that the actor in those days was seeking something Broadway could not offer."[7] The issues clearly emerging were whether professionals could participate on honoraria, which Kingston appeared to answer in the negative, and, if not, whether the kind of art expression Alice now intended to provide as exemplum for the neighborhood could be created without professionals. *Great Catherine* moved uptown because it was limited in both artistic and commercial success downtown. This was or should have been a useful reminder of the distances both geographical and cultural between the two and that whatever a company chose to import to a neighborhood would have to have the characteristics to succeed there.

The opening and the closing one-acts on this program got most of the public attention, but the middle play, *The Queen's Enemies*, got most of the Neighborhood Playhouse effort. It had a larger cast than the others, it was performed in elaborate costume on a full set equipped for special effects, and it featured Alice's return to the stage. The casting emphasized Alice's personal connections with Dunsany, which were very advantageous to the company as his work became better known in America. When *The Queen's Enemies* opened, Dunsany's work was simultaneously in production at Stuart Walker's Portmanteau Theatre, one of the forerunners for all little theater in the United States. The Neighborhood Playhouse trumped all the others by having the only Dunsany world premiere.

However advantageous Dunsany may have been for publicity purposes, he was not easily promoted as a social activist or his work as something likely to advance the civic purposes of little theater or the social ones of the Henry Street Settlement. William Butler Yeats, who produced

Dunsany at the Abbey Theatre in Dublin, published his work through the allied Cuala Press, and even managed to enroll Dunsany as benefactor, several times characterized Dunsany in variations of the phrase "very nearly very good." On one such occasion, writing to Gordon Craig, Yeats said of Dunsany: "He is splendid for a scene and then all goes to pieces. But what is good in his work is nearly as good as it can be. It is all worked out of time and out of space. Impossible cities, and impossible wilderness, and people with wonderful names, invented by himself, but alas! It is a great misfortune to be born to the Peerage, life is too pleasant for him. Fifty pounds a year and a drunken mistress would be the making of him."[8]

Yeats would be produced later by the Neighborhood Playhouse, and Dunsany would be revived. But in 1916 there was a New York audience that concurred with Yeats's sense of Dunsany's work. Of the Stuart Walker production of his *Gods of the Mountain* that opened at the same time as *The Queen's Enemies, The Theatre* magazine said that Dunsany "has the trick of writing in what may be described as the fifth dimension."[9] That review, like others, focused on the fantastic dimension, at best aesthetic, at worst irrelevant, of what Dunsany referred to as his "fables." The Dunsany-Shaw program featured what the press described as "the foremost Irish dramatists," but both the Shaw and Dunsany works were very selective representations of things specifically Irish. While the Dunsany productions played in New York, newspapers there were filled with reports on the executions or the releases from internment of the Irish nationalists of Easter 1916. As Yeats put it, Dunsany was "too pleasant" to be representatively Irish at the time, and the Lower East Side portion of the playhouse audience, whose interests were guarded vigilantly by Lillian Wald, was not likely to be interested in anybody's "fifth dimension."

Both Shaw and Dunsany were identified by place—Ireland—while their work was place-less, or at least in reference to no place, and so an alternative to identity as defined by place or origin. That was not consistent with the settlement and playhouse ideal of integration of history and assimilation. An antidote to place must have had its attractions for the neighbors of the Neighborhood Playhouse in particular, as they were rooted in minority cultural identity and urban ghetto. The unintended effect of what Alice brought to the neighborhood, performance of Irish dramatists whose work was without reference to locality, may have been to please an audience oppressed by place. But the more ambitious agenda for the playhouse and the settlement had been to integrate identity into American life, and momentary escape from that effort would not satisfy a determined activist such as Lillian Wald.

The Queen's Enemies, an Egyptian fable, was not totally without relevance to the program or to the audience. It was consonant with a program featuring strong women and antiwar sentiments. As she enters a stone vault beneath the Nile, the queen is introduced by a lament: "If they could see my tears they would never permit such woes to be borne by one small woman. But they only look at men and their horrible wars. Why must men slay one another and make horrible war?" The men and rivals begin to enter, down steps at stage right, for they have been invited to a banquet. In processional movement, and at the Neighborhood Playhouse to original chamber music, the various Egyptian warlords enter, dine warily, and then move to an offstage room stage left. In the printed text, the queen, chanting, slowly exits up the steps:

> I have prepared a sacrifice to god. Men speak of other gods: there is only Nile. I have prepared a sacrifice of wine—the Lesbian wine from fairy Mitylene—to mingle with your waters till you are drunken and go singing to the sea from Abyssinian hills. O Nile, hear me.[10]

Then, as critic Clayton Hamilton described the performance, "The river rises, and pours through a grating in the wall of the underground temple. In utter darkness, we hear the gurgles and the gasps that mark the drowning of the incarcerated enemies of the Queen. Then a sudden torch appears upon the outer stairs. The Queen ascends serenely to the upper air. She has no enemies anymore; and she will sleep in peace."[11]

Dunsany's stage directions for the flood seem to imagine a water effect with gauze, as in old melodramas. But the Neighborhood Playhouse production, much to his delight, contrived a more vivid effect with its new lighting console, and the lighting operator, unusually for the time, was given a separate credit on the program. The photographic record

4. *The Queen's Enemies* downtown in 1916, with Alice Lewisohn, right, as the queen and George Abbott, left, as one of the twin dukes of Ethiopia.

shows the set to have been a detailed mock-stone backwall with hiero-glyphics, downstage column for depth, and a cluttered forestage of banquet props, all designed, as the program noted, to suggest "an early dynasty." Alice, in a robe with bare shoulders and a serpent headpiece, appears in photos as beautiful and supremely confident in a stylized regal role directly antithetical to Kingston's portrayal of a Catherine from ordinary life. In her memoirs years later, Alice's account of the production omits the fact that when it transferred uptown, the role of the queen was taken over by the young Catherine Nesbitt. Alice had retired from the professional stage ten years earlier, in 1906, when the heiress identity was revealed, at age twenty-three, as "Eleanor Leigh" in Sarah Cowell Le Moyne's *Pippa Passes*. When the queen, at age thirty-three, stepped out of Dunsany's play, the reviews of the uptown transfer praised how she had "created beautifully the role of the little queen when the production was made in Grand Street." But they had even higher praise for Nesbitt.[12] The

5. Alice Lewisohn in costume for *The Queen's
Enemies*, 1916.

memoir suggests that for Alice the downtown obligations were greater
than the uptown ambitions and the mixed results of the transfer uptown:
"This Broadway misadventure was a timely reminder that our way was
not along the thoroughfares, but in lonely bypaths, coping with the
many-faceted problems knocking at our door."[13]

   This was not the last "misadventure" or the end of debate over the
organizational function and relative benefits of the conflicting playhouse
roles as epitomizing either professionalism or education. The debate derived from an important conflict in the Neighborhood Playhouse, which,

like all nonprofit cultural institutions, was confronting issues on revenue means for noncommercial ends. Alice's unannounced resolution in the summer of 1916 was to create on Grand Street an "atmosphere for those who desire to forget themselves in the pursuit of an art expression," which would seem to invite recreation more than reform. The opening program of 1916–17 was not conspicuously activist, although the antiwar sentiment was not without significance in the United States in 1916, particularly on the Lower East Side, which in the era of "preparedness" was associated and justifiably so with sedition and resistance. But the production advertised instead what it called "Dunsany's Celtic imagery," "poetic feeling," and "the poet who retires to the realm of fairy tale."[14] On the basis of this production and others, the very influential journal of advanced thought on theater of the time called *The Drama* celebrated Dunsany for epitomizing "the little group of dramatists who have created an international interest in Irish drama" because of its "insistent note of lyricism . . . willful aloofness from the mechanistic aspects of life, and a feeling for its ever-present wonders."[15] So what comes to identify one group of "Irish dramatists" is absence of praxis and presence of wonder, including a Celtic ethnicity that was acceptable and unthreatening in a place, lower Manhattan, that was an intense locality very familiar with dangerous ethnicities. The great final productions of the company, *The Little Clay Cart* and *The Dybbuk,* would restore the focus on specific cultural identities and express that focus in cultural identities less accommodating than Irish.

Testing goals and importing quality had the effect of bringing in new parties to the internal debate. Some merely passed through: in *The Queen's Enemies,* George Abbott, three years after his New York stage debut and fifteen before his great successes in Broadway farces, appeared as the second of the twin dukes of Ethiopia. But some additions to the company became fundamental influences on its management. The Shaw-Dunsany program had the interesting effect of bringing formally into playhouse roles Aline Bernstein, costume designer for *The Queen's Enemies,* and Albert J. Carroll, who played small roles in both the Dunsany and in *Great Catherine.* Aline Frankau Bernstein had turned thirty-six years old during the run of performances. Carroll, only twenty-one at the time of the program, had come to New York from Chicago in search of a stage career, and had first entered the playhouse orbit by performing in educational dramatic "interludes" during film evenings at the theater. He would become professionally known for *The Grand Street Follies* before, during, and after the formal end of the Neighborhood Playhouse. He shared with Agnes Morgan and Helen Arthur a commitment to professional theater and its benefits for performers and audiences alike. These six—the four N.P.H. women, Carroll, and Bernstein—were primary directors, formally or informally, of the future of the Neighborhood Playhouse. The financially independent ones were a minority of two. So when Alice determined to use professional means for settlement ends, she had indeed set "many-faceted problems knocking at our door."

Even after the success of two Lord Dunsany programs, the Neighborhood Playhouse scarcely "sold out" to uptown glitter. Rather, it began to address as a company the many issues raised by its success, and in this process it began to rechart its future. The company's powers of self-critique can be seen both in comparison with comparable contemporaries and in the kinds of programming that followed Kingston's Shaw and Lewisohn's Dunsany. The Washington Square Players had opened in the same month as the Neighborhood Playhouse's opening season, and its famous corollary the Provincetown Players opened in New York City in the same month as the Neighborhood's third season. While *Great Catherine* and *The Queen's Enemies* program was in rehearsal as the season opener on Grand Street, Provincetown made its New York debut on November 3, 1916, with O'Neill's *Bound East for Cardiff* in a brownstone building on MacDougal Street in Greenwich Village. The group had been in evolution during summers in Provincetown, Massachusetts, with some overlap of the Washington Square Players, including Susan Glaspell and Jig Cook. Among the distinguishing features of the new company were that it would be solely amateur, because, as Glaspell described Cook's convictions, "the gifted amateur had possibilities which the professional may have lost." Provincetown did not have organizational affiliations like the Neighborhood Playhouse's with the Henry Street Settlement. Glaspell quoted Cook's belief that "To me my own nature is more fascinating than Rousseau's, revealed in his 'Confessions,' or Goethe's in his 'Poetry and

Truth,'" and also his absolute confidence in his new group: "There are more interesting things latent in their minds than they have yet written or acted. Their hope is greater than it was in the beginning."[16]

The Provincetown project took shape from principles different than the Neighborhood Playhouse or even Alice Lewisohn's private revision of them in August 1916. In September 1916, Provincetown members gathered at John Reed's house in Cape Cod and passed a series of group resolutions, such as "Organization is death!" Others included "the resources of the theatre . . . shall be placed at the disposal of the author" and "the author shall produce the play without hindrance, according to his own ideals." The first Provincetown expressions were by O'Neill, who as a matter of organization insisted on the name "Playwright's Theater" for the original improvised and unlicensed playhouse. The company brought to the Greenwich Village neighborhood O'Neill's *S.S. Glencairn* sea plays, including *Bound East* and also, by the beginning of 1917, *Fog*. The opening production of *Bound East,* with makeshift scenery, costumes by Jig Cook's mother, and bench seating for 140 summoned to the "club" by circulars, was attended by the nationally celebrated actor James O'Neill, Eugene's father, whose presence underscored the contrast in performance between the commercial stage and the bohemian one. O'Neill biographers Arthur and Barbara Gelb surmise that the showcase for the playwright satisfied Eugene, at least, while "the under-rehearsed actors were barely competent by professional standards."[17]

The Provincetown Players were certainly an influential literary company simply on the basis of staging the first Eugene O'Neill productions. But O'Neill's own success would eventually break up the company in 1920, when the downtown production of *The Emperor Jones* was celebrated sufficiently to move with great success to Broadway and thus to alienate purists of the company. As the Washington Square Players closed and reopened as a more commercially competitive Theatre Guild in 1919, so the Provincetown Players closed for a "sabbatical" in 1922 and reopened in 1924 as an uptown entity led by O'Neill, Kenneth Macgowan, and Robert Edmond Jones. By contrast, after its success uptown, the Neighborhood Playhouse, anchored by both its building and its principles to Grand Street, honored standing commitments while contemplating evolution. Decades later, in her memoir, Alice Lewisohn characterized the principal innovators at this juncture in American theater history. For Alice, Washington Square had "their intellectual outlook and interest in glittering innovations" and Provincetown was "dedicated to authorship . . . a source of inspiration to personalities." Neighborhood, however, was "experimenting toward a synthesis of expression . . . was neither a place for the intellect alone, nor just a laboratory in experimental drama . . . [but] potentialities which belonged to the function of theatre."[18] It was an ambitious foundational agenda that she and her company evolved in negotiation and experimentation and did not abandon as quickly or as completely as their contemporaries did theirs.

Unlike Washington Square and Provincetown, the Neighborhood Playhouse made exploring both a local and a general audience a priority, and at times this could be one of the least glamorous of the potentialities of theater. In the fall of 1916, after its successes with mainstream theater audiences and recognition in the New York press, the continuing cultivation of the Lower East Side audience began to provoke some defensiveness within the company. All reviewers alluded to the remoteness of the Neighborhood Playhouse and its exotic audience. Soon after the opening of the Shaw and Dunsany program, Rose Schiff, chair of the Neighborhood Players, wrote to the *New York Times* to protest what she took to be the patronizing tone of reviewers not familiar with the Lower East Side. "Is there any worthy reason why critics persist in disparaging the locality of the Neighborhood Playhouse?" she asked in print. Offense had evidently been given to reviewers by hats that were not removed and by apples eaten during the performance, so Schiff responded that "it is far from good taste for those who are versed in the superficialities of etiquette to make comment upon them and especially openly to criticise them."[19] The presence of the Jewish audience was in fact a considerable achievement given the cold local reception originally given the Lewisohn "heiresses," and the company, even while sorting out priorities, managed to remain true to its project of engaging the neighborhood.

The programming in the 1916–17 season engaged both uptown and downtown audiences and balanced several theatrical functions that the theater hoped to synthesize. Despite a delayed opening because of the

success of *Great Catherine* and *The Queen's Enemies*, the following production, Chester Bailey Fernald's *The Married Woman*, opened with full participation from the settlement clubs. It was a slight play, in which an
unhappily married woman contemplates—inconclusively—an old lover.
It was performed on weekend evenings while matinee time was given
over to revivals of old festival performances such as *Hiawatha*, now almost
ten years old, by the "Junior Players" and dance programs by the "Junior
Festival Dancers." Wilfred Wilson Gibson's play *Womankind*, not performed since the Clinton Hall days before there was a theater at 466
Grand, was restaged by club members and alumni in January 1917, with
readings of poetry by the playwright. These works were given time equal
to Dunsany or Gertrude Kingston on the playhouse stage, though not in
the New York press.

In the 1916–17 season, several important elements of the playhouse
mission were reaffirmed, if not resolved, by the spring production of *The
Kairn of Koridwen*, a "Dance Drama in Two Scenes" set to music by
Charles T. Griffes. The original production had been in evolution since
the previous summer, when Irene Lewisohn contacted Griffes, a few
months after his performances at the piano for *Petrouchka*, about composing musical accompaniment for a dance she had already planned. *Kairn*
was a story derived from Édouard Schuré's *Les Grandes Légendes de France*
about "Druidesses" who are discovered in worship of "Koridwen," god-
dess of the moon, by a male warrior. One druidess, Carmelis, is charged
to kill him, but instead spares him and poisons herself before she is discovered by the other druidesses of Séne. The opening required dance by
the ensemble of Festival Dancers, including Irene as Carmelis and
Blanche Talmud, a genuine company discovery through settlement activities, as the head druidess. The program distributed to the audience
explained, "The ceremony, accompanied by rhythmic movements, describes the circle of the universe and unfolds to them the three planes of
existence. One by one they respond to the spell, and interpret in esoteric
language the principles of their faith—individuality and universality, liberty and light."[20] The second scene was built around Carmelis prophesy-
ing the warrior's great future and then releasing him by boat before
ending her own life with a potion of hemlock. The lighting effects were

again given separate credit, and the design plans of the production, by Herbert Crowley, who a few years later would marry Alice, were on display in the lobby.

Neighborhood Playhouse programs credit the 1913 pageant as the first of its "Lyric Dramas," but *Kairn* was the production that brought dance and festival principles to the priorities of the repertory at 466 Grand Street. It gave Irene, aged twenty-four when *Kairn* opened, a lead role, a director's role, and a management role equal to Alice's. She was quite specific in her instructions to Griffes, who was told to create an "exact musical counterpart" to her own "carefully clocked libretto of movement." The dancer and the composer had an ongoing argument over whether a conductor would be used, and when *Kairn* finally opened on February 10, 1917, with a conductor, Griffes, at the piano, she battled him over the tempo. Helen Arthur managed that artistic dispute and also contentious union negotiations encountered for the first time when the production requirement of a large number of professional musicians coincided with contemporary labor organization. In reviews, the dance was rather less positively received than the music, which was analyzed in detail by the influential critic Paul Rosenfeld and considered of importance by even more mainstream a critic as A. Walter Kramer. "Mr. Griffes has written a tone poem in the ultra-modern idiom, one of the first works by a native American in this daring style to have public performance," Kramer wrote in *Musical America*. "Whether the general public approves of it musically or not, one must confess that it has the quality of compelling attention and of stimulating the imagination."[21]

However mixed the reception, in February 1917, or on the second anniversary of the opening of the theater, *Kairn of Koridwen* established in the Neighborhood Playhouse programming both dance and participatory elements essential to the Lewisohns' original plan and, ultimately, to the company's greatest successes. The full program included "Three Dance Processionals" by the Junior Festival Dancers before the main program by the Festival Dancers, and in this differed from the kinds of programs like Kingston's that imported art to the settlement instead of creating it there. Dance as taught and studied in this context was a new and important extension of settlement ideals. The dance historian Linda Tomko, writing specifically about the Neighborhood Playhouse, argues that in this instance "female settlement workers took advantage of the cultural moment to introduce and develop new dance practices":

> A specific conjuncture of people, theories, and events positioned women settlers to develop dance practices as direct forms for engagement with pressing Progressive-era problems of immigration, ethnicity, and urbanization. At the same time, the vaunted flexibility of settlement methodology and the cultural staging ground afforded by "residence" in urban neighborhoods empowered women settlers to exceed and refigure public sphere identities for themselves as aesthetic workers and also as social welfare laborers.

The result, apart from the experience of creating the productions and experiencing them, was development of a succession of important dancers emerging from the Lower East Side. Irene's favorite student was Blanche Talmud, a performer at the Neighborhood Playhouse including *Grand Street Follies* from 1925, whose own classes in "Interpretive Dancing" created a next generation of Jewish women choreographers such as Helen Tamaris, Anna Sokolow, and Edith Segal, all of whom worked on Broadway musicals as well as dance programs. Settlement student time in the dance studio provided the kind of personal affirmation that was quite close to Lillian Wald's goals and quite distant from Alice's creation of a Dunsany program. Tomko has collected recollections of the classes and rehearsals. Tamaris recalled that "Miss Talmud was tall and slender as a reed and spoke just as Miss Lewisohn did in a soft gentle voice. . . . We danced in a circle facing each other—and Miss Talmud would say—'The Grieg Music,' or 'Now we'll have Chopin.'" Sophie Bernsohn Finkle, a Festival Dancer in productions in the 1920s, told Tomko, "There was no ballet, of course. It was modern dance. You closed your eyes and had a good time. Technique came later."[22] This was an especially liberating experience in the setting of the Orthodox Jews who had objected to the chorus of girls in bare feet when *Jephtha's Daughter* opened the theater building. Though *Kairn* was not acclaimed, the most important of the later productions of the Neighborhood Playhouse, such as *The Little Clay*

Cart or *The Dybbuk,* would descend from elements integral to it and absent from the Shaw/Dunsany kind of program: designed by movement as much as by text, created in and from the settlement setting, and reflective of Irene's vision as well as Alice's, it managed to combine the "ultramodern idiom" with broad settlement participation.

The competing visions and obligations that would characterize the progamming of 1916–17 season and the three years that followed it are all evident in the close of the third season. The series of productions that followed alternated between distinct senses of mission and audience without any synthesizing vision of theatrical or institutional function. The first program that followed *Kairn* was an unlikely linking of an antiwar piece called *Black 'Ell,* a slight comedy of old age from the prolific Alvarez Quintero brothers of Seville, and a revival of *A Night at an Inn.* The program opened on March 24, 1917, and *Black 'Ell* had been published only a month before. It was printed in the February issue of *The Masses,* the proletarian politics and culture magazine edited by Max Eastman, spouse of Crystal Eastman, who had been president of the American Union Against Militarism since 1915. As the United States neared commitment to the war, the magazine had abandoned class critiques for a variety of antiwar polemics, including a satirical "Preparedness" issue in the summer of 1916. *Black 'Ell* was a direct pacifist appeal to the damaging human costs of war beyond combat casualties. In it, a patrician English "hero" returns from the front shattered by the experience of killing, and the kindly housemaid, whose own son has been reported dead, turns vindictive: "I wish black 'ell to them wot killed 'im, and if there's any justice in 'eaven, God'll give it to 'em."[23] Its odd companion piece in the program was *A Sunny Morning,* by Serafin and Joaquin Alvarez Quintero, in which the elderly Dona Laura, played by Alice, trades humorous pearls of wisdom with the elderly Don Gonzalez, played by Albert Carroll. *A Night at an Inn,* which closed the program, was now also announced as the first title in a new book series, "The Neighborhood Playhouse Plays."

Black 'Ell was in the Saturday and Sunday evening performance schedule by the Neighborhood Players when the United States entered the war on April 6, 1917, and this clearly pleased Lillian Wald much more than Alice Lewisohn. In her memoir, Wald described entertaining military officers and politicians at a penultimate performance, which came after the declaration of war. She describes how "the play had attracted the attention of pro-militarists; that same evening a group, probably sent to pass judgment, left the theatre with ostentatious disapproval." The next day, the final performance day, the commissioner of licenses banned performance. Wald went to the commissioner of police and promised that if the performance was banned she would greet the audience personally, inform them of the act of censorship, and lecture them on the significance of the intervention. The ban was retracted, although there were many subsequent orders of censorship affecting this theater and others in the war years and immediately following them. It speaks volumes about the evening's triple program and the state of Neighborhood Playhouse programming at this date that Wald's recollection includes no reference whatsoever to *A Sunny Morning* and that Alice's memoir includes none to *Black 'Ell*.

A number of dance programs followed the *Black 'Ell* production, and these had the benefit of maintaining Irene's voice in the programming, bringing in positive influences such as the choreographer Louis Chalif and training new groups of Henry Street Settlement students and a corps of Junior Festival Dancers. However, in the midst of these overlapping dance and lyric drama programs, there was another production that could not be mistaken for make-believe, a fifth dimension, or abstract placelessness. In a guest appearance that was quite unlike any previous celebrity turn, in late April—after the American entrance into the war— the Neighborhood Playhouse hosted the District of Columbia branch of the National Association for the Advancement of Colored People and their production of Angelina Weld Grimké's *Rachel*. The play had been written the year before and remained unpublished. Unlike Grimké's lyric poetry, which had been published, the play, billed as a "A Race Play in Three Acts," presented in very raw terms the subject of lynching and the impact of racial violence on black Americans. The Neighborhood Playhouse program has been lost, but when the same group produced the play in Washington, D.C., three weeks earlier, the program announced that "this is the first attempt to use the stage for race propaganda in order to enlighten the American people relative to the lamentable condition of ten millions of colored citizens in this free Republic."[24] The play, like *Black 'Ell*, emphasized the aftereffects of atrocity: in Grimké's work, Rachel, an African American "new woman" of enormous vitality and potential, on recognizing a lynch-mob murder in her own family's past, vows never to marry or bear children into racist society. Alice's recollection, years after the fact, was only that "a self-made play and production by a group of colored actors from Washington was one of the first attempts of the Negroes to express their values in the theater."[25] A visiting producton could not be extended, but it is significant that when the 1916–17 season concluded by remounting the triple bill, *Black 'Ell* was replaced by a production of Susan Glaspell's *The People*. This was a satire of a publication much like *The Masses,* and the production had moved from the Provincetown Players up in Greenwich Village down to Grand Street. The effect was to replace the politics of the original bill with comedy and programming on atrocity with satire of foibles. The collaboration also had the quality of consorting with the competition uptown, or at least a little less downtown, and asserting their art priorities over social ones.

Compromising programming adjustments were particularly visible at a time of polarized politics. The Espionage Act became law in 1917, and it protected militarism from opposition by mail. It was soon followed by an amendment known as the Sedition Act of 1918, which made resistance to militarism criminal. In this context, Lillian Wald, with Alice as a somewhat reluctant coconspirator, pursued the cause of the American Union Against Militarism. In May 1917, after the American declaration of war, and simultaneous with the Neighborhood Playhouse decision to mount a revival of *A Night at an Inn* and to abandon the productions of both *Black 'Ell* and *Rachel,* the Union announced its "War-Time Program." This took as premise that "America's entry into the world war makes more necessary than ever before all efforts to maintain democratic liberties; to destroy militarism; to build toward world federation and the ultimate abolition of war."[26] It had been a year since the rally at Carnegie Hall where Wald excoriated American presidents current and past, and that year had plainly come to test Alice's commitment to the beautiful over the political. On June 21, 1916, or six weeks after the Carnegie Hall rally, Alice hosted a meeting of the AUAM at her home at 43 Fifth Avenue, and the outcome was a resolution for strong telegrams to President Wilson condemning the planned actions against Mexico. A few months later, minutes of AUAM meetings record Alice reading a response from Wilson about the organization's position on conscription. A year later, after passionate debate over whether pacifism, a position of increasing influence during the war, was in any way compatible with antimilitarism, the more aggressive prewar ideal to which Wald remained faithful, Alice's name remained on the letterhead of the AUAM. In September 1917, the organization, against Wald's advice and threats of resignation, and meeting in Waverly Place instead of at Alice's, changed its name to the Civil Liberty Defense League and so shifted its attention from world to domestic issues. At that point, Alice's name disappeared from its letterhead along with Wald's. But they were not completely removed from the activist orbit. One month after that fundamental division in antiwar activism in American politics of the period, Crystal Eastman, who chose American civil liberties as her primary front, wrote to Wald to ask for a donation and to propose that "perhaps we will be able to come down to some Play House function early in the winter."[27]

It is probably not possible to overestimate either the direct or the indirect cost of Henry Street Settlement stands on principle in this period of suspicion and xenophobia. One indication of the kind of surveillance that might have resulted is the correspondence that came to Wald from Esther Lape, "Adjunct-General's Office," in the state capital of Albany, on May 29, 1917. Lape's letter has been lost, but Wald's response makes clear the justifications required of a public corporation not evidently in compliance with wartime measures. In her response, Wald justified the settlement's "mobilization" response, particularly because "The Neighborhood Playhouse, a theater belonging to the Settlement and run by it, is advertising the State census in its screen and flashing on the same at each performance statements explaining the census, and urging all people to register promptly." Further, the "Nursing Department of the Settlement offers home nursing care to all families of enlisted men in which cases of sickness occur." Thus having accounted for the settlement's contributions toward both the uncounted masses of the Lower East Side and to the counted casualties of war, Wald dismissed the adjunct general's inquiry with the offer that, "if there are any questions you need otherwise which this statement does not make clear, I shall be glad to answer them."[28]

Wald's reference to the "screen" is of course to a cinema screen, and the showing of films in the theater of art was and would be an ongoing debate for much of the history of the Neighborhood Playhouse. To some extent this was a debate of its time. *The Birth of a Nation* opened at the Liberty Theatre on Forty-second Street in 1915 one month after the Lewisohns opened their theater at 466 Grand Street; major theatrical producers such as David Belasco and the Shuberts were linking film and theatre finance; and even performances such as a famous melodrama on Broadway called *The Alien* combined screen and stage effects in the performance of a single drama. But in the early days of film, screenings by a nonprofit, educational organization raised issues not relevant to Broadway. Alice recorded that the first "picture program" in the Neighborhood Playhouse was shown on February 22, 1915, or in the first two weeks of its existence. It certainly served the purpose of audience development, especially of children, the principal beneficiaries of the Henry Street Settlement. Alice described a playhouse packed with children at admission of five cents (*The Birth of a Nation* opened at $2.00) to see motion picture clips of a dog at play, a cat with a litter, and similar subjects. Movie programs became the weeknight offerings of the playhouse when the schedules of dramatic and dance productions performed by amateurs were limited to weekends. Friday evening movies became popular as a Jewish family outing, with, according to Alice, "mothers with a shawl over the sheitel, sometimes led by a young Miriam in her American clothes." The 399-seat house allowed up to 600 for the children shows, Saturday "Children's Matinees" built around film were introduced, and the audience became regulars. "Some of these youngsters established a banking system at the box office, bringing a penny at a time for deposit until their capital had accumulated to five cents," Alice wrote in her memoir. "Frequent were the visits of these anxious young depositors to Miss Kaplan, the Treasurer, to check their balances."[29]

While they were in the house, the children also watched various "interludes" of drama or dance. This fulfilled the mission of introducing the children to the arts, even as a captive audience, and also had the pragmatic effect, by testing the cast, of building and training the house company. Some aspiring professionals such as Albert Carroll made their first appearance at 466 in the interludes of a film program, and playhouse discoveries such as the dancers Blanche Talmud and Lilly Lubell developed their stage experience before audiences more or less lured in by the likes of Douglas Fairbanks and Mary Pickford. But as film took on more of the characteristics of popular entertainment, the conflicts in this programming between audience development and audience education, between the movie clips and the interludes, between art and commerce, became more evident. In the summer of 1916, drafting a brochure for the new season, Alice wrote that film, especially in conjunction with children's entertainment at matinees, "gives the Playhouse a wider connection with the life of the neighborhood." A sentence later she referred to "those people who enjoy this short and inexpensive form of entertainment." A report on the playhouse drawn up a little later, in fall of 1916, for the Henry Street Settlement suggests some of the underlying artistic resentment at film's popularity: "the purpose of continuing the Motion Pictures is to give a standardized performance for Five cents."[30] During the stage success of *Great Catherine* and *The Queen's Enemies* in the fall of 1916, extended performances downtown before the transfer uptown postponed film programs at 466, and the local audience was vocal in its disappointment.

In spring 1918, a report on the popular children's matinees was prepared by Grace Mills, house manager from opening until official appointment of Helen Arthur to the role later in the same year. She reported fourteen Saturday matinees with a collective attendance of 6,043, an average of 431, and overfilled houses of up to 700. "The attendance at the Saturday matinee is controlled almost entirely by the kind of picture which is presented," she wrote. "If a picture in which Mary Pickford or Marguerite Clarke appears is given, the attendance is always sure to be very large. I cannot feel that matinees of this sort serve any particular purpose, except that of amusement."[31] Helen Arthur, in this role, would have a greater tolerance for amusement but also a lower tolerance for what the theater purists here refer to as "standardized performance." Increasing regulation of the film industry in New York City, and increasing control of film production by a smaller group of financiers, would create additional friction between high art and popular entertainment on Grand Street. Doris Fox Benardete, who was with the playhouse during the rise and fall of film's role within it, recalled that "restrictions established in 1920 by the Picture Managers board requiring moving picture houses to exhibit assigned and designated programs could not be tolerated by the Lewisohns, who chose always to have a free hand in determining what their audiences would see. With the establishment of such restraints, the directors felt that the Neighborhood Playhouse, forced to become only another local moving picture theatre, would serve no useful purpose."[32] The Lewisohns would eventually abolish film from 466 Grand Street, but they could not do so easily, and film would remain a good indicator of relations between the playhouse and the neighborhood.

"The Directors" had not by any means forsaken their idealism as they became better acquainted with barriers to it both internal and external. Their fourth season of 1917–18, the only full wartime season, was built around a fall production, *Pippa Passes,* and a spring production, *Tamura;* both followed from Alice's earlier resolution to introduce the neighborhood to high art of impeccable pedigree. This, the programming insisted, was what Benardete termed, in paraphrase of the Lewisohns, a "useful purpose" for the playhouse. The two principal internal productions of 1917–18 successfully advanced the case that the educational goals of the settlement and its playhouse might in fact be best realized by art rather than either politics or amusement.

Pippa Passes was very deliberately modeled on the Broadway matinee production of 1906 that featured Alice, under an assumed name, in the supporting role of young bride to Sarah Le Moyne's principal role of Monseigneur. Le Moyne had become a very active volunteer in dramatic activities at the settlement, particularly in voice and diction coaching. She appeared in a Browning program at the conclusion of the first season in the new Neighborhood Playhouse, and then she had died in that summer of 1915. She had been as powerful a mentor to both of the Lewisohns in arts as Lillian Wald was in politics. By the fall of 1917, she was memorialized at 466 in the "Le Moyne Club," a fund-raising, advisory group organized around "hostesses," or benefactors, who rented an existing staff room for dramatic readings, literary discussions, or purely social gatherings. By the end of the year, rentals proved so disappointing that at a final board meeting Wald "suggested that possibly the Players would prefer to rent the Room only for Saturday and Sunday nights next season."[33] That is, in Wald's estimation the potential for generating support through the image of a stage diva irrevocably associated with Browning was evidently so weak that it had to be coupled with prime weekend theater performances. But in the beginning of the season, Alice expected Le Moyne material and production strategies to have as formative an effect on new students as they had had on her eleven years before.

Browning's marriage vignette presented a parable of art unadulterated by compromise that followed from Alice's standing expectations that everyone on the stage and watching it be prepared, as she wrote in her draft mission statement of 1916, "to dedicate themselves to the pursuit of art expression." A passage of the verse that Alice chose later to represent the play suggests how substantial a counterbalance *Pippa Passes* was to film. The speaker is the sculptor and wedding groom Jules:

> Shall to produce form out of unshaped stuff
> Be Art—and further to evoke a soul
> From form be nothing? This new soul is mine!
> > . . . Oh, to hear
> God's voice plain as I heard it first, before
> They broke in with their laughter . . .
> > Stand Aside—
> I do but break these paltry models up
> To begin Art afresh.[34]

The text has origins as remote from "amusement" and from the origins of the neighborhood audience as *A Night at an Inn*, which despite its own exoticism became the first production to be revived at the Neighborhood Playhouse. Like *A Night*, *Pippa Passes* included enough racial undertones in one character's general denunciation of religious people including Jews to suggest something about the producer's remoteness from neighborhood sensitivities. The Lewisohns were intimately involved in the production, and they presented themselves onstage for audience reaction: Irene as the young bride once played by Alice, and Alice as the spectral figure Pippa. Their determination to advance their case for the union of settlement ideals, by casting an amateur in Le Moyne's role of Monseigneur, and of art, by dispensing with incidental popular music introduced in 1906 in deference to Broadway appeal, was as uncompromising as the sculptor's.

Their ambitions were rewarded when, after a full summer of rehearsals, it opened on November 17, 1918. It was so successful with all audiences that it became the first production of the Neighborhood Playhouse to be revived in its opening season. To Alice, the success had less to do with the critical reception, which was positive and respectful though not ecstatic or enthusiastic, or with attendance, though all performances in the initial run were sold out, than it did with creating the playhouse aesthetic from neighborhood resources. In her report to the board at the end of the year, and the end of the *Pippa* revival, Alice wrote:

> The designs were made and the settings designed and executed almost completely over the summer. The play was read and practically cast last spring and a great deal of preparation was underway before the rehearsals began in September. They had to be completely recast on account of enlistment, illness, and changes in the plans of some of the Players. The entire group of players and many of the Festival Dancers were drawn upon for the cast. There had never been quite so much interest in any of the productions on the part of the players as during *Pippa*.[35]

Forty years later, in her memoir, she would remember this production of *Pippa* as proof of "the creative dynamic often referred to as the spirit of the Neighborhood Playhouse, a spirit lovingly guarded by the searching need of the amateur."[36] If art seemed to some vain and vacant in a context of racism and nativism, Alice had with *Pippa Passes* demonstrated in production organization educational and vocational benefits that were not evident to the settlement in the production organization of more explicitly political performances like *Black 'Ell* or *Rachel*. The remarkable quality of social activist goals in competition with artistic ones in at this period, which are epitomized by the record of the Neighborhood Playhouse, was how competitive they were, how they improved each other, and how together they constituted an extraordinary civic debate.

In her report at the end of the year, Alice observed that "the third season of the Neighborhood Playhouse seemed in many ways the least eventful," by which she meant it lacked the high profile productions like Gertrude Kingston's and *A Night at an Inn*. At the same time, she believed that in this season "there has been a steady and growing interest on the part of the audiences and greater ease in the facility and organization of the productions."[37] But both the theater's relation to audiences and the means of production can be seen in retrospect as issues in these opening seasons rather than as strengths, and they can be seen as especially prominent issues in the principal production of that spring of the third season, in 1918, of *Tamura*, a Japanese Noh drama.

In London during the previous year, the Lewisohns had seen productions of W. B. Yeats's "Plays for Dancers," such as *At the Hawk's Well*, which were performed in parlor settings with the Japanese dancer Michio Ito. Ito came to New York in the fall of 1917 and would remain based in the United States until the 1940s. According to Doris Fox Benardete, Ito eagerly joined the Lewisohns because he saw only high art universal values at their neighborhood playhouse: "'Art,' he said, 'knows no nationality. It is the link that will eventually bind all men in the bond of understanding.'"[38] Alice's account, also in retrospect, is rather different: "his contact with the West, via Dalcroze in Hellerau, had deflected his interest from his native culture. Western art, Western ideals, Western music were firing his imagination."[39] The production is a good example of the more complex relations of art and culture than Benardete or Alice recognized, or at least admitted. Here, the artist ostensibly not recognizing nationality introduces Asian aesthetics to Western context, does so in the new world after having done so previously in Europe, and brings both immigrant consciousness and Japanese culture to a neighborhood fully familiar with the first through a distinct and well-defined racial identity of its own. He also does this stimulated by Western culture and so to some degree seduced away from his own, as in the dilemma of assimilation. The complexity of the cultural transaction was reflected in the distinct accounts it produced in participants. Alice claimed that the power of the Noh drama was that it "had nothing about it that could tie it to anything the audience might recognize as familiar"; Irene's notes on the performance script open by explaining that "this play is to be re-garded as one of those dealing with the pacification of the country and the driving out of evil spirits."[40] In *Tamura* there was an opportunity to achieve both high artistic ambitions and cultural commentary on the world war joined by the United States twelve months before and not brought to armistice until six months later.

6. Michio Ito in costume for *Tamura*, 1918.

The production was celebrated for its stage presentation in movement, music, and chant of the texts that had been in some literary vogue since being edited and published by Ezra Pound and then adapted by Yeats. The first part of the drama presents a Boy in conversation with a traveling Priest, Waki, danced by Irene. In the second part, the Boy returns a war hero, leading the Priest to pray for peace in a dance to percussion music suggestive of war. The Priest is rewarded with the appearance of Tamura, an ancient apparition, danced by Ito, who restores peace. But the aesthetic of the production was effective enough for the composer Charles Griffes, who had very strong opinions and high standards, to praise it as "a most strange and at the same time wonderful effect."[41] In addition to the talent of Ito and the choreography by Irene, the production introduced stage use of masks long before the Provincetown Players used them in Strindberg in 1925 or O'Neill became celebrated for his use of masks in *The Great God Brown* a year later. While the principal dancers performed in masks, their lines were chanted by members of the chorus, with the priest's lines voiced by Alice and those of Tamura by Ian Maclaren, a professional actor who would join the Neighborhood Playhouse full time when it became professional several years later. The effect must have equaled Yeats's sensation, reported in his influential 1916 essay "Certain Noble Plays of Japan," that as Ito danced one watched him "recede from us into some more powerful life." The Lewisohns knew Yeats's work with Ito from their London visit, and they would open their tenth season at the Neighborhood Playhouse with his work *The Player Queen*. But within the context of the Henry Street Settlement and current mission statements of the Neighborhood Playhouse, they could not have endorsed Yeats's contempt in the same essay for what he called "the common people" or the "mob" who fell so far short of his preferred "aristocratic form."[42]

In retrospect, the tension between service to "the common people" and ambitions toward "aristocratic form" is evident in the notes of the year-end meeting held in the Le Moyne Club at 466 on May 7, 1918. The meeting was attended by Lillian Wald, Rita and Henry Morgenthau, the principal benefactors and volunteers second only to the Lewisohns, and the N.P.H. women to date, whose attendance was recorded as "Miss Morgan, Miss Alice, Miss Irene, Miss Arthur." There was a great deal of success to note. During the year, a Pitt Street Annex had opened around the corner with direct connections to the playhouse through the back alley. That provided new rehearsal, shop, and storage space that made tighter performance scheduling possible and no doubt pleased the professional ambitions of Agnes Morgan and Helen Arthur. Students in the Neighborhood Playhouse drama clubs had been used in productions by both the Provincetown Players and the Washington Square Players, and students from the dance clubs had received scholarships to private, elite dance schools and companies uptown, which must have been considered success in the philanthropic plans of Alice and Irene. Lillian Wald could take satisfaction in the fact that the season had opened with a suffragist benefit that raised $850 in a single performance and that by its end Winthrop Ames, the leading little theater producer in New York, had joined with the Neighborhood Playhouse to produce "a theatre experiment" for the War Service Entertainment Committee. All were involved in preparations for the annual end-of-the-year festival, in this case a Pentecost festival, with settlement students and amateurs performing orchestral music, operetta, "a performance which the Players and Festival Dancers are working up by themselves," and an open workshop in the annex "so that the parents of the children will have an opportunity of seeing this side of the work."[43]

However, the actual programming of the season continued to pit competing visions of artistic and theatrical ideals against social, activist ones without resolution. For the May 1918 meeting, Alice provided "a general report for the season" that recorded but did not address conflicting interests that she had hoped, in mission statements and revisions of them, to resolve. In addition to the principal productions, *Pippa Passes* and *Tamura,* the most publicized events had been celebrity appearances by Edith Wynne Matthison, in a performance of Shakespearean roles, and Yvette Guilbert, in a medieval French play with songs. At the other end of the spectrum, the playhouse hosted the Yiddish Players and the Workman's Circle. The latter, while its work was "produced in a very crude and simple manner, have always made an appeal to the audiences," Alice's report noted. The company had also provided a program for the Menorah Society: the original program, Alice's report explained, was dropped "because of the uncertainty of the draft and the large number of men [in wartime] it required, and also because of general sentiment on the part of the players that it did not present the finer side of Jewish character." On the continuing popularity of films, Alice reported with satisfaction that "this is the first season in which it has not been necessary to substitute a motion picture on any week-end night for a regular performance." Evidently not solely intent on recruiting the neighborhood ethnicity, she did record of *Tamura* and its slighter companion piece *Fortunato* that "as a result of this bill many Japanese and Hispanic people come regularly now."[44] Caught between her intentions to improve the neighborhood and to represent it, and three years after she opened the building with *Jephtha's Daughter,* Alice and company began to represent race and ethnicity from a safer distance, to address local issues indirectly through more innocuous, for the time and the place, exoticisms and ethnicities than Jewishness.

The company programming got consistently weaker as it became more aestheticized: the 1918–19 season at the Neighborhood Playhouse did not open until Thanksgiving, it included only two principal productions, and the numbers of guest productions declined to a single one, the [Isadora] Duncan Dancers, which performed outside the usual calendar in early October and during the summer. This was a season in which New York's mainstream, uptown theaters hosted a hit from Chicago called *Friendly Enemies,* which, at the time of Armistice, presented in comic fashion German (i.e., Jewish) Americans fighting on both sides of the war. New York's downtown theater season included the opening of the Theatre Guild, fashioned out of the failed Washington Square Players, and a satire by Sinclair Lewis called *Hobodemia,* in which the bohemians prove their narcissism.

In this context, the Neighborhood Playhouse's principal contribution was *Guibour,* a medieval miracle play not remarkable for relevance or transcendence of narcissism. The play served as a vehicle for Yvette Guilbert, who provided the text from an authentic fourteenth-century source called *Un Miracle de Nostre Dame,* took the title role, cast members of her entourage in salaried supporting roles, and offered Alice the role of her daughter and Irene that of Our Lady. Taking place during the Hundred

Years War, the narrative follows Guibour, wronged by small-town gossip, from the arranged murder of her son-in-law to the execution pyre to an act of clemency from Our Lady. Guilbert's reputation at this time was built on provocative cabaret songs from the Latin Quarter, and later she would be known as the woman whose portrait hung in Freud's study at 19 Bergasse. Her role in *Guibour* allows her to represent evil:

> Lordings, kill me a man. That is my will. Albeit he is a friend of mine and one well loved. Dig deep in my purse. Line your wallets till they bulge. The man whereof I speak has cost me my fair name—because of him I am the scorn and mock of everyone. My heart is broken with sorrow and grief has withered me. I cannot speak to you of this in seemly wise, my words to will, my head is fire.

Without actual contrition, or even rationalization of her act, she is bound to the funeral pyre outside the church when Our Lady, played by Irene, in the stage effect of a statue coming to life, steps down from her pedestal to march through the crowd: "Friends, ward off the fire from my loyal servitor. Let not the flame come nigh her. Guibour, courage, keep a stout heart, your prayer is heard; neither fire nor torment shall have power to harm you."[45] As a result of the miracle, the neighbors of the town are filled with clemency in place of spite.

The production is notable for being the only full one at the Neighborhood Playhouse designed by Robert Edmond Jones, who was in the beginnings of his great design career. His work had been followed closely in New York since the opening of his design for Granville Barker productions in the old Wallack's Theatre in 1915, one month before the opening of the Neighborhood Playhouse. His work there was notable for geometric designs in place of realistic ones and lighting without footlights; both were styles favored by the Lewisohns. At the time of *Guibour*, Jones was between a production of *Hedda Gabler* with the stage diva Nazimova and a celebrated ballet-pantomime in medieval romance style called *The Birthday of the Infanta*. Later, of course, he became more closely associated with the work of Eugene O'Neill and the Shakespeare productions of Arthur Hopkins, including those parodied in *The Grand Street Follies*. The vision that he brought consistently to all design for the stage was later articulated in writing: "Think of this moment. All that has ever been is in this moment; all that will be is in this moment. Both are meeting in one living flame, in this unique instant of time. This is drama; this is theatre—*to be aware of the Now*."[46] This passage is from an essay, "Art in the Theatre," that acknowledged influence from William Butler Yeats's "Plays for Dancers," those performed by Michio Ito, and also the Abbey Theatre of Dublin's first New York tour, which also influenced the Neighborhood Playhouse's continuing infatuation with Irish things, or at least writers.

However, the contexts of these productions often conspired against a Pateresque conception of art as a living flame, and the remoteness of work from context was especially difficult to maintain in a spectacle, like *Guibour*, which portrayed neighbors being transformed before an audience

7. The Robert Edmond Jones design for *Guibour*, 1919.

of neighbors at the Neighborhood Playhouse. Like *Tamura,* also a drama literally remote from Grand Street, *Guibour* invited contextualization by the audience into terms of World War I and pacifism. The continuing audience at 466 could also make connections between this production and previous ones of females in scenes of violence in *Rachel* and the building opener, *Jephtha's Daughter.*

If the audience was slow to contextualize, some stood ready to help. The files for the *Guibour* production include a broadside, apparently distributed independently, that quoted passages of Guilbert's many antiwar statements, including:

> This war! It is the failure of man, the proven failure of his civilization, the frank avowal that his poor instincts have remained in their brutal, primitive condition—the cruel piteous admission as to that single motive, which still fascinates him and which is sufficiently intoxicating to rally men in their thousands to the banner of one sole cause—that of murder.[47]

The actual program notes, by contrast, emphasized the production's ritual qualities and its image of "so picturesque an episode of French Life in the Middle Ages."[48] The directors of the Neighborhood Playhouse consistently located the value of *Guibour* in terms reminiscent of Jones.

But that appears not to have been the full power of *Guibour.* After closing at 466, Guilbert and the whole company and design moved uptown to perform a benefit for the Visiting Nurse Service of the Henry Street Settlement in March. The event raised $1,800, a considerable sum, from an audience of benefactors who, however comfortable in the settings of a Broadway theater, were at least half conscious of the social welfare purpose of the event and the antimilitarism of the performance in addition to the "one living flame" and the "picturesque episode of French Life." One trivial indicator of the full tension between the art and activist identities of the Lewisohn theater enterprise at this point in 1919 can be seen in the publication of *Guibour* as the second of the Neighborhood Playhouse Plays begun with *A Night at the Inn.* For *Guibour,* the series inexplicitly and pretentiously became known as the "Neighbourhood

Playhouse Plays" and the place of production the "Neighbourhood Play-house." The Anglophilic affectation did not endure.

There was only one other major internal production in the spring of 1919: a program of original one-acts built, like *Guibour,* around strong female figures. The opening dramatic plays were *Everybody's Husband,* on freeing a heroine from an arranged marriage, and *The Noose,* on a wife's denunciation of her politician husband's toleration of racial lynching. The closer and featured act was *The Last Megalosaurus,* a pantomime on cave-men and cave women at war. The general critical reception was fatigue with feminist programming and disappointment with design quality, previously, and especially through Robert Edmond Jones, a trademark of the company. The *New York Times,* a staunch supporter of the Neighbor-hood Playhouse, ran a notice that opened, "Woman reigns triumphant in the bill of one-act plays which the Neighborhood Playhouse in Grand Street has put on for a series of Saturdays and Sundays. Three times is Mere Man flouted and scouted." The reviewer, John Corbin, reported general audience delight with some cave-people business such as mixing cocktails in coconuts, but found the overall effect "quite out of tune with the militant mood which dominates the Neighborhood Playhouse."[49] It is unclear from the review if he was referring to a militant feminist agenda inside the playhouse or to the militant class and ethnographic struggle outside the playhouse as most evident to occasional uptown visitors to Grand Street.

For what it lacked in strong dramatic programming in the spring of 1919, a spring that included no festival, the playhouse substituted a series of lectures on "The Relation of the Arts to the Theatre." The project had begun the previous fall with a demonstration of the theater's state-of-the-art electrical lighting. The plan was very directly to find occupations for the house on off nights other than movies. In late summer, Helen Arthur wrote to Lillian Wald to apologize: "Today at the meeting we neglected to tell you that next Tuesday evening on the stage and in place of the movie that Agnes Morgan will give a demonstration of the technical side of setting a stage. She will try to make it as amusing as possible." In the kind of correspondence that suggests distance rather than intimacy or solidarity, Arthur also offered, "I thought perhaps some people from the settlement might be interested" and reported a plan for fifty-cent tickets, the price of the balcony for a theatrical program. Across the bottom of her typed letter, she clarified, in handwriting, the policy on house complimentary passes: "Irene says this doesn't mean the household—they are invited."[50] Agnes Morgan and Dennis Sullivan, the lighting operator, gave demonstrations in fall, and in spring the series was fully launched with twelve lectures by speakers associated in one way or another with the playhouse: Alice and Irene, Robert Edmond Jones on "Costume and Color," Helen Arthur on "The Aesthetic Side of Business Management," and, to the largest house, Guilbert on "The Art of Interpretation." *Theatre Arts Magazine,* the leading proponent of little theater, found the series to be a model for the rest of the country. In an editorial feature, the magazine complimented the company for a series intended "to augment the cultural background of the young people who are acting and working in the various groups of the Playhouse, to furnish an artistic stimulus for them, and to demonstrate anew the value and necessity of a correlation of all the arts in the work of theater." It also praised the earlier lighting demonstrations for attracting an audience "whose only connection with the Playhouse was their constant attendance at its motion pictures" and then showing those unsuspecting moviegoers the power of theatrical "technical exhibitions": "Such is the appeal of 'behind the scenes.'"[51]

For all the success of the lectures, the following season, 1919–20, the Neighborhood Playhouse's sixth, reached a programming nadir that not coincidentally coincided with newly dismal relations with the Henry Street Settlement. This occurred at a time when the broader settlement movement itself was in flux. The chilly relations suggested by Arthur's letter on "some people from the settlement" was evident in the fall of 1919 at a higher level. On November 17, Wald wrote to "Dear Alirene":

> A gentleman sitting next to me at the Playhouse Saturday night observed that there ought to be something on the program to indicate its connection with the Henry Street Settlement. He very intelligently remarked that it might be considered money making in the view of the large audiences, but that it was even more important to suggest to sluggish minds that there was a social movement back of all the performance.

To this end she suggested "one line somewhere on the program" that acknowledged the Henry Street Settlement. "If you two think there is any question of the propriety of this," she wrote in the same letter, "we can discuss it." Alice and Irene's response is not archived in the correspondence. Evidently it was one of resistance, because five days later Wald again wrote to "Dear Alirene" offering flexibility on a point that had apparently progressed to discussion of settlement clubs and activities: "On further thought, I think that you are right and that reference to the classes could not be exact unless we went into great length about it."[52] The competing interests of the enterprise are evident in the distinctions between the "large audiences" and the "social movement," and in the rhetoric of strained relations. Wald nicely rebuts the sentiments of "some people" with her own disdain for the "sluggish minds" of an upscale and uptown audience that could be oblivious to the social needs of those who did not visit but lived on the Lower East Side. But in the exchange of correspondence a lack of collective vision is apparent at the outset of the theatrical season.

The sixth season for the Neighborhood Playhouse was, of course, already laid out by November, and the strained relations could indicate recognition of the coming season as a disappointment and a diminishment from previous years. The single full dramatic production, *Mary Broome*, a play by Alan Monkhouse, was mounted by Ben Iden Payne, the British theater producer of Shakespeare and adaptations of writers such as A. A. Milne, with his own touring company. Late in the season, in May, a dance drama directed by Irene and a folk drama without a director credit was staged. In between, however, there were a series of visiting productions and rentals including amateur companies such as Yvette Guilbert's students and a group from Carnegie Institute of Technology, now Carnegie Mellon University. The lack of independent programming and the absence of a Neighborhood Playhouse performance agenda was especially conspicuous in comparison to the direct competition. The Theatre Guild, financially stronger since its successful production of St. John Ervine's Irish drama *John Ferguson* during a stagehand strike in the previous year, took over the Neighborhood Playhouse's speciality of Orientalism with its production of John Masefield's *The Faithful*. The Theatre Guild would enjoy no great box office success in a quick succession of productions in large theaters, but its artistic ambitions remained intact. The Provincetown Players took over some of the Neighborhood Playhouse's female presence by producing plays by both Edna St. Vincent Millay and Djuna Barnes, and the company also began to realize the sensational reception and commercial success of its productions of Eugene O'Neill, beginning with *Beyond the Horizon* in February 1920.

In contrast, the Lewisohns seem to have built their season around a fall visit to New York by Lord Dunsany, to have done this without the agreement or even the active participation of the rest of the producing staff such as Agnes Morgan and Helen Arthur, and to have been motivated more by author idolatry than any new synthesis of performance attendance and social goals. The notion of the British peer playwright appearing on the lower East Side neighborhood around Grand Street titillated the *New York Times* and the mainstream press in general. Coinciding with the revivals at 466 of both *A Night at an Inn* and *The Queen's Enemies* during a fall 1919 visit to New York by Dunsany, the *Times* ran a feature in its weekly magazine on "Lionizing a Lord in Grand Street: A Neighborly East Side Affair in Which an Eighteenth Baron Dunsany Distributes Autographs on the Sidewalk." The feature focused on the contrast of the aristocrat visiting the slum rather than on any catalytic effect the social intersection may have created:

> It was almost furthest east on Grand Street, where the population is about as foreign as it ever gets even in New York, and the exact spot on the rather wet sidewalk where the member of the peerage stood was just in front of the Neighborhood Playhouse, where these foreigners—or some of them under judicious guidance—make amateur dramatics seem to touch human life more nearly than usually happens with the professional article in the regions about Times Square. Drama seems to come natural with them, somehow.

The fact that the playwright was Irish enhanced the contrast for the *Times*, which ended the story with the observation that the "other eminent Irish dramatist, Bernard Shaw, a large part of whose fame also has been made in America, could not match [the contrast], even approximately."[53]

The Dunsany visit to New York had been planned by the peer in spring 1919, and it was very much because of the Neighborhood Playhouse. Dunsany was in correspondence with Alice, and in spring 1919 he proposed a visit to the playhouse as payback for the successful earlier productions of his work. Explaining that he was going on military leave and so would not be sent by the War Office, Dunsany assured Alice, "Do not doubt my gratitude. I ought to go to the Neighbourhood Playhouse first, and see Stuart Walker second, and then perhaps go and gaze at the Statue of Liberty or the Flatiron Building or whatever shows newcomers go and look at."[54] When he arrived, he found the playhouse production schedule abandoned in order to present, on October 16, 1919, a revival of his two plays in the Neighborhood repertory, along with an intervening performance by the Festival Dancers and the Balalaika Orchestra of Russian folk dances.

In Alice's account, the theater was the beneficiary of the playwright and not, as in Dunsany's letter, the reverse. Ultimately, she felt that the event failed, and she cast her account of it in the metaphor of "the privilege of introducing parent [Dunsany] and offspring [Neighborhood Playhouse]." The relation was in fact the reverse: Dunsany's work would not remain on stage, in the United States or elsewhere, despite the compelling productions of the World War I years, especially those at 466. His popularity was in fact related to the fantasist quality of his work, and after the early twentieth-century stage popularity, his remaining audience would be mostly readers of his prose exercises approaching science fiction. For Alice and, oddly enough, for a general audience at the time, the otherworldly, fantasist quality of Dunsany's work was associated with his Irishness. She lamented her own performance before the playwright, in particular the apostrophe to the Nile when she drowns her guests at the end of *The Queen's Enemies*. Alice believed that her performance of the speech as drama rather than poetry, or the shift from "the author's emphasis upon poetic color [to] the director's responsibility to the dramatic tension," disappointed: "*The Queen's Enemies* proved to be a stab in the back to Dunsany's Celtic imagery." In the memoir written years later, she gave considerable space to the contrast between Dunsany's "poetic feeling" and the performance's "pull of dramatic tension" and repeated the paternal metaphor: "I have asked myself if the poet who retires to the realm of fairy tale is not attempting to protect his dream children from the definition of the here and now."[55] This is an extraordinarily submissive reading of the performance of the execution of misogynist militarists by a woman warrior.

The contrast between aesthetic fantasy and gritty details was always part of the enterprise of the Neighborhood Playhouse. The Playhouse achieved its first public success through Dunsany's work, and even in celebration of it, the pragmatic and quotidian consistently penetrated the barrier of "poetic feeling." Even in the first Neighborhood Playhouse production of *The Queen's Enemies* in 1916, the press searched beneath the celebrated Celtic illusion for its activist opposition: "Alice Lewisohn is arresting and altogether charming as the little queen—the first important woman's role in any play by Lord Dunsany."[56] As it happened, revivals of that play during Dunsany's visit coincided with the first efforts toward labor organization of stagehand staff inside the enterprise. Unionization was a prominent issue in the theater industry at the time, and labor organization had special resonance to the socialism-literate Lower East Side. *The Queen's Enemies*'s special lighting effects required a new chief electrician for the house lighting system. Doris Fox Benardete's history of the company locates in the hiring of "Mr. Sullivan" a new element of tension in the company. Sullivan brought necessary skills, union membership, and a new pay scale for the stagehands. This launched a pattern of regular "conflict with various theatrical unions over the Neighborhood Playhouse wage scale." Benardete recalled of Alice and Irene in 1918: "Their attitude appears to have been that, inasmuch as the little theatre was non-profit-making, those who worked for it should contribute free as much of their service as they could; on the whole that was, when salaries were involved, the state of affairs that prevailed down in Grand Street."[57]

The tensions and contrasts involved in the Neighborhood Playhouse's success with and dependence on Dunsany helps illustrate some of the broader issues confronting both the productions at 466 and theater practice outside the mainstream in New York at that time, including the femininization of "little theatre" (Alice as "the little queen") and its opposite, advancing unionization (the ominous "Mr. Sullivan"). In these, as in other dimensions of theater practice in urban context, there is a less than perfect match between the interests of the playhouse and the interests of the neighborhood.

In the regular revivals of Dunsany in place of original programming, the Lewisohns, in opposition to Agnes Morgan and Helen Arthur, became party to the odd history of Irish drama abroad in which the best intentions to present a revealing and instructive example of national and regional cultural fracture were undone by "artistic" success. There have been many histories of "how the Irish became white" or the evolution of "Celtic" tropes and images into American popular culture.[58] In the context of Grand Street in the early twentieth century, there is an especially sharp contrast between the cultural situation of Russian Jews and the politically innocuous exoticism and ethnically inoffensive foreignness represented on the stage in a work of Irish playwrights. The special popularity of Irish culture, a phenomenon of the early twentieth century and the early twenty-first century, is indicated by the Neighborhood Playhouse's first production of Dunsany's work in 1916 as an aesthetic exercise particularly Irish and entirely untouched by events and conflicts surrounding the contemporary Easter Rising in Dublin in the same year.

It should be said that Alice and Irene's infatuation with Dunsany, and by extension the work of other Celtic fantasists, was not exceptional. For example, in the influential journal of advanced thought on theater of the time called *The Drama*, Dunsany was usually celebrated in terms that echoed Alice's sense of him as the poet of fairy tales. For Helen McAfee in 1917, in an article given the sweeping title of "Lord Dunsany and the Modern Drama," Dunsany is seen as epitomizing "the little group of dramatists who have created an international interest in Irish drama" because of his "insistent note of lyricism . . . willful aloofness from the mechanistic aspects of life, and a feeling for its ever-present wonders."[59] There was some counterargument. Louise Bryant, writing in *The Masses* on "The Poets' Revolution," found the interest in Ireland in a doomed uprising fueled equally by the Irish labor movement and the Celtic revival and found the model of Ireland to be the "Ancient Irish law [that] placed the blood money for a poet so high that it could only be paid by the death of the murderer."[60] But for the most part, the more general perception of what was of interest in Irish arts was more consistent with Alice's emphasis on its "Celtic imagery" and "poetic feeling." Alice had more influence than many, and she linked the Neighborhood Playhouse, at a moment of institutional weakness, to one of the less stimulating dimensions of that amply available theater fare known as the Irish Play.

This kind of programming was chosen against considerable pressures placed on the playhouse by its neighborhood, both the literal locality and the cultural ambience as context for theater practice. Pressure against "poetic feeling" came from what Doris Fox Benardete called "unpleasantness over money."[61] In November 1919, after the Lewisohn-Wald exchange of letters on the "social movement" or lack of it in performance, and also after the Dunsany visit, an unusual business meeting brought together the "Producing Staff," the Neighborhood Players, and the Festival Dancers, along with choral groups, for a unique meeting of the entire ensemble. The agenda had nothing to do with artistic vision and a great deal to do with labor management. Helen Arthur gave an overview of the financial situation and its heavy reliance on volunteer contributions of labor, talent, and revenue. Then the "N.P.H. Women" left, and the remaining ranks of actors and dancers elected a "Committee of Five" to represent the whole to the management. This group made written recommendations in one week and met again with the management in two weeks. At that meeting, the majority opinion of the group recommended increasing the size of the company so that productions could be in rehearsal and performance at the same time. Further, they recommended that "the amateur standing of all players was to be kept and no professionals were to be engaged for any parts." The minority report was given by one Tobias Bennett. His proposal was for "a small repertory company, playing every day in the week and receiving a small stipend a week as a scholarship." The producing staff of Alice and Irene and Agnes and Helen acceded to the majority with the addition of adjustments to the rehearsal schedule to allow greater amateur contribution. However, "with reference to the plan for next year, the Producing Staff suggests that the money allowed to the full-time playing group be given in the form of scholarships to be awarded annually." Thus was the "unpleasant-ness over money" first introduced into the company plan as salary compensation in the disguised form of fellowships or honoraria.

Additional pressure on any commitment to "poetic feeling" over "social movement" came in the form of the new agenda of the settlement movement. In the context of the Lusk Laws, the Sedition Act, and the Espionage Act—tests of loyalty introduced during and after World War I—the settlement movement as collectively represented by the United Neighborhood Houses newly set its priority on "Americanization." A December 1919 draft of a position paper filed in Lillian Wald's papers has the title "What the Settlements Stand For." It laid out a new and more assertive premise: "It cannot be too strongly stated that every Settlement is a constructive force, in its neighborhood, standing for progress by the orderly process of law, and against sedition and lawlessness. Among the foreign born of our cities, the Settlements stand for Americanization in its deepest sense." While noting that "there is diversity in the work of the Settlements," and that "many are striving to foster the cultural arts," the paper set the higher priority on the effort to insure that "the present economic strife must give way to an orderly democratization of industry." In conclusion, the paper used rhetoric very like Wald's own on the opening of the Neighborhood Playhouse in 1913: Americanization "means also a desire on our part to preserve and perfect all the historical, cultural and other contributions, which our new citizens may have to make. It is idle to talk of 'citizenship classes' 'Speak English' drives or other mechanical devices, unless these efforts are vitalized by the determination of America to welcome the new-comer by according him justice and opportunity."[62]

This powerful agenda would take considerable time before formal approval by the organization. But the draft in Wald's papers and its resonance against her well-known positions indicates an even more powerful competition for Alice's and Irene's vision of the role of art and beauty in the neighborhood and in the institutional auspices of the Henry Street Settlement.

4

1920-1922

New Plans, Salut au Monde, *and* The Grand Street Follies

The Neighborhood Playhouse opened the season with professional actors on salary for the first time in 1920. The settlement volunteers, the temporary workers, the children, and the club members all continued, although now in a supporting role within the ensemble. Ideally, this hybrid arrangement would be mutually beneficial for the professionals, who could link their commitment to art with independence to pursue it full time, and for the amateurs, who could now work in close quarters with a higher level of expertise. The new organization resembled the form of the plan of August 1916 by which art would be brought to the neighborhood rather than discovered within it. The distinction between professional arts and amateur arts was measured by all the company directors in terms of the superiority of the former, the inferiority of the latter, and the vast distance between the two. As Alice wrote in retrospect in her memoir, "Working with actors who though personally sympathetic were geared to the needs of Broadway made us increasingly conscious of the cleavage between their theatre and ours."[1] The de facto professionals Agnes Morgan and Helen Arthur believed that the great distance was between the inferior means of Grand Street and the superior ones of Broadway. For others, especially those most associated with the Henry Street Settlement, and presumably Lillian Wald, the distance separating the neighborhood and its superior ethos of reform from Broadway and its inferior culture of commerce was not great enough. Between the two visions was the

Lewisohn one of an ideal integration of production quality and neighborhood participation.

The decision to hire professional actors to remain on salary in a repertory company had been made the previous spring and summer. Alice's choice of the opening production for fall 1920, *The Mob,* by John Galsworthy, was a particularly aggressive pursuit of her new professional-amateur model. Few plays could better represent an internal "cleavage" or more prominently foreground all the issues implicit in "their theatre" and "ours." In fact, the choice of production and its relation to the audience mirrored quite well the last time the Lewisohns had done Galsworthy. When they had mounted Galsworthy's *The Silver Box* at Clinton Hall in 1913, that play contrasted sharply with their previous production, *The Shepherd,* whose success inspired the company name the Neighborhood Players. Galsworthy's "well-made" parlor drama about a British playboy's abuse of class power reflected artistic ambition and the theatrical professionalism of Agnes Morgan more than the neighborhood solidarity and Henry Street ideals represented better by Dargan's version of Tolstoy adapted by Alice and Irene for recent immigrants.

In the second Galsworthy production, a sensational dramatization of a principled parliamentarian attacked in a searing final scene by a mob, the distance between the professional, assimilated, and lawful spheres of the Neighborhood Playhouse enterprise and its amateur, immigrant, and potentially lawless counterpart were evident in the single production and not just in the totality of a repertory of plays. The third act of *The Mob* is set at the stage entrance of a theater where the heroic Stephen More, departing from an antiwar speech, is forced to flee from a surly Cockney crowd of thugs lurking in back alleys reminiscent of the ones outside 466 Grand Street. In the final scene, the mob stones and then actually penetrates More's upper-class residence, assaults him, and in mob-frenzy kills him. As they enter the drawing room, Galsworthy's direction, a strong evocation of class hatred, reads, "The din of execration swells."[2] In this production, the mob was played by the amateur, immigrant, and newly subordinate members of a previously egalitarian company. The tensions of the new professional-amateur organization of the Neighborhood Playhouse apparently fueled their performance as they attacked Ian Mclaren, lead professional, in the role of Stephen More. Alexander Woollcott in the *New York Times* commended the hostility of the "local talent" of the "whirling, shouting bunch of hoodlums who swarm up onto a table and kill him."[3] Even Alice, in her memoir, remembered that "the drama taking place behind the scenes contributed to the heightened tension and fervor in the playing." Her gloss on the content of the play can hardly be read without reference to the conflicts in the company, or between the neighborhood and the playhouse. "In contrast to the undisciplined outbursts of *The Mob*," she wrote, "the main characters of the play were typical of a sophisticated stratum of English society."[4]

Doris Fox Benardete, always more of a pragmatist than Alice, in her own retrospective described some of the organizational tensions reflected in the parallel disgruntlements of the stage mob and the neighborhood amateurs. To Benardete, backstage and box office manager, the introduction of professionals was a logical next level of development only made possible by the superior performance standards attained with effort by the amateur company over time. In her account, over the years amateur productions had "developed a technique and an assurance which emboldened [the directors] to attempt more subtle and more involved productions." The productions they aspired to perform were the play scripts of the well-known, and largely British, playwrights: in this context Benardete mentions *The Mob*, which opened the 1920 season, and Harley Granville Barker's *The Madras House*, which opened the 1921 season. For the Galsworthy play, the directors also encountered a standard licensing contract for a professional playwright that limited performance to professional, and so royalty-producing, productions. Benardete admired the decision to introduce the professional actors who would meet the licensing criteria and felt that, in the context of the company on the Lower East Side, greater professionalism in the performance of intellectualized drama rather than entertainment insured that the Lewisohns remained "in the forefront of the revolt against the commercial theatre."[5]

However, the role of amateurs represented part of the idealism of the Neighborhood Playhouse and the entire little theater phenomenon of which it was part. Speaking of Jig Cook and the Provincetown Players experiment, Susan Glaspell, in her account of the period, *The Road to the*

Temple, recalled that Cook "believed that the gifted amateur had possibilities which the professional may have lost." Cook, at least, relished the disorder—in Glaspell's term, "intensity"—incumbent on the nonprofessional theater: missed rehearsals, performances of cut scenes or earlier versions of them, improvised departures from play script, curtains held for cast latecomers, just "bad acting," etc. Cook preferred the provisional nature of what was accomplished: "in the theater for experiment you may do things which in themselves are not worth doing . . . a thing that was on its way to something else."[6] Of course, the Provincetown Players would face the same issues of professionalism, opt for uptown productions for larger audiences, and close in 1922 to emerge reorganized into the Provincetown Playhouse with alternative idealisms. The other of the three companies to emerge in 1915, the Washington Square Players, had by this point, 1920, already reorganized into the Theatre Guild, expanded, and moved uptown. While the Neighborhood Playhouse was performing John Galsworthy on the Lower East Side, the Theatre Guild was producing a Russian-Jewish shtetl tale called *The Treasure* uptown in the Broadway theater named for David Garrick.

The shift to a hybrid professional-amateur company structure had a variety of effects on operating procedures. In the fall of 1920, when the company put Ian Maclaren and Albert Carroll on salary, it also hired its first paid staff publicist, Helen Rosenthal. The company entities were formalized into the professional-amateur Neighborhood Playhouse Acting Company and the amateur Festival Dancers. Alice's recollection was that "this did not materially change the organization" and was, instead, "a daring experiment." It was in fact both significant change and experimental. No doubt this created both tension and some disorder: the next of the many Neighborhood Playhouse prospectuses and statements of "new plans," the one that would publicly describe the new structure, did not appear until the following fall, in 1921. Among the material changes brought about by the new structure was a radical alteration of the weekly performance schedule. Performances were previously mostly weekend events; now the new degree of professionalism included a weeklong evening performance schedule that moved stage rehearsals into afternoon times not possible for amateur and otherwise employed casts. The purely dance or "lyric" performances filled empty weekend stage hours and could never be convincingly described as equitable with the acting company stage time or visibility. Season subscriptions were also introduced in hope of matching continuing salaries with predictable ticket-sales revenue.

One conspicuous casualty of the new performance schedule was the cinema, which had been a popular offering since the opening of the building in 1915 and a calculated dimension of its mission. The film screenings stopped when *The Mob* began weekday evening performances, and Helen Arthur gave Lillian Wald a long, handwritten account of the film program (which was filed for Wald with material for an article on Jane Addams and Hull House in Chicago). Helen wrote that "our programs were consciously 'educational.' There were travelogues with slides, short movies of animal or plant life-sciences and rather ancient films of historical romances or dramatizations (rather feeble) of well-known stories." These shorts were organized into a program that included live performance: "There was always in the program what we called, a little too elegantly, 'an interlude'—we all loathed the word 'specialty' and so our special number—sometimes a play, sometimes 'readings,' sometimes 'musical or dance numbers' went under the title of 'interlude'—but it was always *called* by the audience 'the speci-*al*-i-ty.' "

With three shows on each of three evenings, the programs were reaching an audience of up to 3,000 per week, although many of those were repeat and in some case constant attenders. They also included piano music programs performed by Lilly Hyland that were much more extensive than simple film overture or accompaniment. Helen described how the regular audience especially prized the opening of the film season, which preceded the theatrical one. In September, she wrote, it took resolution to leave her summer vacation home "as the day of the opening grew hotter and hotter and as our hilltop seemed so much more desirable than the smelly corner of Grand and Pitt." Once in the city, however, she described in her unedited account how "I saw the same faces that I had seen the last night the year before, and as the first audience filed out—I said to an old woman with a sheitel (is that the way it's spelled?) 'Did you enjoy the performance?' She looked at me and said so simply, 'Well, I waited all summer for dis.' "

The development of the film industry itself made it difficult for the Neighborhood Playhouse to maintain a program. There was the increased commercialization and monopolization of the industry by people Helen referred to in her account as "persons of no taste, when the best is said of them": "The thing that sickens me is their insistence that wealth is the important thing in life—the utter vulgarity of the producer's point of view gets frightfully under your skin after you've seen one hundred movies. I detest censorship but I hate the stupidity of commercialism and then too there is the subtlest kind of propaganda in pictures."[7]

In addition to a dearth of material suitable for Neighborhood Playhouse purposes, there were increasingly strict labor laws for film theaters that made it difficult for part-time operations to compete in this new and highly competitive market for mass entertainment. In Alice's account, "Almost overnight, the market had become glutted with a cheap, standardized type of picture. Stakes had gone up in the movie race. The exchanges not only quadrupled their rates for pictures but found that they could control the stakes more easily by instituting a 'service'" that included not just the programs of films but delivery of them to theaters. She admitted "a certain ruthlessness in denying what had been deliberately stimulated as a standard for wholesome entertainment."[8] However regretfully, film programs ceased at 466 Grand Street in September 1920, and with them the most popular part of the playhouse function for many in the neighborhood. Doris Fox Benardete quotes verbatim a letter of complaint received at the playhouse about "the sudden change from a cozy motion picture house." Anticipating a defense, one Milton Sokol wrote, "Your answer to me will probably be that look at the finer things they are producing at such low prices, but I'll bet and win that out of an audience maybe you'll pick out a handful from the neighborhood I can tell by the cars outside."[9]

While not a shameful embrace of commercial theater or complete surrender of earlier idealism, it was not evident whether the idea of a professional repertory company of actors represented a pragmatic compromise or a shrewd strategy. Ever the pragmatist, Benardete recorded how, because the emphasis would be on limited-run performances, the actors chosen for the professional company had to be selected for "complete adaptability" rather than for perfect fit with a single role. The adaptability of the cast would not naturally qualify them for all the new, more ambitious series of plays that the directors planned to attempt. The new routine of evening performances and daytime rehearsals for the next production also conspired against extended runs for successful plays, which would displace a fully rehearsed production on the Grand Street stage, or transfers uptown with an unchanged cast, who could not then simultaneously perform downtown. The issues surrounding transfers uptown, which were much easier to achieve under the company's structure when it produced, performed, and moved *The Queen's Enemies* in 1916, continued to frame internal debate from the introduction of the professional players in 1920 until the close of the Neighborhood Playhouse in 1927.

There were many good reasons for choosing *The Mob* and producing it under these new auspices. Alice felt that the collision of the various forces on either side of the "cleavage" was preferable to slow transition. For her, "*The Mob* offered a unique opportunity not only to initiate a professional course but also to reconcile amateur and professional in their relation to the playhouse." In retrospect, she thought the "worst fears of the amateur were never to be realized" and the "drastic change" was accomplished with the outcome that "the Playhouse had not abandoned its personality or direction."[10] Internally, the professional dimension had the benefit of linking the interests of the "N.P.H. Women" in higher production values, and Alice and Agnes Morgan, whose visions differed increasingly over time, codirected very satisfactorily. Even Irene, who could easily have resisted promotion of the dramatic priorities over the dance ones, found the production completely compatible with Neighborhood Playhouse goals. On a full page of notes for future reference, she typed a single unrevised sentence: "I learned from 'The Mob' what the thrill of a production might be, in actual music, symphonic values what the thrill of a production might be."[11] The production was beyond doubt a critical success, and happily the introduction of the publicist, who brought critics to the performance, coincided with the kind of strong, professional performance that kept them coming back. Publicity was further aided by a visit and speech from the stage by the playwright, and Galsworthy, like Dunsany before him, extolled the merits of the Neighborhood Playhouse.

Perhaps above all, *The Mob* appeared to represent a high art advancement of political positions consonant with the playhouse, the Henry Street Settlement, and Lillian Wald, although there were tensions in this context as well. Galsworthy had first titled the play "The Patriot," and its first production in 1914 was a success at the very estimable Manchester Repertory. The text is intentionally vague about the particular piece of political legislation that places the parliamentarian in a dilemma, but the conflict between his pacifist views and the military fervor of his colleagues is suggestive of the Boer War. At the onset of World War I, Galsworthy withdrew the play as unproductively inflammatory in wartime. The central character certainly has some of the intentionally inflammatory steel of Lillian Wald, which she did not temper during wartime. As the conflict between denunciation of war and temptation to remain silent develops in the opening act, Stephen More rehearses a speech that could have been delivered by Wald: "I cannot sit silent to-night and see this begin. As we are tender of our own land, so we should be of the lands of others. I love my country. It is because I love my country that I raise my voice."[12] However, while the subject of the drama, resistance to militarism, would certainly be endorsed by Wald as consonant with settlement ideals, the treatment of the subject, like the notion of suppressing it during war, probably would not have satisfied her. The treatment also resonates oddly against the production setting of Grand Street. By changing the title from "The Patriot" to *The Mob,* Galsworthy, as others have noted, shifted the subject from the courage of his hero to the villainy of the masses. In consequence, as noted by the journal of the little theater movement, *Theatre Arts Magazine,* the play becomes "an attack on the mob, rather than upon imperialism."[13] The New York *Dramatic Mirror,* a much more politically conservative and even reactionary publication, rather enjoyed the notion of mob evil being dramatized on the Lower East Side, or, as its critic put it, in "teeming, mob-filled Grand Street."[14] The "cleavage" Alice hoped to rectify with this production was between professional and amateur theater, between the personal goals and professional ambitions of the directors and the institutional goals of their program, between the subscription audience and the neighborhood audience, and between the mainstream critics who constitute critical success and the journal critics more likely to represent artistic success.

Two different voices help suggest some of the contesting forces within the box office, critical, and perhaps artistic success of *The Mob* as an opening to the company's seventh season, or about the midpoint in the life of the Neighborhood Playhouse. The first is the reaction of Lillian Wald to the introduction of professional players. It was recorded much later, in the second of her memoirs, but her positions are unvarying and this statement probably accurately reflects her reaction in the fall of 1920. She welcomed "the full-time professional actor, with his specialized training and experience." However, she welcomed the professional-amateur structure not for the access to new plays it provided, which was the chief attraction for Alice. For Wald, the professional was welcome for the influence brought to bear on "the majority of the Neighborhood Players [who] had neither the maturity nor the qualifications for sustaining major roles." Extending her thought to the other leaders of the Neighborhood Playhouse effort, she explained that "the professional alone, it was thought, could not express the Neighborhood Playhouse idea: the amateur, too, was essential. Both had a part in the new development."[15] She sought, then, a multidimensional structure to the sole end of developing the students of the Henry Street Settlement. The proportions and relative priorities within the "Neighborhood Playhouse idea" was an as yet unsolved problem facing her, Alice, and the other directors.

A second commentator helps suggest the anti-professional model in much more practical terms than Susan Glaspell. During the run of *The Mob*, Thomas H. Dickinson, an aggressive and frequently abrasive proponent of little theater who would later hope to influence the Neighborhood Playhouse, published in *Theatre Arts* an open letter "to the little theatre directors of the United States." In it he listed some of the principal playwrights who had succeeded in creating a culture of amateur theater in England. Many are Neighborhood Playhouse names: Yeats, Dunsany, Shaw, Brighouse. Some are names in the immediate future of the Neighborhood Playhouse: Harley Granville Barker, Arnold Bennett. However, in addressing the American directors, Dickinson summoned forth these names to warn the directors that "it is easy to go back to Wilde and Shaw and the English comedians and new masters. Your audiences expect some of this from you." In place of that easy route, Dickinson proposed that "nothing will give your work character and standing in the community quicker than the production of new works by local audiences. Not only does this appeal to local pride, but it is almost the foundation stone of your efforts." In addition, Dickinson warned against "the crowning fault of the American little theatre director": envying and seeking professional approval, especially by imitating "the ways and interests of the professional theatre" and "copying the methods of publicity of the professional theatre."[16] Wald certainly would have been comfortable with his recommendation. However, as a missive to the little theater directors of the United States, this position does not recognize the specific context of little theater in New York City, with its surfeit of professional resources not equaled in other locations. Nor does it recognize the specific needs of a theatre operating in conjunction with a settlement or a funding model based on philanthropy. The task for the Neighborhood Playhouse was to find the relative proportions and priorities—between new work and recognized "masterpieces," professional and amateur performers, local and metropolitan audiences—that would exploit New York City theater culture in order to advance the social aims of both the theater enterprise and its sheltering organization.

Such a resolution was not found quickly under the professional-amateur model. In fact, after *The Mob*, the season 1920–21 became a near-disaster that nearly forty years later Alice would recall as a winter when openings were faced as "dreaded doom." The first of the subsequent productions was *The Whispering Well*, by Frank Rose, a British playwright and Labour MP much in the vein of Galsworthy or Harold Brighouse. The Rose play was, in fact, brought to Grand Street by Whitford Kane, who imported his own production of Brighouse's *The Price of Coal* to the playhouse in its second season in the fall of 1915. In the meantime, Kane had evolved from the protector of "real Ireland" works to a performer in David Belasco extravaganzas such as *Dark Rosaleen* cited in *Theatre Magazine* for celebrating "Celtic Types" that "at least, serves the most useful purpose of bringing together a group of diversified Hibernians that are a constant delight to eye and ear."[17] Perhaps in 1920 Kane was returning to artistic ideals after a term in commercial theater. Perhaps Agnes Morgan and Helen Arthur felt he could have the kind of positive effect on the amateur company that Alice sought in Ian Maclaren. In any case, *The Whispering Well,* a "Lancashire fairy play," about a weaver outwitted by the devil, failed to sustain the kind of illusion that succeeded in Dunsany, failed to attract even negative notices, and left Alice convinced that the company was unforgivably "guilty of sheer banality . . . adding complacency to artificial simplicity."

The holiday season was covered with a revival of *The Mob,* but February 1921 brought another "dreaded doom" in the form of *The Great Adventure* by Arnold Bennett, which was compared unfavorably to its American premiere in 1913 and to a subsequent American film. Even the Neighborhood Playhouse's own mailing on the representation of a painter seeking shelter from his own fame would only go so far as to call its new semiprofessional company "very capable."[18] In meditating on what she called "'mis'-productions" and a professional staging that failed to meet earlier amateur standards, Alice concluded, "One has done his best and in the end the play, the audience, or the production fails."[19] However, it was equally possible to convict the company, especially so unique, strangely situated, and consequently so closely watched a company as the Neighborhood Playhouse in this transition. Together *The Whispering Well* and *The Great Adventure* represent a failure of programming vision that is larger than a single production. The Neighborhood Playhouse had vacillated in programming before and always to negative effect. In the case of the winter of 1920–21, the failures may have confirmed Thomas Dickinson's dire warnings that fall of "aping the ways and interests of the professional theatre" without attention to the context of little theater, and, in the case of the Neighborhood Playhouse, of its unusual cultural and geographical situation. Bennett was among Dickinson's names of British stage luminaries who, whatever their merits at home, had no relevance to the American stage, especially to little theater or, in a common British usage, "subsidized professional theatre." Another name Dickinson advised America to avoid was Anne Horniman, Whitford Kane's patron. A third was Granville Barker, who against all odds would salvage the season of "dreaded doom."

Granville Barker has become generally recognized as one of the leading theater practitioners of the twentieth century, although he was not self-evidently so in 1921, when the Neighborhood Playhouse first produced his work. By that point, he was known as the distinguished playwright of works such as *Waste* and *The Voysey Inheritance* and an actor-director with a particularly long and rich association with Bernard Shaw. That alone would make Granville Barker a broader theater influence than the playwrights previously produced at the Neighborhood Playhouse, Bennett or Brighouse, or those who visited 466 Grand Street, Dunsany or Galworthy. Granville Barker had long associations in London with the Stage Society, a venue for productions beyond the long reach of the censor. He had been codirector with J. E. Vedrenne of the Royal Court Theatre, which introduced repertories in unconventional formats including weekday matinees. From 1904 through 1930, he had been instrumental to the extended evolution of a prospectus for a British national theater. He was, then, no stranger to the kind of institutional planning and replanning characteristic of the Neighborhood Playhouse enterprise.

That enterprise had been a direct beneficiary of Granville Barker's pivotal American visit in 1915–16, after which he returned to Britain for the war effort. His influence had been a critical part of the multidimensional theater context of New York at the moment of birth of the Neighborhood Playhouse, the Washington Square Players, and the Provincetown Players, and also the professional-amateur dilemma confronting the Neighborhood Playhouse in 1920. In 1915, in an unsigned column almost certainly also written by Norman Hapgood, the editor, *Harper's Weekly* extolled the Granville Barker ideal as the solution to the professional-amateur alternative confronting Alice as "cleavage." For *Harper's*, "The Barker Season," in advance of its opening, was declared as:

> what our professional managers and our amateurs have failed to do, because [Barker] was better at business than the one group and better at art than the other. Where the professional manager said, "We must find what the public wants," Mr. Barker said, "We must find good plays." Where the professional manager said, "We must spend more money," Mr. Barker said, "We must get better results." . . . Where the amateur said, "We must elevate the public to great drama," Mr. Barker said, "We must interpret great drama to the public." Where the reformer said, "We

must teach other people to appreciate the value of fine art," Mr. Barker said, "We must teach ourselves to appreciate the value of hard work." . . . He justified his faith by his works.[20]

As it happened, Granville Barker did not get a theater in New York. Before he left, he famously worked in another style entirely by staging *The Trojan War* and *Iphegenia in Taurus* in the Yale bowl, which seated 70,000 in New Haven. When he left New York, he notoriously did so with a new American wife, Helen Huntington, who was previously married to one of his own benefactors, Archer Huntington. Granville Barker's original plans for the season included an American premiere for his own play *The Madras House*, but that plan did not survive the frenetic season. The play would wait until the fall of 1921 for its American premiere, which was at the Neighborhood Playhouse.

1920–21 had opened well with *The Mob* and then dissipated into failures that must have seemed an indictment of the new organizational model. However, the end of the season was a triumph that vindicated the professional-amateur model and did so in association with Granville Barker. He had previously produced his own play *Harliquinade*, cowritten with Clayton Calthrop, as a curtain-raiser for *Androcles and the Lion*, but in New York during "the Barker season," it had been replaced, fortuitously, by *The Dumb Wife*. So in the spring of 1921, the Neighborhood Playhouse mounted as its final production of the season the American premiere of *Harliquinade* with a very slight one-act called *Innocent and Annabel* by the popular (and recently deceased) American playwright Harold Chapin. No rationale for the choice of this play appears in the Neighborhood Playhouse Gift archive in the New York Public Library. Nor does any press coverage comment on the decision to base an evening on a curtain-raiser. But the result was extremely gratifying for what *Theatre Magazine*, in reviewing this production, called "the Lewisohn Players at the Little Theatre on Grand Street."[21]

To explain the nature of the play, most reviewers cited a line from the program: *Harliquinade* "isn't a play at all—it's an excursion." The Barker-Calthorp conceit was that players representing different eras would collectively illustrate some single, intrinsic quality of theater. The opening scene was in classical Greece, where Mercury debated Charon on the nature of illusion. The play then proceeded through sixteenth-century Italy and eighteenth-century England with appropriate changes of costume as actors made transitions between roles, such as Mercury of Greece (Albert Carroll) becoming Harliquinade in Italy. The fourth scene, set on "the day after tomorrow," was set in the "Bronx Art Theatre," a name change for the New York production in order to feature what was perhaps the only theater location more unlikely than Grand Street. The audience was assisted by two actors, Whitford Kane as Uncle Edward and Joanna Roos as Alice Whistler, who resembled Lewis Carroll's Alice as drawn by Tenniel. They remained on stage throughout, positioned stage right and stage left at the bases of the proscenium, and explained the narrative in direct address to the audience and sounded gongs for transitions. To the reviewer for the *New York World,* this was "after the fashion of the old French theatre." *Harliquinade* does not seem to have resulted in any astonishing revelations about theater or theater history, but it did succeed as novelty of high design. For the *World* reviewer, "once in quaint Grand Street, you turn into the little Neighborhood Theatre, and there you will embark upon as fantastic and as alluring a trip into lands you have never seen as you could wish to take." That review was given the headline "Audience Goes on Trip to Fairyland."[22]

Harliquinade had the merit of vindicating the theater organization and at the same time illustrating well several issues it faced in the immediate future. The praise of the production was greatest for Joanna Roos, who, at age eighteen, was a professional product of the Henry Street Players and its workshops led by Yvette Guilbert. The production thus integrated settlement ideas with the newer element of theater professionalism represented by Whitford Kane and Albert Carroll. It was codirected by Alice Lewisohn and Agnes Morgan and thus united two wings of "N.P.H. Women." The different settings were illustrated in dance and so represented a coproduction of the Neighborhood Players and the Festival Dancers. The weekly performance schedule also linked the distinct dance-drama operations: *Harliquinade* played five performances per week, and on weekend evenings the theater featured a well-received dance, or "lyric," program, *The Royal Fandango.* However, despite the insertion of

8. Albert Carroll in costume and on set for Harley
Granville Barker's *The Harlinquinade*, 1921.

the Bronx Art Theatre, the production lacked local resonance and critique, as distinct from celebration, of theater. As in the manner of *Guibour*, it could be said that the production organization integrated settlement ideals and allowed the actual content of production to indulge in remote aestheticism. The *New York Times* terms of praise were the entertainment tropes of "gay diversion," "amusing," and "charmingly mounted." The treatment of the glories of theater left the *Post* reviewer dunned down to "the level of ordinary propaganda." The real integration of settlement ideals and theater ideals would be a successful organic company production that engaged through actual places and not only fantastic ones, as in *The Dybbuk* on opening in 1925.

The degree of success of the "trip to fairyland" also led to the first transfer of a Neighborhood Playhouse production uptown since *The Queen's Enemies*, and so the Broadway identity of the Lower East Side company was associated again with abstract charm disassociated from place or neighborhood. Paired with *A Night at an Inn*, *Harliquinade* opened at the small Broadway Punch and Judy Theatre in June, which added summer performances after the end of the season rather than altering a repertory schedule. The *New York Dramatic Mirror* found the Broadway version "so near to reaching the summit of artistic achievement . . . by that indefatigable little band of workers at the Neighborhood Play-house."[23] Alice's recollection, however, was that "*Harliquinade* was packed and sent to the Punch and Judy Theatre, only, or perhaps quite naturally, to be ignored in the confusion and glamour of the 'Great White Way.'" The transfer failed, but transfer to larger audiences and greater publicity remained a temptation for the company, including the produc-tion that immediately followed *Harliquinade* in the next season, Granville Barker's *The Madras House*. Years later Alice realized that "the theatres of Broadway, even the charm of the Punch and Judy, were merely houses or caravanseries for selling wares, while the audience, to a large extent tran-sient comers, had no relationship to distinctive values." She claimed that this was "obvious from the start," that transfers failed because of "ab-sence of spiritus loci," and also recollected years later that the obvious "had apparently to be tested again and again to actually 'take.'"[24]

Even before *Harliquinade* moved uptown, efforts continued to resolve issues surrounding the new professional-amateur organizational model and to define a corresponding financial model. In the summer of 1921, several new steps were taken that allowed release of "The Purpose and the New Plans of the Neighborhood Playhouse" in the fall, for the new season, or about a year after such a mission statement should have been created, adjudicated, and approved. On June 14, 1921, a meeting at the Lewisohn home shaped plans on finance issues. With Lillian Wald, Mr. and Mrs. Morgenthau, Agnes Morgan, and the Lewisohns in attendance, Helen Arthur provided a report, accounted for publicity at a cost of $300 per week in the previous season, and concluded that "this had not brought in the desired returns." At this meeting, the directors agreed to raise ticket prices for the coming season from $1.00 orchestra and 50 cents balcony to $1.50 and 75 cents. They also agreed on plans to create a subscription plan, and when the list of addresses was tabulated later that summer it numbered 8,850.[25] After only one year, the first publicist of the company left for marriage. Fortuitously, Helen Arthur was introduced by Kenneth Macgowan, who was working with the Provincetown group through its transition, to Stella Bloch Hanau. As it happened, Hanau was not at all a worker like the first publicist but a very well-connected family woman capable of donating time and perhaps cash. She was a neighbor of Edward Bernays, who revolutionized media relations and taught the first course on the subject at New York University in 1923. For Doris Fox Benardete, clearly a worker in the organization and not a benefactor, "while the Neighborhood Playhouse engaged an ostensibly inexperienced publicity woman, the job was handled most professionally and efficiently because of Mrs. Hanau's peculiar advantages."[26] Whether by superior technique or connections or both, she launched a Neighborhood Playhouse campaign that, like others on the Bernays moel, stressed a bombardment of small press items that created name recognition.

It was at this point in the company history, in the summer of 1921, that Doris Fox Benardete provides more detailed information on the finances of the Neighborhood Playhouse. She reveals that the Lewisohn annual contribution for the coming season was $30,000 and that they were forced to add another $15,000 for overruns that represented an annual $45,000 unnamed, unrestricted, and unendowed gift. "Alirene" was of course the manager of the gift in the context of Lillian Wald's supervision and manipulation by the remaining directors. It was an enormous gift at a time when a professional actor's salary was $50.00 per week and "the manager and the director," presumably Morgan and Arthur, each received $250 per week. It was also a considerable production budget, since the theater building had already been capitalized and was used without rent. Benardete was at this point the bookkeeper, though she preferred the title treasurer. There plainly was some stress among what the *Dramatic Mirror* had called "that indefatigable little band of workers at the

Neighborhood Playhouse." At her most generous, Benardete observed that "the Lewisohns, preferring to continue alone, chose not to ask others to assist them in supporting the enterprise. They dreaded having financial aid from persons who might be lacking in understanding or sympathy for their project, or perhaps even worse—from persons possessing both who might desire to introduce their own ideas."[27] While their degree of control remained uncompromised, what the Lewisohns and the Neighborhood Playhouse lacked was a sustainable financial plan that was diversified beyond a single-donor expendable gift. At the midpoint in its life, the Neighborhood Playhouse was in a position to test whether this commitment to independence represented vision or vanity and also whether the evolving mission would or would not benefit from anybody's ideas but their own.

By September 1921, "The Purpose and the New Plans" had been printed for public consumption, but many of the internal financial matters remained unresolved. On September 22, at a staff meeting for which the unrevised minutes appear to be in Alice's hand, the only subject was decreasing expenses in order to supplement salaries. Irene stated that "it was found impractical to increase the weekly salary and we wish to consider salaries as a drawing account and anything that comes in above the endowment is to be placed in a cooperative fund—to be divided among the permanent company." Among the suggestions to decrease expenses and so to increase contributions to the cooperative fund were reductions for the cleaning women, for "Hymie the messenger," and for telephone calls. Helen Arthur announced plans for installation of a "coin box telephone" and defended Hymie.[28] In a less generous mood, Benardete attributed financial issues to "the incompetence with which the directors attempted to cope with [them]." Of the Lewisohn sisters at this time she wrote, "Generous as they were, the sisters seemed not to understand that people who work for a living must earn enough to live on." She provided examples of the sacrifices made by festival volunteers from the neighborhood, by cleaning people working for a weekly $15, and by box office staff working for only one dollar more. Helen Arthur came under particular criticism by Benardete because "no one who worked at the Neighborhood Playhouse made much money, but Miss Arthur always managed to appear as if she did." Helen "never pretended to be a democrat": instead, she would arrive at the theater in late afternoon by taxi, and have the box office pay the fare and count it toward "beer and pretzels for the cast" and other petty cash items that were never expended as such. In this account, the Lewisohns, at least, "tried to act like ordinary mortals," and traveled by subway and bus, though of course "when they got home they always had Miss von Nagy, their companion from childhod, to stroke their neck and shoulders." Helen Arthur did not seem to Benardete as comparably economical: "Helen tried to hide extravagant production costs from the Lewisohns, delayed payment of accounts, and then bounced checks: then the treasurer [Doris Fox Benardete] got the very devil from the creditor and the Lewisohns, if they heard about it, and Miss Arthur."[29]

The tensions between directors, between directors and staff, and between the playhouse and the neighborhood are all evident in "The Purpose and the New Plans of the Neighborhood Playhouse" when it was formally released to announce the eighth season, which would be at once the most successful to date in critical terms and also prelude to sudden sabbatical for all operations. Like the other Neighborhood Playhouse statements of purpose, the 1921 one attempted, but never quite succeeded, to synthesize aesthetic interests and community ones. This was the purpose of the opening sentence of "The Purpose": "The Neighborhood Playhouse has for seven years pursued a two-fold purpose—to offer opportunities for aesthetic expression and training to gifted amateurs and to bring to the community, side by side with this, the more finished workmanship of maturer artists of the theatre." The implicit issue being defended is the introduction of a professional corps within the company, but that change was only one level of division that operated on both personal and institutional levels.

Alice, clearly the author of the statement, foresaw a synthesis that had not yet been reached: "The Playhouse feels that this combination of the enthusiasm of the amateur with the craftsmanship of the professional has a distinct value in its future development, offering, as it does, possibilities of experiment in many directions and emphasizing in particular that bond of fellowship that draws together artist and artisan, student and craftsman, through their common love of the theatre." This "distinct value" was quite different from those of 1915 when Lillian Wald welcomed the theater because "what will seem best to-night has been woven out of the traditions of our neighborhood, and . . . the music and the dance and the color are part of the dower brought to New York by the stranger." However, in 1921, the new brochure refers to the local audience as "*one* of the most vital and inspiring factors in the development of the Neighborhood Playhouse" (emphasis added).[30] Alice had articulated her dual vision, at least privately, as early as the summer of 1916. But it was publicly unveiled in 1921 in the context of subscription prices that could not possibly have been designed for the playhouse's neighbors, and the artists and the artisans seem linked by something quite the opposite of "their common love of the theatre."

The season that followed the new mission statement opened with the second play produced at the playhouse by Granville Barker, *The Madras House.* It had been performed in London in 1910, and it was the latest of the Neighborhood Playhouse British imports in the line of Shaw and Bennett. Very like Shaw's *Misalliance,* which it partly inspired, *The Madras House* uses the scene of a successful clothier to argue that privileged women were, in fact, more, not less, exploited than women laborers, and, in a very dramatic acrobat of argumentation, that aristocratic British women were more, not less, exploited than the women of the Muslim world. The partners in the firm are estranged and meet only to contract its sale to an American, Mr. State, who "has the instinct for turning money over and the knack of doing so on a big scale." State plans to franchise the Madras House and so to capitalize on the buying power of "The Great Modern Women's Movement." The prime operating partner, Huxtable, who was apparently played by Whitford Kane to great effect, embraces manipulation of women but resists the Americanization of British drapery practices. The distant partner, Constantine Madras, finds that this confirms his worst views of British society and reveals that he has previously converted to Muslim belief because the British "attitude towards the other sex has become loathsome to me." In a third act scene that features women modeling revealing gowns, Constantine is able to declaim his point about the female fashion set being the "kept women" of "an industrial seraglio."[31]

9. Whitford Kane and E. C. Carrington posing on the rooftop terrace of 466 Grand Street in costume for *The Madras House,* 1921.

Played as an arch comedy of ideas, the production was the kind of success in which, as Alice recalled, "the popularity of *The Madras House* threatened to swamp the playhouse." Popularity was not her goal, and she genuinely regretted, then and later, a success of the "craftsman professionalism" without much evidence of "the enthusiasm of the amateur." The play had opportunities to connect to the idea of a theater on the Lower East Side. In Alice's words, the opening curtain on the seven Huxtable single daughters succeeded as an oppressive, bourgeois "vault of Victorian chastity,"[32] and the second act presented the back room of the kind of business well known on the Lower East Side as "the rag trade." Apart from the Edwardians in decline, the cast also included strong women, especially Miss Yates, who refuses to reveal the identity of her seducer and is quite happy with the prospects of an independent life as a single mother.

In what was intended as a glowing notice, Kenneth Macgowan welcomed *The Madras House* as proof that "there are just five houses in New York where a first night has a distinctive intellectual quality." The others were the theaters of Arthur Hopkins and David Belasco, the Theatre Guild at the Garrick, and the Provincetown Players, which would close at the end of this season and later reopen with Macgowan as partner. Adverting to the remote location, Macgowan praised the play and the production for a "curious mixture of wit and understanding, sociology, philosophy, and sophomoric precept. . . . There is at last an audience in New York and in the little playhouse on Grand Street for this very unusual farce."[33] When, after sixty-four performances that disrupted the repertory schedule, the directors, against previous solemn vows, again chose transfer uptown to the National Theatre in January, *The Madras House,* like *Harliquinade* the year before, attracted ecstatic reviews and almost no audience in the higher stakes of the larger theater, with its "absence of spiritus loci." The business meeting minutes record that on February 28, 1922, at the Lewisohn home, "after discussion of the Uptown production of 'The Madras House,' it was moved by Mr. Gibbs [accountant-manager], and seconded by Miss Wald, that in the future no Neighborhood Playhouse productions be taken uptown unless under different auspices. This motion carried." The same minutes record for the first time discussion of an end-of-the-year "burlesque," which would evolve into *The Grand Street Follies* of 1922.[34]

In the winter of 1921–22, the Neighborhood Playhouse was not only performing British wit, which was not at all as unusual as Macgowan suggested and could hardly be described as innovative or experimental. But its programming was veering from the artists to the artisans, from professional to the amateur, and from uptown to downtown audiences, without finding a single, integrated vehicle for its single vision. Success disrupted ideal institutional development. In December 1921, the *Green-*

wich Villager features a gossipy note that began with how "Sir Herbert Tree [was] once asked the question: 'When is reportory [*sic*] theatre not a reportory theatre?' And answered it by: 'When it's a success.'" The inference drawn was that "this seems to be the danger of the present situation at the Neighborhood Playhouse," because it extended *The Madras House* on Grand Street and postponed planned openings.[35]

One departure from the American infatuation with Shaw-Barker-Bennett was the opening of "Midweek Interludes" featuring "The Color Organ" or "The Clavilux" played by Thomas Wilfred. Seven years after construction of the theater at 466 Grand Street with the concave stage rear wall for light projections, the design was revised. A keyboard was installed in the pit that operated backstage lenses that rear-projected images onto an onstage screen. In *Theatre Arts Magazine*, a photo spread of the clavilux explained in captions that the instrument was a new and "happy union of art and mechanics in the age where science has seemed to be, if not the enemy, at least the rival of creative art." The magazine found it impossible to photograph the "mobile color" images that the instrument projected, but it featured a piece by theater critic Stark Young that described the experience of watching it: "you sit within a darkened theatre before the space in which the light will play. There is a complete silence; and presently you become aware of a proscenium opening. Impalpable forms appear at the sides; they are pale, almost white, they move in a slow, waving rhythm like soft curtains. . . . What we see is impossible to describe; this mobile color is a new art and we have no images of speech for it."[36] The instrument also had its witty detractors, such as the original *Life* magazine: "There was also an organized claque in the back of the house, personal friends of the color green, who applauded vigorously every time it was shown, doubtless in an attempt to impress the management so that green would be given a larger part in the next composition. And after the performance a line of middle-aged admirers were seen standing at the stage-entrance waiting for the red to get its make-up off and to go out to supper."[37]

After demonstrations, the clavilux was used for "midweek interludes" that fell between the dramatic productions of the weeknight professional players and the dance performances on weekends. Clavilux was incorporated into adaptations of Irene's *Dance Patterns* and Agnes Morgan's version of a short story by Leonard Merrick called "The Suicides of the Rue Sombre." Its full value would become evident later that season in the adaptation of Walt Whitman's *Salut au Monde*.

Some of the counterforces and decisions facing the company can be seen in the context of minor productions and publicity that preceded *Salut*. In January 1922, in *Theatre Arts Magazine*, the theater historian Oliver Sayler published a piece equally extreme in praise and in blame. First, he repeated some of the quotations that had been circulating in Neighborhood Playhouse publicity. These include some distinctly odd forms of praise, such as Mrs. Fiske's, "Rare good taste prevails everywhere—good taste, good sense," or William Archer's, "perhaps the most delightful of New York sideshows." But Sayler's real focus was on where he thought the directors had wandered from their purpose:

> Their field for service was their own particular community. They would assist that community toward esthetic self-expression, and to that end they established a workshop for all the arts of the theatre and classes in acting and dancing, while for example rather than for intrinsic reasons they brought in to the theatre noteworthy and stimulating plays and players and artists from outside. If they gave some of those plays, such as Dunsany's and Galsworthy's, and some of those artists, such as Guilbert and Ben-Ami and Tony Sarg and Wilfred, a definite momentum toward larger goals and a wider audience, so much the better. And if they attracted patrons from uptown and out-of-town, and students of the theatre arts from everywhere, they would be cordial hosts. But their charge was the Ghetto and their mission its esthetic self-development.[38]

The directors, of course, did not envision their role as service. Nor did they believe promotion of Yiddish theater through Jacob Ben-Ami or the kind of design associated with Sarg, later known for stage marionettes, was peripheral to their mission. Most of all, they differed on whether "esthetic self-development" could come entirely from within, an assumption by Sayler consistent with the convictions of Lillian Wald. The Lewisohns and the Morgan-Arthurs were themselves transplants to "the Ghetto," and so they naturally believed in a more complex interaction.

The company celebrated its seventh birthday on February 12 by launching weekend matinee performances by the Festival Dancers specifically scheduled for children home on holiday from school. However, only two evenings later, having vowed not to export productions uptown, for the first time they imported a production not under their auspices from Broadway. This amused the *Metropolitan Guide,* an entertainment journal that greeted the transfer of a Charles Vildrac play, *The S.S. Tenacity,* as directed by Augustin Duncan and designed by Robert Edmond Jones, from the Belmont uptown to 466 in these terms: "This anniversary," or the seventh birthday of the Neighborhood Playhouse, "will mark an occurence [sic] new, we believe, in New York theatrical history. We are accustomed to having plays move uptown, from the highways and byways, to Broadway. But the reverse process is unique."[39] At the same time, the company was also affiliating with that most contra-ghetto company, the Theater Guild, for a production of Shaw's epic *Back to Methuselah* uptown at the Garrick. Shaw's play uncut includes five complete dramatic acts, running something on the order of twelve hours, tracing the history of civilization from Adam and Eve into the distant future. To produce it all in three performances, Lawrence Langner of the Guild called in Alice and Agnes Morgan to stage the first episode, *In the Beginning.* Langner, in comments reminiscent of the leering in *The Madras House* but without the irony, was delighted when Adam and Eve in flesh-colored tights (the costume design of Lee Simonson) entered before an audience of "prim social workers from the Neighborhood Playhouse, who brought with them an atmosphere of Social Welfare and Higher Morality not usually associated with the theatre."[40] The production was not a critical success, because of its length, nor a popular one, because tickets were sold only for the complete three-episode performance and, almost ten years in advance of epics like O'Neill's *Mourning Becomes Electra,* no satisfactory meal schedule had been incorporated into the performance one.

Almost simultaneously with its Theatre Guild collaboration, the Neighborhood Playhouse entered into emulation of its other principal rival, the Provincetown Players. After moving *S.S. Tenacity* downtown in February, Augustin Duncan mounted at 466 in March his own production of O'Neill's *The First Man*. Mailings and programs for the play all used different graphics than the ones the playhouse had used consistently over seven years, and Duncan's use of the theater consisted only of facilities, not personnel, but preproduction publicity insisted that *The First Man* was part of its subscription series. The production, which opened on Saturday evening, March 4, was also timed to coincide with the Provincetown Players production of *The Hairy Ape,* which opened the following Friday. Unfortunately, it also coincided with a week for O'Neill that his biographers term "ghastly" even by the standards of O'Neill's frequently epic difficulties. O'Neill's troubled relation with his father, the great melodramatist James O'Neill, had ended with his death in 1920. As he was writing in *The First Man* about an iconoclast's ambitions and his wife's death in childbirth, O'Neill's mother died in California in 1922. She was there managing her husband's real estate investments in the company of Jamie, Eugene's elder brother. Jamie was in recovery from years of alcohol abuse but relapsed while transporting his mother's body back east by train. During rehearsals, O'Neill was getting intermittent communications about Jamie barricaded in his coach with prostitutes. Arthur and Barbara Gelb report that "after a couple of weeks he could see that *The First Man* had some glaring weaknesses and that the production was not going to overcome them. Mentally abandoning *The First Man* . . . he devoted himself entirely to *The Hairy Ape*." The train bearing his mother's body was still west as *The First Man* opened, and arrived in New York the same night *The Hairy Ape* opened.

The playwright's decision, of course, was not good for *The First Man,* Augustin Duncan, or the Neighborhood Playhouse. George Jean Nathan called the play "one of O'Neill's worst full-length performances" because it was little more than "aping the technique of Strindberg."[41] For the Neighborhood Playhouse, however, the problem was aping the technique of the Provincetown Players. A later mailing read, "Knowing *The Hairy Ape* you will surely want to see this other play." The lobby of 466 was given over to an exhibition because "it is especially fitting that these Provincetown painters should place their latest work on exhibit in conjunction with the latest play of their fellow townsman and artist." The *New York*

Sun recognized a dislocation of place in the play, which ends with debate over the fate of the infant:

> The great aunt promises to take the baby away to the pure air of the country. We don't know where she was going to take him, but we suspect that is was somewhere near Provincetown, Massachusetts.
>
> What the child needed, we guess, was sea air. And that seems to be what the playwright needs for the play. That Old Devil Sea is a good friend of O'Neill's, and his plays never seem quite happy when they are far away from it.[42]

The playhouse couldn't succeed even with a high probability project like O'Neill when the subject, the ethos, and the production management were all so far from 466 Grand Street's mission, participation, and direction. *The Hairy Ape,* which is partly set at sea, was a success consistent with the Provincetown Players' record and vision while downtown. Uptown and out of context it was less successful, and a road tour was cancelled. By the end of the year, the Provincetown Players would break up, largely over the issues surrounding O'Neill's successes and uptown transfers, the issues only temporarily resolved at the Neighborhood Playhouse by the motion seconded by Lillian Wald. By the end of the season, the Theatre Guild was also giving the public what they wanted in an Arnold Bennett play called *What the Public Wants.* This was the configuration of the three companies described at the time by the angry theater historian Oliver Sayler: "The Guild on its record is not an experimental theatre. It has taken no more chances than the average earnest Broadway producer, not as many as Arthur Hopkins, the Neighborhood Playhouse, the Provincetown Players, or its own earlier self, the Washington Square Players."[43]

One factor that may help explain the Neighborhood Playhouse spells in winter of 1922 of Guild collaboration and Provincetown envy may have been the long project that would open in April as *Salut au Monde.* Underway for so long that it revived some of the founding principles, *Salut,* the final production of the year, also successfully integrated the dual aims of the "New Plans" announced at the beginning of the season: "to offer opportunities for aesthetic expression and training to gifted amateurs and to bring to the community, side by side with this, the more finished workmanship of maturer artists of the theatre." From the earliest festival performances before the building opened at 466, the Lewisohns had considered creating a festival out of the inclusive ethos of Walt Whitman's work. By the spring of 1918, they had developed a conception that incorporated music by Edward MacDowell and Marion Bauer. At that point, it appears that they began to feel that the previously composed music would not suit the originality of the conception. At the same time, Charles Griffes, who knew MacDowell and Bauer and who had collaborated with the Lewisohns the year before on *Kairn of Koridwen*, became, according to his biographer, "passionately concerned." There was some hesitation on the part of the Lewisohns, likely because Griffes's European influences seemed distant from Whitman's Americanism. Griffes seemed aware of this: later he would write to Bauer, who was delighted to be outside the project, "But oh! What will you Whitmanites say!" Eventually the commission was made to Griffes: $450 for the composition and also conducting with piano at fourteen performances. The terms repeated those of *Kairn* and did not improve despite the success of the earlier show. By comparison, in the spring of 1918, Griffes got the same lump sum for recording six pieces, a much less time-consuming project, and with those compositions he would also receive royalties. According to the Griffes biographer, Edward Maisel, by the time of the signing of the commission, Griffes "was already some way along in his sketches to the libretto, which, like the earlier Lewisohn production, effloresced into murky cosmism in some passages and offered splendid opportunities for imaginative feeling in others." While a great deal had been composed, two years later, in the spring of 1920, the whole remained unfinished when Griffes died of pneumonia at the age of thirty-six. According to Maisel, in his final illness Griffes refused the Lewisohn request to consider a successor for the project. After his death, they did assign Edward Ricketts, who reported to Maisel that the final score was a first act by Griffes, a third act by himself, and a second from "various sources" to evoke different world religions.[44]

The earliest, handwritten (presumably by Irene) sketch of how they would treat Whitman's poem begins:

PROLOGUE:

SCENE: steps rising on either side of proscenium. The Poet, dressed to suggest WW—in soft shirt open at the neck a long cape and large slouch hat, is standing on the center of stage with his back to audience. Figures suggesting forms of nature appear on the top of the steps at either side. They come down and as the leader reaches the Poet, says:

CHORUS: Oh take my hand WW.

WW gives one hand—then the other—then speaks:

Such a gliding wonder

Each sharing the earth with all.[45]

This kind of abbreviation of Whitman's long lines is typical of the rest of the script. Whitman's "Salut au Monde" opens:

O take my hand Walt Whitman!
Such gliding wonders! such sights and sounds!
Such join'd unended links, each hook'd to the next,
Each answering all, each sharing the earth with all.[46]

In the poem, an earth force of vague origins takes Whitman on a global tour. The poet-persona recites a litany of what he sees and hears, good and bad, from prisons and slave ships and workers and scientists, all the time attempting, much like the Neighborhood Playhouse, to integrate oppositions. In some notes for a meeting on November 13, 1921, early in production planning, Alice wrote, "Not greatest lit[erary] effort. Seemed to interpret so much of the present day philosophy. Man's place in the universe. Drama of human life thru cosmic life rather than cosmic life thru the human personality." In notes for the meeting, she also scribbled that it was three years since the death of Griffes (it was two) and the hundredth anniversary of the birth of Whitman (it was the 102nd). Never much concerned with details, she was stimulated by the task of expressing the cosmic, and in Whitman's text she had found a superb vehicle for festival expression. Among her notes were the underlined words that this text is "the scheme of *our fest.*" While using as lead actor Ian Maclaren from the players, the production was conceived as a festival and performed on the in-house dance schedule of Saturday and Sunday nights only. In her notes, Alice recorded her conception that "Salut seemed to embody the vision of world brotherhood so necessary to project on the heels of the World War."[47]

When the curtain rose for the first of eight performances, the choruses on steps left and right embraced Walt Whitman, played by Ian Maclaren. His first line about the gliding wonder brought forth an image of the globe projected by the clavilux. It was an opening effect that was praised by the *Brooklyn Eagle,* which had its own history with Whitman: "In act I there is an adaptation of an idea which the Neighborhood Playhouse has used before this—the color organ. Walt Whitman, looking out into space and time, sees the great circle of the world, on which in an endless stream flows a stream of every-changing color. The audience follows it breath-

10. Cast montage before the clavilux rear projection for *Salut au Monde,* 1922.

lessly, as if watching the development of the plot of a melodrama."[48] In the second of three parts of the performance, the Lewisohns interpolated scenes to enact brief references in the poem to world religions. In the stage version, dances presented priests in Hebrew, Hindu, Greek, Muslim, and Christian contexts with Rickett's musical settings. Whitman's chanted lines were replaced by songs, and the singers, in particular, fully fulfilled the playhouse's foundational ambitions. The Hebrew interlude of "Kol Nidre," the Yom Kippur prayer, was sung by Sol Friedman, a long-time amateur Henry Street Players veteran in his first professional appearance. The Hindu song was performed by Basanta Koomar Roy, an immigrant to the Lower East Side from Bengal. The Greek song was sung by an amateur from North Carolina seeking stage time in New York, and the Muslim number was performed by a Persian studying at Columbia University whose professor documented Rickett's ideas. Their songs were staged to dance by both the Festival Dancers and the Junior Festival Dancers. The third and closing part, which returns to the poet's summation, came down from stage to house for an audience processional. The archive register of productions lists for *Salut* a full cast of 26 men and 56 women, and a sold-out orchestra held 300. The procession was led from stage by Jacob Tobin, the African American doorman of the Neighborhood Playhouse, whose participation especially pleased Lillian Wald: "the enthusiasm reached the colored porter, magnificent in form, who asked to march as the representative of his race, with naked thorax."[49]

Salut au Monde was universally praised and drew conspicuously greater numbers of visitors from uptown. It also fully succeeded in the terms of "experimental theater" demanded by Oliver Sayler and others. For Stark Young of the *New Republic, Salut* was "one of the most important events of the theatre year because . . . it is an experiment in terms of poetic idea interfused with and commented upon by light, music, and dance forms; it attempts, in sum, to establish a rhythm out of a synthesis of all these elements." That quote was edited by Doris Fox Benardete for her history of the company. But as a participant, her enthusiasm was clearly based less on critical praise for synthesis of dramatic elements than on the actual experience of synthesis of the playhouse company. She reiterates several times that "everyone connected in any capacity with the Play-

11. Ian MacLaren in costume as Walt Whitman for *Salut au Monde*, 1922.

house who had any ability or talent was engaged to make *Salut au Monde* the unique achievement it became." While recognizing the contributions of the directors and some of the other artists she considered management, such as Aline Bernstein, Benardete filled her history with long rolls of the names of unknown staff people who contributed to the production: "Polaire Weissman, Martha Mabel (known as Dixie) Moore, Jane Didesheim, Susan Friedberg, Florence Levine, Ella Markowitz," and so on.[50] In 1922, after seven years of intermittent victories and repetitive failures, *Salut au Monde* restored to the Neighborhood Playhouse the communal exhilaration produced earlier by events like the 1913 pageant before the theater building was opened or the *Jephtha's Daughter* production that opened it in 1915.

That was a brief moment of communal exhilaration that could not easily be sustained, and the remaining weeks of the 1921–22 season, from that moment of high success, brought a quick series of events leading to a hastily planned suspension of operations. The show that followed *Salut au Monde* was *Makers of Light,* by Frederick Lansing Day. It had less to do with the clavilux or stage design than it did with psychological realism as practiced by George Pierce Baker's workshop at Harvard or his students, including Lansing Day, Eugene O'Neill, and Agnes Morgan. *Makers of Light* opened on May 23, and four days later, on May 27, the core business committee of Lillian Wald, Rita Morgenthau, Helen Arthur, and Agnes Morgan, and Alice and Irene convened to assess the first professional season. The minutes were recorded by Irene. The good news, according to Agnes, the pragmatic stage manager, was that the inaugural "union crew worked out very successfully from a technical angle." The bad news, according to Helen, was that *The Madras House* and *The First Man* had broken even and every other production had lost money. The notes record that "the situation as a whole is about what it was last season notwithstanding the subscribers and the raise in prices of tickets." To judge from the minutes, the Lewisohns were silent throughout the meeting, and the subtext of the meeting seems to have been that their productions, such as *Salut,* were running greater losses than those associated with Morgan and Arthur, such as *Makers of Light.* The heightened stage festivals had higher production costs than more "realistic" productions, and even the importation of productions such as *S.S. Tenacity* or collaborations such as *Back to Methuselah* could not fund productions with elaborate sets, original musical scores, or large choruses, which, even if mostly volunteer, created substantial overhead in costume fabrication and rehearsal time. Transfer uptown had not proven successful in the case of *The Madras House,* and apparently was not even considered for *Salut.* That meeting ended at 11:30 P.M., and it was continued five days later. The conclusion reached was that cost reduction was not possible and significant new financial support would be the solution: "if it is right to subsidize the public to this extent, it is also necessary to find new sources of income." Donors with the potential to be the first significant ones other than the Lewisohns were discussed.[51]

Further discussion at the double meeting was given to "the burlesque," which since *The Silver Box* in 1913 had been a traditional company celebration at the end of the season. When burlesque was discussed at the final business meetings, the possibility of extra, external performances was introduced at first only as actor benefits. Alice later gallantly claimed that "our subscribers were the actual cause of the accident of *The Grand Street Follies,*" but fiscal anxiety had to be part of the motivation for the "First Edition" in June 1922, after the record of the first professional season. In an undated first draft of Alice's memoir, she sets a darker scene than in the published version. "We were sitting gloomily about the dining table of the Neighborhood Playhouse restaurant, wondering how in thunder we were going to conjure up the special invitation production promised to the subscribers," she wrote. "The thought weighed like a machine gun on our minds. And suddenly, in one of those lucid moments which occasionally present themselves, I said, 'Why not invite the subscribers to our perennial burlesque? Why not include them in our family party?'"[52]

This solution to programming promises and fiscal shortfall was not entirely unprecedented in New York theater. When the inaugural, public *Grand Street Follies* of 1922 opened on June 13, it had been preceded by a week by the well-known *Ziegfeld Follies* uptown at Times Square. That 1922 edition featured sketches by Ring Lardner, an appearance by Will Rogers, and music by Victor Herbert. It was greeted by the *New York Times* as the "blue-blood among the revues" with "loud rejoicings over its beauties, which nearly always manage to be more striking than ever before" and "a paucity of the extremely humorous."[53] After it opened in 1922, the *Grand Street Follies* would be joined by the *Greenwich Village Follies,* already a summer perennial. Though in this year staged on Christopher Street, the *Greenwich Village Follies* had already evolved into a poorer cousin of its uptown, Belasco cousin: the *Times* welcomed it for "melody and beauty pre-eminently" and only after that for "novelty, burlesque, and comedy."[54] The Neighborhood Playhouse promised instead, in its pre-publicity, "a travesty on the Neighborhood productions."[55] For the opening night, subscribers-only program, this included the subtitle "A Low-Brow Show for High Grade Morons" and the notice "Send Your Enemies, If Not Your Friends." The first extended skit was a parody of *The Madras House* in which the "kept women" of the "industrial seraglio" took center stage with Helen Arthur as Turkish Delight, Agnes Morgan as Oriental Dream, and others, all performing for a very confused Sol Friedman as Granville Barker's ultraperceptive Constantine Madras. The next number parodied both the clavilux and *Salut au Monde* in a staging of "What Whitman's" hitherto unknown poem "I'll Tell the World." In the next parody of "Royal Fandango," which had been revived in 1921–22, Irene and Blanche Talmud danced Torero and Prince opposite Dan Walker and Albert Carroll as the Gypsy and the Lady with a Fan. The self-parody took aim at both the dramas of the season, such as *Makers of Light* under the title "Making Light of Day," and the lyric programs, including *The Green Ring*. After an ice cream intermission on the rooftop garden, the company looked uptown, with Albert Carroll performing John Barrymore, Pavlowa (in the spelling of the day), and Irene Castle.

The inaugural *Grand Street Follies* combined elements of anarchy and spontaneity with informality and ensemble performance that set it aside from *Ziegfeld, Greenwich Village,* or other follies of that summer and later ones, such as *The Garrick Gaeities.* The result was legendary, and in fact threatened to become the sole legend of the Neighborhood Playhouse. Two years after the company ceased to exist, Joseph Wood Krutch celebrated the 1929 edition as "scarcely more finished than that for 1922 . . . it occasionally crosses over to the wrong side of the mysterious line which separates the careless spontaneity of the best burlesque from the embarrassing antics of the funny man who half realizes that he is only making a fool of himself."[56]

Even in 1922, the tension between parody and ambitious intentions was evident. Alice later celebrated the annual editions as the fulfillment of festival intentions and an extension of a company-defining success such as *Salut au Monde: "The Follies* was one of the most refreshing and releasing experiences of each year, relieving by the bubbling delight of its preparation whatever intensity and strain the repertory might have exacted. All departments, lyric, dramatic, classes, and staff, were called upon to participate. From a practical angle it enabled us to keep the company intact."[57] She does not mention that she personally never participated in any stage or credited offstage capacity; Irene, onstage in the first edition, would not be in the second or later editions. Regarding later editions, Doris Fox Benardete recalled the tension among directors immediately focused by the success of the *Follies*. "What hoax was being played upon the directors of the Neighborhood Playhouse?" she asked. "The sisters who had devoted their lives and their fortunes to advance art, what irony must they have had to face when it was not for their art the public yearned but for the hilarious burlesquing of art by their director and their manager."[58]

More than irony was evident even in the inaugural year of the *Follies*, 1922. The show opened on June 13, and on June 20 a typed announcement on Neighborhood Playhouse letterhead was distributed internally and signed, "Faithfully Yours," by Alice, Irene, Helen, and Agnes. It announced a meeting four days later and stated, "We hope you will surely be present as a matter of vital importance to every member of the Playhouse will be discussed."[59] No minutes were kept of the meeting. Two days after it, the *New York Times* announced "The Neighborhood to Close for Year": "The cessation of public activity for a year, it was declared yesterday, is made necessary by the fact that the time will be required to develop the possibilities and potentialities of the Playhouse. The intervening year will be devoted to 'the formation of a permanent company of players and dancers; further experimentation in pantomime and lyric drama; finding new material; and an expansion of the workshop.'"[60] All those things, of course, had been accomplished in the previous year of professional players and subscription sales. The subscribers themselves were a major concern over the remainder of the summer. An eight-paragraph, heavily edited draft of a letter to subscribers, dated July 14, stressed past accomplishments and an unshaken intention "to continue experiments in the lyric drama and to revitalize, through some new mode, the spirit of the ancient ritual festivals. The production of *Salut au Monde* indicated infinite possibilities in this synthetic art form."[61] Four days later, Lillian Wald wrote to "Ailrene" to state that "the signature ought to be one person, the Chairman of the Committee, Alice. . . . She might sign it 'For the Committee of the Neighborhood Playhouse, Faithfully yours.'" The letter to subscribers that finally emerged, on August 29, declared "the postponement of further productions until the Fall of 1923," and it was signed, without name or names, as "Faithfully Yours, the Neighborhood Playhouse.[62]

5

❧

1922–1925

The Lessons of the East and The Little Clay Cart

Only in an ideal world could the entire reason for a sabbatical year in a theater company be to "develop possibilities and potentialities." A sabbatical, in fact, might cease such development and at best would limit it. A more likely scenario was sketched out in reference to the lives of many performing arts enterprises by Alice Goldfarb Marquis, in her book *Art Lessons*. Generalizing on the "drama of institutional theater" as a non-profit enterprise, she described the beginning, the middle, and the end: "Act one features a brilliant, charismatic individual with exciting new ideas and the drive to realize them. In act two, community leaders join local drama buffs to provide what they believe is generous support for the talent in their midst. Audiences flock in, awards and honors accrue, everyone rejoices that the institution will endure and prosper forever. On the crest of success, production costs rise. Deficits loom. In act three tragedy closes in."[1] On the sabbatical announcement, the drama of the Neighborhood Playhouse might be said to follow this scenario up to a point. The charismatic Lillian Wald launched the theater with enthusiasts Alice and Irene Lewisohn, and their ample honors appeared to represent sustainable success to others. Their story differs from the scenario at this moment in the company history because they did reopen after the sabbatical, in fall 1923, which was a revival not equaled in the parallel cases of the Provincetown Players and the Theatre Guild. Moreover, the success of the Neighborhood Playhouse could have been sustainable and not inevitably tragic. In the end, however, the Goldfarb scenario prevailed.

At the end of its second act, the Neighborhood Playhouse had fallen victim to the rising costs that underlay the decision to close for one year. A style of fiscal management that was at best inefficient had been evident at least since the adoption of the professional model. Apart from the personality conflicts such as that between Benardete and Helen Arthur inside the company, there were important contexts for the enterprise that could have made it better informed. The first was its operation as a philanthropy. The transfer from a Gilded Age of philanthropic excess to one of progressive social constructivism had become complete since Alice and Irene had succeeded their father Leonard as administrators of the family philanthropy. The philanthropy trends in the 1920s moved, as Kathleen D. McCarthy has documented in her book *Noblesse Oblige,* away from "progressives" micromanaging their gifts in the fashion of the Gilded Age benefactors. Instead, in the new trend, "experts were, in effect, to serve as liaisons between donor and recipient, interpreting the needs and capabilities of both for the benefit of society as a whole." Among the great managers of this new relation was Jane Addams in Chicago, whose work was known and emulated by Lillian Wald in New York. Among Miss Addams's greatest benefactors was Julius Rosenwald of Sears, Roebuck, and Company who was of the same generation of German Jewish immigrants as the Lewisohn brothers and whose philanthropy continued much longer than Leonard's and evolved much more fully into the progressive model than Adolph's. By the 1920s, Rosenwald was proclaiming the difficulties of directing wealth and the necessity for professional interveners who could provide "scientific inquiry." Further, Rosenwald was opposed to any enterprise funded solely by single benefactors, which he declared "too autocratic."[2] Neither the difficulty of disbursing gifts effectively nor the needs for professional assistance were understood by Alice and Irene, whose single-benefactor funding continued to rise to higher levels almost in direct proportion to their disagreements with the theater professionals in the house, Agnes Morgan and Helen Arthur. Nor were those lessons of a new age in philanthropy communicated to them by Lillian Wald as effectively as they were to Rosenwald by Jane Addams. The sabbatical, however, with its suspension of productions for retrospect and exploration, did offer at least an opportunity to contemplate the funding model.

A second dimension of fiscal policy that makes up the "drama of institutional theater" is the external context, with its pricing and competition systems that intersect with the independent company. The systems are in fact less tragic and more remedial, but here, too, Alice and Irene, for all their dedication to ideals, had no expertise and sought none. The timing of the sabbatical, in retrospect, proved to be the ideal moment for new productions. A large part of the Neighborhood Playhouse audience came from uptown, and the boom decade of the 1920s, especially the mid-decade years, was a period of significant opportunity in total theater activities, both in new productions and length of productions. The Neighborhood Playhouse pause for "potentialities" in 1922 deprived it of the opportunity of a season at a theater-industry peak. The window of opportunity would close at the end of the decade, when theater industry would face emerging threats that included greater film-industry competition and costs driven higher by organized labor.[3] The pause in 1922 also followed a significant crest in the company's individual popularity, with the recent critical and popular successes of *Salut au Monde* and *The Grand Street Follies*, and so it halted audience development at a moment when the company was in a position to capitalize on success.

In this complex of problems caused by success, the Neighborhood Playhouse was not alone. For many years, William Baumol and William G. Bowen were among the most cheerful of those students of performing arts who "don the inherited mantle of the dismal scientist." Using economics rather than aesthetics, they studied how "the objectives of the typical nonprofit organization are by their very nature designed to keep it constantly on the brink of financial catastrophe." This drama of nonprofit institutions unfolds as the quality of services provided, including production values in theater, prevail as goals in themselves, with rising costs proportional to success. *Salut*, for example, sets a level of success, produced by higher investment, that consequently sets the bar higher for subsequent investment to maintain the institutional mission. Baumol and Bowen report that in the dismal-scientist view, "the likelihood of surplus funds is slim indeed. These goals constitute bottomless receptacles into which limitless funds can be poured." In the case of nonprofit theater, the great organizational goal of reaching audiences that might otherwise not experience theater make it even more difficult to achieve balance, let alone profit. The lesson, for Baumol and Bowen, is that "the desire to provide a product of as high a quality as possible and to distribute the product in a manner other than that which maximizes revenue combine to produce a situation which is unusual in yet another respect. For such an enterprise a substantial increase in the demand for its product may well worsen the organization's financial health!" This was the dismal fiscal phenomenon faced by the Neighborhood Playhouse as well as other nonprofits including theater then and now. If there is a tragedy in the organizational system of nonprofit theater, it is the inevitability that, facing loss generated by success, the institution cannot revise its strategic plan. The two economists describe this in either grudging admiration or exasperated incomprehenson: "the organizations cannot simply refuse to expand their activities in response to an increase in demand. By such a refusal the organization would renege on its fundamental objectives."[4] Though they had little expertise in management and philanthropic strategies, the Lewisohns were determined to refuse to renege on founding principles.

In nonprofit theater of the early twentieth century and since, two strategies have been frequently employed to contain costs while preserving mission. Both were adopted by the Neighborhood Playhouse and its colleague institutions, and both failed. In *Theatre in America*, published in 1968 and not followed by a lot of research in the same area, Jack Poggi assumed his mantle of dismal scientist to explore the unpopular subject of "the impact of economic forces" in American theater from 1870 to 1967. He prefers the term "noncommercial" to "the art-theater, or little-theater, or experimental-theater movement in this country."

Using as example the New Theater, viewed by the Neighborhood Playhouse founders as a prototype, Poggi documents how the repertory system, adopted on Grand Street in 1920, had been proven problematic at best by 1910. The difficulty faced by Lee Shubert, Winthrop Ames, and the thirty benefactors of their New Theatre on Central Park West was that the repertory system introduced the disadvantages of paying for the downtime for leading actors and also of fixing an irrevocable scheduling limit to the most successful shows. The second of these disadvantages, capping successful runs, had the additional effect of alienating playwrights who "preferred to take their work to commercial managers for consecutive runs."[5]

In Poggi's account, a further adversarial trend faced by the Neighborhood Playhouse as it contemplated its potentialities in 1922 was the general decline of the little theater movement since the Lewisohns' first efforts at the beginning of the century. Poggi's history is of the divergence of the most successful actors, directors, and managers, figures like Agnes Morgan and Helen Arthur, into professional theater endeavors, and the remaining amateurs, like the Festival Players, into a club context that suggested not so much "amateur" as "unprofessional." He cites as notable exceptions to the trend in the 1920s the Provincetown Players, the Theatre Guild, and the Neighborhood Playhouse. On the first case, he cites the company history by Helen Deutsch and Stella Hanau from 1931, which explained the great success of Eugene O'Neill's *The Emperor Jones* in 1920, its transfer uptown, the subsequent commitment of O'Neill to uptown, professional talent, and the company's decision to suspend activities for the 1922–23 season, which was also the Neighborhood Playhouse's sabbatical year. Unlike the sabbatical group, the inactive Provincetown Players never resumed in the same form: in 1923 it was reorganized as the Provincetown Playhouse with new priorities more compatible with uptown success. The Guild, at the same time, had a longer history of uptown transfers and had already moved premises from downtown to the Garrick Theatre on Thirty-fifth Street. In 1923, it defined itself in terms of a new theater building rather than a new company organization and launched a public bond drive that capitalized the Guild Theatre on Fifty-second Street in 1925. The uptown setting proved unpopular with artists, the company had to redeem the bonds, and so, in the words of the designer Lee Simonson, "began to adopt the Broadway technique." The history of movement uptown was, to Simonson, "the metamorphosis of the Theatre Guild into a producing organization indistinguishable in taste and method from many of the Broadway management."[6] In the case of the two contemporaries most like the Neighborhood Playhouse, both repertory and transfers uptown proved to be the path not to solvency but to extinction.

The building at 466 Grand Street was not completely dark for the season of 1922–23. Uptown, the season was notable for being the winter of the antithesis of little theater in the spectacles of John Barrymore's *Hamlet* and David Belasco's *The Merchant of Venice.* Downtown, at the Neighborhood Playhouse, there were occasional rentals, and it opened in late winter for *The Little Legend of the Dance,* a return of the Festival Dancers for a children's production of a story by Agnes Morgan choreographed by Blanche Talmud. The season also proved a boom one for the dramatic clubs in the settlement, though they did not perform in 466. The *Henry News* reported that "Henry Street has its playhouse but the large number of girls and boys who are club members are not able to participate in its finished productions. We are trying to fill the gap between the two by club plays at house parties."[7] In addition, while the Lewisohns traveled, a lecture series was developed as a means of cultivating benefactors. Helen Arthur cleared the series with Lillian Wald in early fall by approval of a draft invitation from Helen signed "Faithfully yours." There would be four lectures in the adjacent rehearsal hall and shop on Pitt Street, giving patrons a more intimate scale and a backstage ambience. A subscription to all four lectures cost $5.00, and, as per Helen's memo, "for outsiders the price is Seven Dollars and Fifty Cents," when admission to full performances was $1.50. The speakers represented fairly well the tangled and sometimes conflicted ambitions of the enterprise. In November the speakers in the "lecture course" were Stark Young, one year into his long tenure as theater critic at the *New Republic,* and Minor White Latham, the Elizabethan scholar already known for her book *Puck* and in a few years to be better known for *Elizabethan Fairies.* After the holiday break, the course continued with Dhan Gopal Mukerji, a Hindu folklorist who talked about the Indian legend of *The Little Clay Cart* almost two years before the Neighborhood Playhouse production of it, and Norman Bel Geddis, the stage and later industrial designer who would become well known for his collaboration with Max Reinhardt and Aline Bernstein on *The Miracle* at the Century, the new identity of Winthrop Ames's failed New Theatre on Central Park West. The mix in the lectures of establishment critic, academic scholar, South Asian folklorist, and designer represents both a version of the Neighborhood Playhouse most likely to appeal to benefactors and also real organizational options and decisions to be made. No notes survive in the Lillian Wald archive on the success or failure of the series.[8]

Meanwhile, on sabbatical, Alice and Irene had embarked on a grand tour sketched out in an itinerary filed with Wald and largely executed as planned across the post–World War I national alignment. The route was from Genoa to Naples and then "four to six weeks in Egypt (and Palestine)." January and February were spent in India and Burma for research on *The Little Clay Cart*. The return was through the Persian Gulf with stops in Mesopotamia, Beirut, and Greece. The summer address was Paris and London, and the contact throughout was the Farmers Loan and Trust Company in Paris. The itinerary plan ended with "home. . . ."[9] It was the same winter that Jig Cook and Susan Glaspell closed their theater and settled in Crete, where they delayed return until the Provincetown Players was essentially abandoned and left for reorganization. Alice and Irene's version of sabbatical was more luxurious, ambitious, and ultimately more profitable for their theater. In her memoir, Alice later wrote that the purpose of the journey was to address the fact that in recent years the theater mission "appeared in patches like a grandmother's quilt, joined together with bits from a bag of old remnants. . . . To go on repeating the gestures, stemming from forms grown threadbare and tarnished, seemed hopeless. How [to] find a way to those roots which, we felt, could alone answer the need of theatre of our day?" They hoped to find their way in "the atmosphere of the East which had given birth to ritual art."[10]

The roots they sought were found in the concept of little theater that had launched their project, and these were rediscovered in the East, through research for *The Little Clay Cart*, which would restore the Neighborhood Playhouse mission by replacing repetition with original theatrical value. One record of their rediscovery was an article, "The Little Theatre in Egypt," published in the *Atlantic Monthly* the summer after their return and bylined "Alice and Irene Lewisohn." It was a literal and no doubt idealized description of theater as practiced in Egypt. It was written without exegesis or generalization: the implications for New York were only implicit in subtitles such as "The Great White Way of Cairo" and "The Little Theatre of Sudan." The essay opened:

We sat in a box reserved for European visitors, sipped our Oriental coffee and smoked, while the orchestra was tuning and the audience assembling. Opposite us, the Moslem bourgeoisie deposited their yashmaked harems behind a long screen of Nottingham lace curtain and then seated themselves below with the unveiled ladies of their acquaintance. Below us was the pit where gathered the rank and file of the audience, completely native in *tarboosh, kufieh,* and *galabya.* Above us, packed to overflowing, was the gallery, for this was a gala night when Nunyra, the idolized singer of ballads, of opera, of lieder, was to appear.

This Egyptian setting could not be a better analogy for the Neighborhood Playhouse, with its bourgeois and rank-and-file audience, with its meeting of American and Eastern European decor and dress, and, on founding, the insertion into that mix of idolized divas of European traditions such as Yvette Guilbert or Gertrude Lawrence or Ellen Terry. In the article, the narrators see the lack of vision and patchwork repetitions in this opening "Great White Way," and so they trust themselves to guides of the most remote "Little Theatre." These include dance-theater performances, first on the Nile and then in the Sudan: "On leaving the Theatre of the Nile, we began our Assuan seminar under the Nubian professorship of Bogadi Mohammed Ali. Within thirty minutes of our arrival we were in our knickers, galloping on spirited beasts over the Nubian desert sands, past the granite quarries with the unfinished shaft for a new temple, then Pilae romantically rising from the Nile, its pylons half visible, gracefully lifting their petaled capitals like colossal lotus flowers." This arousing scene is followed by others as provocative, including an introduction to "the mysteries of the Dervish" by "Ali, our irrepressible donkey-boy." In the Sudan desert, actually in "what later appeared to be the community bed," they discover "Little Theatre rarefied to its ultimate purpose": "First, the audience is sharing directly with the performers in the creation of the production; second, there is no physical convention of proscenium or setting to separate the audience from the stage; thirdly, and most important, there is the rare and personal sensation that the moment belongs to you alone—that for you alone the gate of illusion is momentarily opened."[11]

There was no likelihood that the lessons of the desert could reverse the proscenium and Western theatrical conventions at 466 Grand Street. But the lessons of group participation and the sensation of illusory forms were useful references back to the festival as performance and that sense emerging in Alice's much revised and ultimately suppressed "Statement Aug. 1916" that the root principle was "to create an atmosphere for those who desire to forget themselves in the pursuit of an art expression."[12] The problematic relation between "art expression" as release and the imperatives of social activism and settlement ideals remains. The difference between the unarticulated notes on purpose in 1916 and the published lessons of the desert from the trip of 1923 is the recognition of audience as a priority above the artists—"that the moment belongs to you." It is a clarification that makes possible rapprochement between the agenda of the settlement and the theater within it. Unsurprisingly, the performance realizations of this clarifying vision would ultimately be set in Eastern contexts: *The Little Clay Cart* and *The Dybbuk*. Unsurprisingly, it would take some time to extend the clarifying vision from the founding sisters to the company, and so the sabbatical did not immediately resolve the conflicts of the group enterprise. In a less polished version of the lessons of the sabbatical, unpublished and unedited notes for company meetings that appear to be Irene's manuscript with Alice's notations, "returning from a pilgrimage in the East," the more symbiotic relation of audience to artist is explicit and not fictionalized: "We have come back with no new light in our hands and are not filled with manuscripts, but our minds are haunted by a firmer belief in our early inspiration, by a clearer vision of the future, and, through our wider contacts, a humbler realization of our place in the theater of life."[13]

What they found on return to New York was an equally clear but rather different vision of the future of the Neighborhood Playhouse. The greatest influence on this vision was the appearance in New York in January 1923 of the Moscow Art Theatre uptown at the Al Jolson Theatre. The repertory of Russian plays performed in Russian was received with universal acclaim and publicized for the technique of acting as derived from Konstantin Stanislavsky. In theatrical trends, the Stanislavsky method was another validation of "realism," simplicity, and sincerity over melodrama or spectacle, and so it resembled other international influences on American little theater such as the Abbey Theatre of Ireland. The Moscow Art Theatre technique differed, however, in that it could be taught and so replicated. One dimension of the MAT sensation in 1923 can be seen in the contemporary academic reception of it, of which A. L. Fovitzky's *Moscow Art Theatre and Its Distinguishing Characteristics*, published in advance of the company arrival in New York, is representative: "Many will naturally claim that the Moscow Art Theatre is not alone in its talent for simplicity and sincerity of performance, and it is indeed true that many other theatres of Europe and America are noted for the simplicity and truthfulness of their acting; yet to Stanislavsky belongs the peculiar honor of having devised and introduced methods of performance which, until he did so, were unknown."[14]

The method became extraordinarily well known in the United States as "The Method" as propagated by members of the company who stayed behind, such as Maria Ouspenskaya, and adherents such as Lee Strasberg or Stella Adler who evolved the method through organizational bases such as in American Laboratory Theatre, Group Theatre, and elsewhere. The method required long processes of rehearsal and collective psychological exploration as well as individual self-examination. As put in the first program for the American Laboratory Theatre, in an editorial called "Collective Education in the Art of the Theatre," method training consisted of discovering "the 'tone' of the play [that] is the harmonious blending of the actors' spirits as expressed in sounds which constitute the music of speech. To evoke this harmony, the regisseur has to understand the subtle psychologic make-up of his group, namely the mental qualities of each actor, his emotional disposition, his comic or tragic potentialities, the peculiarity of his relation to his fellow-players." Then, the regisseur may "arrive at the best results achievable through a harmony of their blended spirits."[15] A distinct difference between the visions developed in 1922–23 by the Lewisohns and by the Morgan-Arthurs, who would advance "The Method," was that the first focused on the catalysis between player and audience and the second on the player-to-player relation.

The author of that note was the leading regisseur in America at the time, Richard Boleslavsky, who would also direct the production that reopened the Neighborhood Playhouse after its sabbatical. He had been a member of the Moscow Art Theatre company from 1906 to 1919, when he left the Russian Revolution and trained in documentary filmmaking with military troops in Germany. Reversing the direction of the Lewisohns, he arrived in New York with his wife for a production of *Revue Russe* in October 1922. When the MAT arrived in January 1923, Boleslavsky rejoined the cast of the Russian productions. He also began a series of lectures at the small Princess Theatre in midtown that established him, with Ouspenskaya, as the chief proponent of the Stanislavsky method in America. According to a contemporary journalistic account, "During the engagement of the Moscow Art Theatre, Boleslavsky held courses in its theory of the theatre. This engagement coincided with the Sabbatical year the Neighborhood Playhouse had granted itself while it laid out a plan for the future, and several members of the staff of the Neighborhood Playhouse were Boleslavsky's pupils."[16]

The cast on sabbatical was scarcely the whole of Boleslavsky's audience, and Boleslavsky had many projects in hand other than the Neighborhood Playhouse group: in particular, cultivating Miriam and Herbert Stockton, who would fund the American Laboratory Theatre later that year, and also directing a major production, *Sancho Panza*, in a Times Square theater in the coming fall. But an unlikely partnership of Boleslavsky and six members of the Neighborhood Playhouse did develop in the summer of 1923 by virtue of a gift from Mrs. Willard Straight, a new benefactor in the Lewisohns' absence, and arrangement by Helen Arthur for a country home in Pleasantville to the north of Manhattan. As Boleslavsky became the first teacher in America of the Stanislavsky method, so actors from the Neighborhood Playhouse became the first pupils of the method. One was Aline MacMahon, a graduate of Barnard College rather than Henry Street, who was already a Broadway veteran before being recruited for the Neighborhood Playhouse by Rita Morgenthau. Soon MacMahon would be stolen back to Broadway by the Shuberts, but in 1923 she had been a company member since *The Madras House*. She left an oral history in which she remembered being "lucky enough to spend a summer with Richard Boleslavsky" and misremembered that he "first came over with the Moscow Art Theatre" and that it was the Lewisohns who "subsidized a small group of actors, six of us, to go off to Pleasant-ville." However, she cherished the good fortune to be with "Boley" be-fore the method "developed into all the nonsense and all the things everybody says." Years later, she said:

> I would also like to say for posterity that I don't think it matters what you believe in. You can believe in [Lee] Strasberg if you like, you can believe in Ouspenskaya, you can believe in any of them. If you believe hard enough to concentrate when you're acting, that's what really counts. If you go to the American Academy of Dramatic Art, if you play in the Irish theatre, which is the loosest theatre I've ever seen in my life, it doesn't matter if that is what you believe in.[17]

What mattered most at the end of the summer of 1923 was belief in the transformative power of the method and the decision to test that power on a very "loose" program of two Irish plays, W. B. Yeats's *The Player Queen* and Bernard Shaw's *The Shewing Up of Blanco Posnet*.

When the company reassembled in the fall—the Lewisohns from the East, the Morgan-Arthurs and the company from Pleasantville, Boleslav-sky from uptown to downtown chores—an initial task was the letter to subscribers announcing the resumption of productions. The manuscript product of what must have been an intense exercise in committee writing was lodged in the Lillian Wald papers and labeled in large script *"The Last Draft"* in Helen Arthur's hand. The opening to "My dear subscrib-ers" was cursory: "After a year of rest and relaxation—with its opportuni-ties for study, for wider contacts, and most of all, for reflection—the Neighborhood Playhouse is to begin its tenth season." It was followed by a Lewisohn paragraph inspired by the visions of the East: "It may not be amiss at the outset of our reopening to restate our point of view and the aims of our theatre. The Neighborhood Playhouse has always included in its vision of the theatre many forms of interpretation other than the one of purely dramatic situation." The letter to subscribers goes on to list as accomplishments the lyric dramas, festivals, Japanese Noh productions, and the color organ in contradistinction to "the more realistic forms of the theatre." A subsequent paragraph expresses the view of the managers who stayed at home and explored the visions from Moscow:

In the further development of this permanent group we believe that a style and a technique will eventually grow out of our own necessities, but we recognize in the method recently exemplified by the Moscow Art Theatre principles of acting invaluable to our stage. Therefore we welcome an association with Mr. Richard Boleslavsky, Regisseur of the First Studio of the Moscow Art Theatre, and announce as the opening production "The Player Queen" by William Butler Yeats and "The Shewing-Up of Blanco Postnet" [*sic*] by George Bernard Shaw, on the preparation of which he and a group of players have been at work in the country during the summer. This experiment of a production in the slow, organic method of rehearsal work after the principles of the Moscow Art Theatre was made possible through the understanding and generosity of Mrs. Willard Straight, and the Neighborhood Playhouse is happy to be able to complete the experiment by providing the plays with a setting and a home.

It would seem possible, by means of a principle of "organic method," to find some shared ensemble capacity for both festival and dramatic work. But the company divergence over principles such as amateur and professional and the artistic and organizational priorities embedded in each had only increased during the sabbatical and the relocation during it of different company parties to different hemispheres. On a less exalted level, it probably goaded Alice and Irene to have Mrs. Straight mentioned in the letter and to have it signed with Helen's customary expression, "Faithfully yours."[18]

As in the case of Augustin Duncan's *The First Man* at 466, the reopening night of 1923 featured a printed program that did not use the distinctive Neighborhood Playhouse graphics. It introduced the audience to the playwrights, noting that Yeats had recently been awarded the Nobel Prize for Literature and reprinting a brief note from Shaw to Leo Tolstoy to accompany a presentation copy of his play. It also quoted Boleslavsky on the choice of plays: " 'The Player Queen' because it is poetic and fantastic and of no world; and 'The Shewing-up of Blanco Posnet' because it is realistic and of our world . . . creating characters in two plays so diverse offered the actor a genuine opportunity for the development of his technique.''[19] The program also carried an advertisement for the new company devoted to the technique, then announced as the Laboratory Theatre. It did not in any way contextualize the two plays by Irish playwrights, which were having their American premieres.

Yeats's play had been in composition and recomposition for more than ten years. It was fantastic in that it placed actions in an otherworldly setting, much in the way of Dunsany, but the connecting allegorical references to contemporary social trends were evident. In *The Player Queen,* an actual queen chooses a cloister life over the court and is replaced by a vulgar actress. It is one of Yeats's many disillusioned denunciations of what he took to be contemporary cultural and social degradations. It had been produced in Dublin late in 1919, where the pageantry pleased and the general thrust either baffled or dismayed: memorably, the *Evening Telegraph* reported that at curtain in the Abbey Theatre ''a great many people, it was clear, were conscious of an unpleasant taste in the mouth.''[20] The Shaw play, also first produced at the Abbey Theatre, in 1909, was set in the American West and, like other Shaw works done previously at the Neighborhood Playhouse, reversed types, in this case proving the horse thief to be kinder of heart than the town minister or judge. But Shaw had specifically written it to challenge the censorship powers of the British lord chamberlain by inserting comments on a prostitute and the deity that were proscribed. Banned in London, it played in Dublin, outside the jurisdiction of the lord chamberlain, where it was enthusiastically received, and so, to Shaw's mind, conclusively proved the remoteness of government authority from audiences and so its irrelevance. Neighborhood relevance could perhaps have been discovered in both plays, but, since the production design was entirely on development of acting technique, here it was the social context of the dramas that was irrelevant. In terms of programming and its relation to institutional mission, the postsabbatical reopening did not progress far from the opening of the 1916 season, the company's third, when the program of Dunsany's *The Queen's Enemies* and Shaw's *The Great Catherine* also suggested a seduction of founding pinciples by artistic celebrity. In 1916, however, the Lewisohns were seduced; in 1923, it was the Morgan-Arthurs. Of the competing visions, the Lewisohn one now seemed most faithful and the Agnes Morgan and Helen Arthur one the most distracted from company foundations.

The Boleslavsky experiment dominated the media view of the production of *The Player Queen* and *Blanco Posnet*. The *New York Times* began its notice of a program "mixed in more senses than one" by calling the Neighborhood Playhouse a "laboratory" that was reopening "cautiously" with the intention "to devote itself primarily to the development of the player."[21] The *Herald* represented the opening as "another novel

12. Esther Mitchell in costume as the "real" queen in W. B. Yeats's *The Player Queen*, 1923.

13. Aline MacMahon as Decima, the "false" queen in W. B.
Yeats's *The Player Queen*, 1923.

experiment" without any history and cited Mrs. Straight's contribution
to help "a group that was just beginning to find itself."[22] The comment,
patronizing in contemporary context, is prescient in retrospect, because
after reopening in 1923 the company would clearly find itself in its remaining four years, and the defining characteristics would not come from
devotion solely to acting technique or to the pedigree of celebrated playwrights. In her memoir, Alice discussed the Yeats-Shaw reopening as "a
serious and determining decision which would inevitably affect the future of the Playhouse." Having been remote from the planning for the

production, she nevertheless credited the intentions and the energies of the company. She did not mention Mrs. Straight. She described the project as representative of a "cleavage which had suddenly assumed threatening proportions" and claimed that "the one chance of restoring equilibrium was to see the experiment through." "Cleavage" was the same phenomenon in the company that she cited on opening the season with professional actors in 1920, and then she favored the professional, uptown quality to the amateur, downtown one. After the postsabbatical reopening, she attributed the limitations of the program to its orientation toward "a contemporary British audience": "One could hardly have expected even a mild interest to be evoked for it by our rather special audience in our time and place."[23] Her memoir took full advantage of its considerable opportunities for hindsight, but the lessons she had learned on sabbatical in the East were immediately, in articles and company memos, also keyed to those concepts of "our special audience" and "our time and place." These were the constants of social context not valued by "The Method."

Ironically, it was not the sabbatical year but the reopening year that would in its programming open the cleavage to its widest. The dilemma of this individual institution mirrored that of nonprofit theater at the time. Having produced in the Yeats-Shaw program of celebrated international authors and a relatively safe ethnicity, Irishness, the playhouse continued its 1923–24 season with a production of a celebrated American author, Percy MacKaye, and, at least on the Lower East Side, a relatively safe domestic ethnicity, that of the American south. MacKaye, a prolific playwright of large-scale pageants, verse dramas, and modest folk dramas, was the theorist of little theater who in 1909 had declared that issues surrounding drama were in fact "civic issues."[24] By 1920, his final Broadway production, a "ballad play," *George Washington*, closed quickly as, according to Gerald Bordman, "reviewers, having had their fill of MacKaye's pretensions, spent a significant share of their notices recounting his history of failure at the same time they expressed their amazement at his continuing ability to find productions." From the Players Club on Gramercy Park, MacKaye maintained his reputation in art theater circles through subsequent careers as poet, novelist, opera librettist, and memoirist until his death in 1955.

In 1923, MacKaye brought to Grand Street a minimalist folk drama, *This Fine-Pretty World*, that emphasized the technique of declaiming backwoods American accents, or at least what New York City thought they would sound like. According to Bordman, the production "received no recognition and so fell permanently from view."[25] What recognition there was found the performance derivative and not in any way associated with the festival ideals of the Neighborhood Playhouse. For Carl Van Doren in the *Nation*, in terms that conveyed disappointment, "the action of the play is content to be as naive as an Irish comedy."[26] Though director credit was shared by Agnes Morgan and Alice Lewisohn, *This Fine-Pretty World* plainly represented the interests of the latter in the little theater literary aesthetics of poetic lines in the context of muted set decoration and restricted physical motion. There were good notices for some of the talent created on Grand Street by the Playhouse, such as Joanna Roos. But in general, the production represented precisely the 1923 decline of little theater described by the economist Jack Poggi in reference to the Neighborhood Playhouse, the Provincetown Players, and the Theatre Guild: shifting attention of professionals uptown and decline of noncommercial production values without their influence. In her memoir, Alice, who in the 1923–24 season was already deep in rehearsal for a spring festival production that would reflect her travels in the East more than the literary environs of Gramercy Park, recalled *This Fine-Pretty World* in terms of institutional decision, not personal criticism, and emphasized reception over technique: "the audience response was negligible, hinting that the confidence of the general public in the Neighborhood Playhouse had yet to be restored."[27]

Early in 1924, during the run of *This Fine-Pretty World*, one of the loudest spokespeople for little theater values directly entered the Neighborhood Playhouse decision-making processes. Thomas H. Dickinson, previously cited as the defender in 1920 in *Theatre Arts* of local values over "British Comedians" and of little theater values over commercial ones, arrived in New York and began to publish reviews and polemics on theater, especially in *American Review*. To Kenneth Macgowan, Dickinson was "a far more powerful factor in our dramatic progress than many realize." Macgowan was especially impressed that Dickinson, while professor at the University of Wisconsin, had created and sustained the Wisconsin Players of Madison and Milwaukee. Dickinson managed the company at least through 1929, the year Macgowan wrote about it, and had kept admissions low while introducing "cultivation of original plays, tours, lectures, a publication, *The Play Book*, and the reading of plays."[28] However, Dickinson's emphasis on authorship, play text, and locality, especially as delivered personally, may have helped tilt the Neighborhood Playhouse balance toward the opposites: production, movement, and cosmopolitanism.

On January 17, Dickinson, from West Seventy-second Street, wrote to the "Misses Lewisohn" at Grand Street to congratulate them (one year early) on the tenth anniversary of the playhouse and to offer his "intimate impressions" of its potential. In a four-page, single-spaced, heavily edited, and poorly spelled typescript, he praised their Lower East Side location as movement "away from the crowded ways of amusement down to the crowded ways of life." He expostulated broadly on theater as a "profession of faith," he laid out his metaphysic, and then he came to his point: "But enough of speculation and theories even though they may not be superficial." He had come to Alice and Irene to make the case for "definiteness": "when I say definiteness I mean definiteness in organizing and stating your position and your program of offerings to the public." Although he said he was writing a history and appreciation of the Neighborhood Playhouse, he seemed unaware that this exceeded all other noncommercial companies in emphasis on mission and vision statements of their plans and goals. For Neighborhood Playhouse definiteness, Dickinson advised: "No program of plays can be complete that does not regard the collaboration of the creative artists of the theater. These are primarily the authors. I should rather call them the composers of the plays. . . . Someone must take measures to cultivate the creative faculty of potential playwrights in the best zones of their activity as this has been done in the more popular zones. No theater is now so well equipped for this service as is the Neighborhood Playhouse." He was making the case for little theater poetic playwrights in local versions of folk drama, much in the vein of MacKaye's *This Fine-Pretty World*. The argument had the positive value of emphasizing work that was at least the same nationality of the audience and not patrician work such as Galsworthy or Bennett or remotely ethnic such as Yeats and Dunsany and Shaw.

But Dickinson's version clearly lacked the "definiteness" of the festival aesthetics and the institutional vision of locality based on participation rather than being the subject of poetic drama. This was the definiteness that followed from *Salut au Monde* and would lead to *The Little Clay Cart* and *The Dybbuk;* it was the definiteness that the "Misses Lewisohn" preserved through the sabbatical and would immediately revive in spring 1924 with a festival program called *Arab Fantasia*, which would not be focused on author, text, or locality. If not directly derived from it, Dickinson's position was not far from the professional position of the Misses Morgan and Arthur. Perhaps coincidently, Dickinson signed his letter to the Lewisohns as Helen signed hers, "Faithfully yours."[29]

The competing visions were not immediately resolved in the winter of 1923–24. At a meeting on January 19 of the four directors, the Morgenthaus, and Alice Beer the costumer, now taking notes, the only direct action taken was to lower ticket prices for the next production, the *Arab Fantasia* principally devised by the Lewisohns. The longest items for discussion appear to have been "shifting emphasis from production expense to royalty, and evolving a method of production that will not demand special scenery and costumes and so release more money for authors and composers." The wording managed to capture Dickinson's sense of the authors as composers of plays and the playwright as the primary "creative artist" of theater. The two sides of the discussion are evident: the Morgan-Arthurs, defending productions of Yeats, Shaw, and MacKaye planned during sabbatical, and the Lewisohns, awaiting the March opening of the result of their sabbatical, *Arab Fantasia*, which was authorless and heavy in scenery and costumes. In a closing item, "it was suggested that Miss Irene write to Mrs. Macy and get an appointment for Miss Arthur to see her regarding playhouse needs."[30] That, of course, would be the continuing effort to diversify the financial support for the playhouse, which was prudent in itself and also using the Lewisohn connections to erode the Lewisohn control of institutional vision. Mrs. Straight does not appear to have continued as a sponsor after the summer of 1923.

In the same winter, Dickinson published a long piece on the Neighborhood Playhouse in the influential *American Review*. It was presented as a "series of impressions," mostly laudatory, but with attention as well to "outstanding anxieties and perplexities." Dickinson located the greatest perplexity in the notion of a neighborhood theater. Acknowledging "the social springs of dramatic art," Dickinson surmised that "if the directors of the Neighborhood Playhouse could agree upon any generalization regarding the first cause of their theatre (they avoid generalizations as a rule) probably it would be that the Playhouse is theatre first, last, and all the time." That sense of artistic mission could be associated with Provincetown Playhouse or Theatre Guild, or some of the next additions to the mix in New York such as the Civic Repertory Theatre. Embedded in this discussion about 466 is a clear bias that the neighborhood theatre, "in the mechanical service of stirring the pot until all the parts cohere," fails as "theatre [a]s the home of beauty," and that, "while clearly dedicated to the service of pure beauty in the theatre, the [Neighborhood] Playhouse, by the circumstances of its founding, and its associations, is bound to the service of social mechanics." Somewhat surprisingly, Dickinson concluded that if an institution chooses to be a neighborhood theater, "the neighborhood in which the theatre is placed should be in fact a neighborhood, with solidarity enough to take and retain impressions. This the East Side is not." His conclusion was based on his perception that the Lower East Side "is landlocked by immigrant peoples, and [it is] as much cut off by the shifting currents of their movement as it is by their alien interests."[31]

In their spring production, the Lewisohns had a vision of "alien interests" as something valuable: much like the Wald vision, this cultural perception saw assimilation as a transaction and the immigrant people as bringing values and not only needs for values. In Doris Fox Benardete's memory, the key to *An Arab Fantasia* was that it "dramatized without dialogue or plot the unfamiliar pattern of the culture and spirit of the Near East." She also documented how the large cast of the production represented a complete cross-section of the professional players such as

Albert Carroll and Aline MacMahon, Festival Dancers such as Blanche Talmud, and amateur players and dancers from the settlement clubs.[32] The script is plainly reminiscent of the spirit of the Lewisohns' "Little Theatre of Egypt" essay. The production opens on bare stage with "sunset glow":

> men's voices rising and falling in the measured lilt of the Koran—nearer and nearer until the men appear. They are dressed in the loose patched blue trousers and turban (once white) that belong to the fellahin. Their dark bodies and feet are bare and the play of their muscles is apparent as they tug rhythmically at a rope. They are drawing upstream an unseen barge piled high with golden grain and long stalks of green sugar cane.

In music and dance, the performance presents four scenes "of Mohammedan life": riverbank, desert, city, and shrine. As climax, the last scene builds toward the dance of the whirling dervishes:

> One by one they fill the floor until the circle is complete. The heads are tilted in ecstasy, the faces assume a rapt expression, the hands are stretched upward and outward to embrace the universe, the feet are turning in pivotal precision, and, finally, an undulating sea of white (skirts) invokes a mood of emotional exaltation. The curtains close slowly.

These scenes, according to the concept statement in the prompt book, would, much as *Salut au Monde* had, address the contemporary urban context, where "the rapidity of motion, penetration of science beyond the human horizon, opening gates to the invisible world, navigation through the seas of space, present a new concept and create another environment for the individual."[33] The spectacle did not intend, at least, to present exoticism in order to revise perceptions of "alien interests"; it intended to represent a new historical and technological environment as an opportunity for a new individualism portrayed in ensemble. *An Arab Fantasia* was a realization of festival principles and so, in Dickinson terms, did not choose between neighborhood and "service of pure beauty" but integrated the two.

The performance did not receive acclaim like *Salut au Monde*, though that as a measure of success would be substituting uptown criteria for neighborhood ones. There was a partner piece in the lyric program, a dance pantomime to Prokofiev music called *Chout* ("Buffoon"). The *New York Times* notice, unsigned but perhaps by a drama critic expecting either uptown "professional" acting or little theater amateur drama values, was disappointed in a lack of clear narrative but did concede that "the two were antipodal but each proved interesting to the highest degree."[34] Fifteen years later, Paul Rosenfeld the music critic humorously recalled his own confused reaction:

> A memory lingers of a stage-design, Esther Peck's, representing the head of a stairway. Wound in the dark draperies and balancing water-jugs on their heads, women were supposed to be descending the steps with sinuous movements and ascending them again. Someone was droning interminable Levantine monodies on a bagpipe or guitar; the bayadères gave me the impression of a number of excessively respectable females taking their good time about going to the well and coming up from it; and *dans l'Orient désert quel devint mon ennui!*

Later, in its Sunday magazine feature, the *Times* recorded that

> twelve young men traveled to that remote region [the Lower East Side] . . . and presented themselves at the door of the Neighborhood Playhouse. They were the graduating class of a Theological Seminary. Presently they were watching the scene in which the dervishes whirl at their devotions. . . . The twelve young divinity students remain, if not to pray, at least to feel something of what the Mohammedan feels. And others who have seen the performances—this sequence of Arab scenes from the bazaar to the mosque—have also felt it.

That served as editorial note to "The Essence of the Mohammedan East," which was bylined to Irene alone. Largely a reiteration of the coauthored "Little Theatre of Egypt," it did in the final paragraphs celebrate the success of *An Arab Fantasia*. "We left our Arab friends filled with a desire to translate in some form a few of these moods," Irene wrote. She cited the technology theme behind the production, but in an internationalist mode that was very different from the emphasis on native American arts favored in the 1920s by journals like *American Review*. Irene stated that the purpose of *An Arab Fantasia* was "to bring to the stage something of the cross currents of East and West still to be caught before the final triumph of Ford car and oil can."[35] The effort, then, was to link the lessons of the East to the lessons of the Lower East Side before they became interchangeable.

When the directors met again on March 30, the focus of discussion had shifted dramatically toward the Lewisohns, certainly on the basis of the artistic success of *An Arab Fantasia*, even though Thomas Dickinson was a guest at the meeting. The unsigned minutes of March 30, 1924, recorded in a style unlike those of Alice Beer from the previous January, state that the meeting opened with a long speech by Alice, who "said that she wanted to remind them again, although she assumed that all the groups understood, of the particular function and needs of the Playhouse and in order to do that she had to present its differences to other theatres and that she assumed that all were agreed on certain fundamental ideas and that we recognized the necessity of not comparing ourselves with other groups as our functions were quite different." The idea above all others was "to expand the idea of Festival further" so that "even *The Grand Street Follies* could be made as much of a Ritual as *Salut au Monde*." Then "Mr. Dickinson was introduced and made a short address." He apparently summarized his own credentials, praised the playhouse, offered to join it, and promised to help with unidentified "problems" "that we were too deeply involved in the more immediate technical problems to handle." Without comment, the floor was taken by Irene, who spoke at length on festival as a collective endeavor and how in *An Arab Fantasia*, "drama lies in mood and therefore each performance is the creation of each individual player because if there is no mood, the drama drops out of it completely." Most of the rest of the meeting was devoted to performance values, especially those associated with the stage crew, in which "there has been tremendous improvement," although "an occasional slip

[or] noise on the stage" was not unknown. There was no follow-up mention of Mrs. Macy. All this was a shift away from previous discussions of the playwright as a primary creative artist and emphasis on text over performance. The clear focus scarcely reflected any of Dickinson's ideas or his influence on Agnes Morgan and Helen Arthur. Nor did there appear to be any lasting influence of Richard Boleslavsky and emphasis on technique of an individual performer. The meeting business concluded with plans for final ballet recitals, the second edition of the *The Grand Street Follies*, and plans for an unidentified fall production clearly intended to fulfill Alice's intention "to expand the idea of Festival further."[36]

In fact, one dimension of Thomas Dickinson's well-intentioned offers to help the playhouse would, if accepted, have aided it considerably. In an earlier work, *The Insurgent Theatre*, which reflected the company only through the end of the 1916–17 season, he identified the Neighborhood Playhouse and the Washington Square Players as "the two most significant theatres in America today." Then, as later, he found the "neighborhood" concept a limitation and a problem unless "the directors of this theatre insist that they are running a theatre and not a sociological experiment station." In this earlier work he admitted that "one notices with a certain humility that in the group that has guided the Neighborhood Playhouse to success there has been no place for a man." However, he was also shrewd enough to see through the image of the theater as "endowed": it had been given a building by the Lewisohns, and it had annual subsidies from the very narrow donor base of Alice and Irene, but it had no capital fund that would continue to provide annual expenses. In *The Insurgent Theatre,* he called this fiscal base "only half an answer."[37] This part of his advice seems to have been muted in 1924, when he was seeking to join the enterprise. Through Dickinson, in spring 1924, an opportunity for broader philanthropic support briefly appeared when a "Neighborhood Playhouse Organization" was planned with, as Dickinson wrote to Alice, "my name added as an advisory member of that Committee . . . [because] wouldn't it be better if my name were not employed in any public way apart from this notation?"[38] That committee was eventually formed, but only as the same group of directors, and the title change did not endure. Dickinson apparently proposed a formal distance of himself from the institutional leadership so that he could continue to wield his influence positively for the playhouse through the *American Review* and other journals. This failed to entice Alice and Irene, who had new confidence after *An Arab Fantasia* and the old reluctance to share benefactress roles, and Agnes Morgan and Helen Arthur failed to promote Dickinson sufficiently.

The relationship seemed to end in June 1924 when Dickinson telegraphed Alice, "Understand your position thoroughly glad to do survey article regret impossible to attend meeting good wishes and bon voyage."[39] It was Alice who was departing for a voyage, leaving Dickinson in Connecticut without ties to the Neighborhood Playhouse. There was no identifiable direct connection, but in 1929 Dickinson, who once wrote about the playhouse that had no place for a man, mounted, through the Provincetown Playhouse uptown at the Garrick Theatre, his own play, *Winter Bound,* about two women who retire to the country to live without men. One cannot endure and, after great debate, leaves to marry a local farmer. It was apparently the kind of play embedded, in text and production, in the Dickinson aesthetic of little theater that matched the Provincetown Playhouse interest in psychological realism more than the Neighborhood Playhouse one of civic engagement. Although 1929 was after its closing, the Neighborhood Playhouse had already, by the time of its meetings with Dickinson, defined an evolving aesthetic that would scarcely have accommodated such a work of drama focused on personal conflict. The company adhered instead to Alice's resolve as expressed at the meeting in March of "not comparing ourselves with other groups as our functions were quite different."

The postsabbatical season highlighted by the Yeats, Shaw, MacKaye, and *An Arab Fantasia* productions ended in May with the second edition of *The Grand Street Follies.* The celebration of the season began, as in the inaugural year, as a fairly intimate celebration of company and audience, with ice cream on the roof at intermission and rehearsal material such as sketch books and scripts for auction to raise contributions to a student fund. All this was announced in a modest playbill. But the spring success was so great that the second edition was revived in the fall, with fewer parts covered by managers and more by the growing professional acting company. Accordingly, the playbill grew into a seven-page program with advertising, company history, and a lengthy essay on William Poel's researches on *Hamlet,* apparently in support of the "Who Killed the Ghost" sketch with Albert Carroll playing "John Barrymore as Hamlet." The festival spirit was not completely effaced by success and professionalism: the enhanced program included a comical verse on exactly how to find the Neighborhood Playhouse:

> Lexington Avenue subway to Spring,
> Going east jitney is caught on the wing.
> Please put a nickel held tight in your mitt;
> Leave the small jitney at corner of Pitt.
> Walk two blocks south on to Grand. "Here's a gay house!"
> Surely it's gay. It's the Neighborhood Playhouse.

The festival spirit, as Alice had said, could include the *Follies,* especially in execution. Though costume and set credit was given to Aline Bernstein, the program could credibly claim that the company was "the first theatre in New York to design and make all its own scenery, costume, and properties" because it had the space, the volunteers, and the students to avoid subcontracting of any kind and instead provide training through the Henry Street Settlement.

The *Follies* targets and the high spirit of carnival in the conception and execution of the self-parody were also genuinely festival in creation of community, including the community of New York theater professionals and the community of the Lower East Side. The prologue of the second edition was a parody of advanced artistic thought, set, like O'Neill's work, on an outbound ship, here the rather more luxurious "S.S. *Algonquin.*" On it, the leading theater critics of the day debate fatuous issues in a comic parody of their petty rivalry. The characters included "Heywood" (Broun), "Aleck" (Woollcott), "Kenneth" (Macgowan), and "Stark" (Young) in masks, by the sculptor Jo Davidson, that made the identities clearer and their infatuation with O'Neill and his masks part of the farce. The program included a parody of a British drama of a type that previously infatuated the Neighborhood Playhouse. In it, actors play-

14. Dan Walker makes up Agnes Morgan for *The Grand Street Follies* of 1924.

ing Eva Le Gallienne and Gertrude Lawrence mingled with the historical characters they had or might have played, such as Joan of Arc and Queen Victoria. The great cross-dressing role in the sketch was Albert Carroll as Emily Stevens, an actress then famous for strong and doomed heroines such as Ibsen's. Stevens visited the performance and was photographed beside Albert Carroll in costume as Emily Stevens.

The history of the playhouse included in the larger program referred to two previous "acts" in the history of the company, the first from the opening of 466 Grand Street and the second from the incorporation of professional actors in 1920. It promised a "third act" with "an enlarged permanent company and with higher aspirations and brighter hopes," and so the opposite of the doomed third act imagined by Alice Marquis Goldfarb as inevitable in company histories. The announcement of forthcoming productions did not resolve the different visions of Alirene and the Morgan-Arthurs: the fall festival production of *The Little Clay Cart* and spring one of psychological drama in James Joyce's *Exiles* reflects in

15. Masked figures suggesting Kenneth Macgowan, Alexander Woollcott, and Robert Benchley "On Board the S.S. Algonquin" in *The Grand Street Follies*, 1924.

inverted form the scheduling and allegiances of *This Fine-Pretty World* in fall and *An Arab Fantasia* in spring in the previous season. However, a possibility of resolution was represented in the second edition of *The Grand Street Follies* of 1924. In the long program of twelve scenes or sketches, the biggest of all were the parodies of the season's productions of *The Player Queen* and *The Shewing Up of Blanco Posnet*, which had been Agnes Morgan's and Helen Arthur's major investment in sabbatical time and in Richard Boleslavsky. The parody of the first, written by Agnes Morgan, was "Play the Queen, or, Old Irish Poker," in which the original False Queen, Aline MacMahon, reprised the role in a send-up "showing unmistakably that there is nothing new under the sun," presumably including theories and methods of acting as well as Yeats's preoccupations.

The Shaw play reappeared in the *Follies* as "The Shewing-up of Jo LeBlanco," by "Gee B. Pshaw," in which the horse thief is replaced by a

16. Renowned actress Emily Stevens visits Albert Carroll's "Emily Stevens" backstage at *The Grand Street Follies* of 1924.

ticket scalper who does less well than Blanco Posnet with a jury, which in the *Follies* version included Cyrano de Bergerac and Harpo Marx. The irony was directed at the significant lack of relevance for the local audience of the plays chosen in consultation with Boleslavsky. In some early performances, there also was a parody of the MacKaye production called "Those Fine Pretty Depths" that was later dropped. Thus, the second edition of the *The Grand Street Follies* was not, as feared by Doris Fox Benardete, a parody of the art ambitions of Alice and Irene. The second edition was a much more barbed self-parody of the ambitions of Agnes Morgan and Helen Arthur, who created it, and an indication that they,

17. Paula Trueman and unicorn in "Play the Queen, or, Old Irish Poker," *The Grand Street Follies* of 1924 satire of the company's own production of *The Player Queen*.

too, could enter into the spirit of festival. The spirit was self-critique to a degree that the *New York Times* commented in an early notice that "the wayfarer who missed so much as a single one of the Neighborhood's productions of the season will find himself sitting silent now and then while his neighbor laughs, and the stray member of the great outside public who sits down before *The Grand Street Follies* will find himself missing a good half of it."[40] However, the focus of self-critique and the festival quality of self-parody would erode in later editions of the *Follies*.

18. The maids-in-waiting greet the unicorn tamer in *The Grand Street Follies* of 1924.

In the enlarged program of the fall revival of *The Grand Street Follies* of 1924, the company set the stage for an "annus mirabilis" that would celebrate the actual tenth anniversary of the opening at 466 Grand Street for that new "Act III." At the outset of the season, the plan included *The Little Clay Cart*, *Exiles*, a revival of *Salut au Monde*, an unnamed "new American or English play," which proved to be Richard Brinsley Sheridan's *The Critic*, and a new edition of the *Follies*. It also set an aggressive campaign for "Ten Thousand Subscribers in our Tenth Year" at new prices of $7.50 for orchestra and $5.00 for balcony. In the plan that was very clearly articulated in the program, the added revenue would be used to enlarge the professional company, enlarge the scholarship programs to "open up new avenues of artistic endeavor for workers," and to "experiment in all forms of drama, dance, music, and the scenic arts." The audience was intended to represent "the East Side and the West, Fifth Avenue, Broadway, and Grand Street alike." Of course, the subscribers were unlikely to come from Grand Street, and the question of audience remained an unarticulated part of the plan of considerable importance. At some point in planning the new season, an unidentified group composed in manuscript "A Condensed Statement of the Program of the Neighborhood Playhouse for the Season 1924–1925." It celebrated ten years of accomplishment in facilities and the "human factor" in the linkage of professional and amateur companies. It also acknowledged that "on the side of the audience not as much has been done": "We feel that our audience is still somewhat in the dark as to the real motives and problems of the Playhouse. It is our hope, during the coming season, to take further steps toward drawing the intelligent members of the audience into an intimate understanding of the problems of theatre as a whole."[41] The statement was never publicly released.

The extended run of the second edition of *The Grand Street Follies* continued into November of the new theater season. When, on December 5, 1924, *The Little Clay Cart* opened to acclaim at the playhouse, the Lewisohns must have felt vindicated by the results of the vow to build the audience and Alice, in particular, by her commitment from the previous March to "the necessity of not comparing ourselves with other groups as our functions were quite different." The success of *The Little Clay Cart* was its difference, from contemporary theater fare and from ordinary notions of little theater that did not achieve festival ideals. The origins of the production, like *An Arab Fantasia*, were from the sabbatical trip by the Lewisohns. As Irene wrote in the program for the opening, "The sabbatical year at the Neighborhood Playhouse meant for two of the directors a pilgrimage to the East for a closer contact with the fountain head of drama, music, and ritual. While in Bombay, we had the good fortune of witnessing a performance of *The Little Clay Cart*, which had long been in the intended repertoire of the Neighborhood Playhouse."

The play is a well-known example of classical Hindu drama that is attributed to a King Sûdraka, described in the Neighborhood Playhouse program as "in the tenth century A.D., and again as far back as the fifth." Apocryphal and popular—the 1924 program included a note by Kenneth Macgowan on a recent unsuccessful production in Dresden—the story of the play follows a series of Hindu conventions such as unity of time and presence of comical characters. In it, using spellings of character names as

19. *The Little Clay Cart*, 1924, as designed by Aline Bernstein.

used by the adaptation by Agnes Morgan and Irene Lewisohn, a Brahman merchant named Charudatta, generous and consequently bankrupt, falls in love with a courtesan of the court, Vasantasena, who is also coveted by the king's son-in-law, Santhanaka, described in the program as a "lisping villian." Vasantasena, with access to the wealth of the court, visits Charudatta, pities his impoverished son's clay cart, promises the boy a gold one, and leaves jewelry in the merchant's home. In a confused assignation, she then meets Santhanaka, repels him, and is assaulted and left for dead. Santhanaka uses the location of the jewelry to frame Charudatta, who is sentenced to death. However, Vasantasena, not dead at all, reappears, and a new lord of the court pardons Charudatta, who joins Vasantasena in marriage, frees her from the courtesan duties, and, in a further act of benevolence, pardons Santhanaka as well. A number of minor characters are reformed by the benevolent unfolding of events, including a Shampooer, played by Albert Carroll, who turns away from vanities and becomes a priest.[42]

Irene reported in *The Little Clay Cart* program being disappointed by the performance in Bombay she had seen with Alice nearly two years earlier because, while "delighted with the opportunity of seeing this play on the Indian stage, we found ourselves, with our Hindu host and hostess, in a wholly European setting": "The settings were of the Mid-Victorian style, with wings and cut foliage, painted gilt Doric columns, plush, fringe, and all the decorative effects of the green baize age. . . . The company, composed of men only, gave a performance very modern in manner, somewhat as, shall we say, Arthur Hopkins might approach Molière!" As a result, the Neighborhood Playhouse production would in development emphasize authenticity and performance style truer to the text and the sources than to contemporary acting style. One of the first efforts to insure authenticity had been to draw up a very long bibliography on Indian history and literature. It was further supplemented with all of Gilbert Murray's translations of Greek plays, H. G. Wells's *Outline of History,* Gordon Craig's *The Art of the Theatre,* Lawrence Linyon's *Court Painters of the Great Moguls,* and Hegel's *Philosophy of Fine Arts,* and an eclectic list of other established authorities in art history, aesthetics, and mythology.[43] It is obviously quite an ambitious bibliography. It is also one that does not escape the intellectual specter of empire, and so it could reasonably be asked of the production whether it was not fundamentally European in conception despite Irene's disdain for such a limitation.

The most extraordinary productions of the Neighborhood Playhouse over ten years were *Jephtha's Daughter, Salut au Monde, The Little Clay Cart,* and, later, *The Dybbuk.* The first and the last had explicit cultural reference to the Jewish audience of the Lower East Side, and this would not be lost on the audience visiting the neighborhood or on the one resident in it. The middle two productions in this select list of the most successful in both critical and popular terms and the most characteristic approached ethnicity by presentation of American diversity and South Asian culture. There are colonialist parallels between the Bombay performance in European style and the Grand Street one under British influence. This appears not to have occurred to Irene in her otherwise perceptive and witty program note, and blindness to the Eurocentric bias would have been a perfect subject for a subsequent *Grand Street Follies* had it been recognized as such and had the *Follies* maintained self-critique as integral to festival. The variation of source material from Old Testament to American poetry to Hindu drama and to Hassidic culture was, over time, an appropriately complex representation of complex cultural transactions. The production history was much more ambitious than a plan of Jewish plays for Jewish audiences. The imperialist slant of the background materials was not as pronounced as it might have been in 1924. The expressed intention was to liberate production style from everything implied by ''Mid-Victorian style,'' and that intention was undeniably realized to at least some significant degree.

The effort toward authenticity was not in vain, even if it was not complete. A particular emphasis was placed on music and instrumentation—the sitar, the esraj, and the tabla—which were given extensive treatment in the planning documents and in the program of the production. However, the effort at authenticity was not solely literal. Among the great artistic successes for the production were the settings and costume design by Aline Bernstein, which drew on the full resources of the settlement workshops. In costume, the effort of the design was toward the atmo-

20. *The Little Clay Cart*, 1924, as designed by Aline Bernstein.

spheric rather than the documentary. For example, according to Bernstein's biographer, for Santhanaka, "Aline was inspired to dress him in bouffant white muslin, with a swishing skirt that fell to the knees and ended just above his leather leggings. The contrast of puffy, frilly white skirt and heavy dark leather was enhanced by the vast quantities of pearl necklaces she draped around his neck, and the dangling earrings with which she mockingly set off his dark, supposed fierce moustache." In the set the effort was also toward stylized evocation, as, for example, in three trees in silhouette, downstage left and right and upstage center. While working on *The Little Clay Cart*, Bernstein was also contributing costume designs to the very high-end and uptown Max Reinhardt production of *The Miracle*, a modernized miracle play at the Century Theatre that would open a month later in January. The result of the two openings in the winter of 1924–25, according to the biographer, Carole Kline, was that "Aline Bernstein's name was definitely and permanently established in the American theatre."[44] By company standards, *The Little Clay Cart* workshop results vindicated the conception of the playhouse with settlement ideals, and in the program the members of the group behind the "Neighborhood Playhouse Workshops" were all given full individual credit. The nature of the collective was evident in a production that Stark Young, in the *Times*, celebrated for "something that our stage, our serious stage at least, rarely exhibits, the pervading sense that the occasion was done *con amore*, always with love and pleasure, by everyone concerned with it."[45]

The performance opened with an attempt to disorient by means of a stage manager who directly addressed the audience. The archived prompt book, originally titled "The Little Cart," divided the action narrative into eight scenes to be played "in quick succession" with "the music between the scenes [as] an integral part of the performance." In the first, "from behind the curtains emerge two handsomely barbed musicians, one carrying a sitar, the other esraj. They seat themselves on the floor, c., and play and sing." After the musical overture, the stage manager enters with the line "Enough of this tedious song, which fritters away the interest of the audience!" The musicians relocate, and, as the stage manager continues to speak, they begin to play again, and the ensemble segues from stage manager frame text to the verse of the traditional drama:

Let me, then, most reverently salute the honorable gentlemen and announce our intention to produce a drama called 'The Little Clay Cart.'
Its author was a man:

> 'Who vied with elephants in lordly grace;
> Whose eyes were those of the Chakora bird that feeds on
> moonbeams.'

Then Charudatta enters, blessing the audience.[46]

The effort throughout was to create a stylized environment unfamiliar to New York expectations. Doris Fox Benardete described "one of the
most amusing devices": "the representation of distance by means of the
players walking round and round in a circle. For the merchant to reach
the courtesan's home, he had in actuality only to cross the stage; but to
create the illusion that he had some space to traverse, he walked round
and round several times. Done with finesse, this primitive device enter-
tained the audience who took no time in accepting it for what it was
meant to signify."[47] The originality of the performance motion and stage
business apparently faded over time, and two years later, on the occasion of a revival of *The Little Clay Cart*, Irene, exasperated two days before
the opening, wrote in rehearsal notes to the company: "Somehow I feel
that we have lost the Eastern atmosphere and quality that must have
that interior feel to it. There is a flow that comes from a more subjective
approach that to me is as yet lacking. . . . Without losing the vitality, let
us add an undertone and vibration that will connect our performance
with the music and give it a more dreamlike, elusive, almost fairy-tale
atmosphere."[48]

These effects and the desire for Eastern atmosphere appear to have
succeeded in the original production of 1924. The focus of the laudatory
reviews was on the successful ensemble creation of a comic and an exotic
artifice. The *New York World* reviewer wrote that "it is unlikely that the
usual terms with which New York drama is labeled may be employed in
reference to *The Little Clay Cart*. It is far removed from common fact."
Basanta Koomar Roy, writing for *Theatre Arts Monthly*, wrote that "I mar-
veled at the way—in far off modern America—the illusions of this ancient
Hindu classic are recreated so simply and so exquisitely." *Theatre Arts*

also gave the production a photo feature that complimented the staging for solving "the difficult problem of extracting the universal out of the foreign and archaic without understressing or burlesquing them." The *Brooklyn Times* specifically related the transformative power of the production to the playhouse neighborhood: "Out of the unwholesome soil of New York's Ghetto there has sprung full bloom an ancient alien flower of fragile texture with a roguish smile upon its petal lips." As the accolades accumulated, there must have been considerable pleasure in the Playhouse that positive New York press notices were matched by positive scholarly responses. The translator whose work was the basis for the Neighborhood Playhouse text, Arthur W. Ryder, wrote to Helen Arthur from Berkeley, California, to waive royalties, to approve of everything he had heard about the performance, and to suggest that the directors copyright their acting text. By January 1925, the company was also getting complimentary letters from organizations such as the Hindustan Association of America, which wrote to Irene to express its "heartfelt appreciation of the Neighborhood Playhouse and its Management for its masterly presentation" and to send a garland "as a token of our gratitude and appreciation to you and to the members of the cast."[49]

The success of *The Little Clay Cart* appears to have energized the Lewisohn sisters in particular. In New York, Irene began to recruit potential benefactors more aggressively. In December 1924, she wrote to a potential patron only addressed as "Mr. Macy," who was probably Carleton Macy, president of the Queen's Borough Gas and Electric Company as well as a number of banking and real estate corporations. His spouse, Helen Lefferts Macy, had been a visitor to the theater. Mr. Macy had apparently not responded to an inquiry by Helen Arthur, and by writing to him Irene was ignoring his disdain and, in an action novel for the N.P.H. Women, directly soliciting the greater male patronage. She promoted the Neighborhood Playhouse as "a real contribution to the community" of greater New York and with some audacity announced that "we now have to seek the support of people with vision like myself." Her vision was, first, of "the training of young people" and only after that "the training of directors." Using as example "the student-like method" of *The Little Clay Cart*, she explained to the head of the utility company, "We believe that bringing art, in this way, close to the life of the community as part of a culti-vated leisure is one of the greatest needs of this very material age." She signed the letter, to which no response is filed, with her name only.[50] Alice, with her own *Little Clay Cart* energy, was in London, and there, on December 15, she married Herbert Crowley. He had designed the Neigh-borhood Playhouse productions as long ago as *The Kairn of Koridwen* in 1917 but none in recent seasons. The *New York Times* identified him only as "an English artist." The news item, placed on an obituary page, noted that "the ceremony was very quiet and witnessed by only a few friends. . . . [Alice] told none of her friends of the possibility that she might be married before she returned, but they were not surprised at the news, for she and Mr. Crowley had been close friends for several years."[51]

Alice's winter trip to Europe permitted her to visit James Joyce in Paris in advance of the next Neighborhood Playhouse production, of his play *Exiles*. The trip also prevented her from being in New York for the tenth anniversary celebration of the theater at 466 Grand Street. The prin-cipal event of the celebration was an address by George Pierce Baker of the "47 Workshop" at Harvard, who wittily reversed expectations and celebrated the Playhouse for inspiring his seminar rather than benefitting from its playwright graduates: "I know that the 47 Workshop is but one of a whole group of experimenting little theatres that has always looked to the Neighborhood Playhouse for inspiration and guidance." It was to be his last winter at Harvard—in 1925 he would move to Yale to create there a degree-granting program in playwriting that Harvard would not approve. His appearance must have come through Agnes Morgan, a product of the workshop. But the object of his highest praise in a speech that was largely ceremonial was *The Little Clay Cart* rather than the con-ventional dramas most often produced and directed by Morgan. He had been to the production twice that winter and said that it "seems to me one of the best pieces of producing I have seen in a very long life of the-atre-going." In this praise, he explicitly endorsed the playhouse concep-tions of festival and ensemble: "such perfection comes only when there is real co-ordination between the different parts of an organization." This was the speech that produced Lillian Wald's thank-you note, quoted pre-viously, that cited the Lewisohn generosity and also warned that "the cost of the Playhouse is greater than they can carry, and we may have to give it up at no distant date if we do not find understanding help."[52]

As at key moments in this company history, great success and elation seemed inseparable from ominous signs. For the anniversary, the *New York Times* praised the playhouse for a long series of "firsts": "the first performance of the music of Charles Griffes, the first use of masks on our stage, the first Dunsany. . . . They have produced for the first time in America Bernard Shaw's *Great Catherine,* Lord Dunsany's *A Night at an Inn, The Glittering Gate, The Queen's Enemies,* Yeats's *The Player Queen.*"[53] The moment of celebration, however, was coincident with the moment of reckoning with fiscal realities. A closing statement for December 31, 1924, itemized the dependence of the company at that high level of success represented by *The Little Clay Cart* on the principal benefactresses. For the previous six months, the Morgenthaus had contributed $1,000, "L. & V. Henry" $1,000, Marianne Moore $10, anonymous donors $300, and "A. & I. L." $10,500.[54] Therefore Lillian Wald's understandable uneasiness about whether the company was more than the Lewisohns could "carry" and presumably whether any stable institution could be sustainable with 82 percent of funding coming from a single private source. Surely a recipient of the balance sheet among other fiscal reports, Alice, on the anniversary, wrote in elation from Provence to "Comrades Dear" in New York. For her, at least publicly, the signs were only positive. "Now it seems as if a new being had [*sic*] taken form expressing a personality distinct and individual yet reflecting the sparkle of that joyous brotherhood of heart and mind—our N.P. family," she wrote from Cassis. Citing the extended season of *The Grand Street Follies,* the success of *The Little Clay Cart,* and the opening of *Exiles,* on which she would have had telegrams the night before, she bragged that "every crack and corner of N.P. seems alight and alive as if festive illuminations were garlanded across the front and a bonfire heralded the opening dooway."[55] Privately, she could not have been unaware that, to some of the directors, the higher production costs of *The Little Clay Cart,* like *An Arab Fantasia,* guaranteed greater financial losses and an unequal distribution of resources over the season.

James Joyce's *Exiles* was a strange choice for an anniversary production: it was distant from the history articulated by Professor Baker and from the values celebrated by Alice. It was also the English-language premiere of the play, which had previously been on the stage only in a German workshop production. Joyce had completed the play years before his novel *Ulysses*, which since 1922 had built a formidable *succès de scandale* reputation, particularly in New York, where it had been subject to lengthy litigation even as published excerpts in advance of the book.[56] *Exiles* had drawn remarkably little production interest. As early as 1915, W. B. Yeats rejected it for production in the Abbey Theatre in Dublin with the often quoted remark that it was "a type of work we have never played well." To this he added, to Joyce of European rather than national aspirations, "It is too far from the folk drama."[57] Someone at the Neighborhood Playhouse should perhaps have said the same. However great the attraction of a world-class avant-garde writer, which would have pleased the Lewisohns, and the psychological parlor-drama form, which would have interested Agnes Morgan and Helen Arthur, *Exiles* lacked the local context that would integrate it into the playhouse, and the directors failed to create one for it.

Exiles is a psychological debate and libidinal contest in the mode of Ibsen between a domineering artist, Richard Rowan (Ian Maclaren), a likeable companion, Robert Hand (Malcolm Fassett), and Richard's wife Bertha (Phyllis Joyce, new to the company). Richard tests Bertha's fidelity, but in the end he remains uncertain of the absolute trust and honesty he thought the test would verify. As Yeats suggested, it lacked the social issues surrounding folk identity and so did not coincide with the interests of his Irish national theater at that time. For the same lack of social context, it had little connection with the Neighborhood Playhouse mission as a theater attached to a settlement house in an inner-city neighborhood. Like Yeats's work *The Player Queen*, or Shaw's *Blanco Posnet*, *Exiles* as staged on Grand Street lacked the playwright's informing context and failed to establish a local one to replace it. An intimation of unconnected intentions was evident when Alice visited Joyce in Paris the winter before the production. She had a theory about the two male characters being "different aspects of one man." In her memoir she reports that Joyce re-

21. Ian Maclaren and Phyllis Joyce in James Joyce's *Exiles*, 1925.

plied that such an "idea had never occurred to him, but it was quite possible." He, however, as an artist, could not be "concerned with the interpretation of his work."[58]

The *Exiles* production was directed by Agnes Morgan and seems in the lineage of "the two famous Irishmen" postsabbatical program of Yeats and Shaw. With them and Joyce, as well as Dunsany, the repertory the playhouse was selecting from Irish drama of the early twentieth century represented a countertradition that throughout departs from the ideals of folk drama Yeats quite properly thought the mission of the Irish National Theatre (one that also excluded a great deal of his own work). The tradition of modern Irish theater of the early twentieth century would have served the Neighborhood Playhouse purposes better. In the works of John Millington Synge, Lady Gregory, Lennox Robinson, and other writers for the "Irish Players" who had great influence over noncommercial theater in New York City in three separate tours around the time of the Neighborhood Playhouse founding, the element of "folk drama," often derived from the verbal and visual emphasis on what came to be called in derision "peasant quality," was compatible with the ideals of a settlement institutional setting. Whether by argument for social inclusion or exclusion, the case could be made that national identity, the advancement of which was sought by the Abbey Theatre, could be integrated into the case for ethnic social integration, the advancement of which was sought by the Henry Street Settlement. Unlike *Salut au Monde* or *The Little Clay Cart*, *Exiles* was not linked to ideas of American assimilation or affirmation of exotic identity and so was not integral to the Neighborhood Playhouse program or the audience it had built for a singular kind of repertory in New York. As had consistently happened in company history, in *Exiles*, professional artistic aspirations—frequently sought in esteemed authors—eclipsed festival values.

Only the second play of the 1924–25 season, *Exiles* promoted itself in the program as "an essentially modern psychological drama." Its critics, however, did not respond with the praise that they had to the essentially fabulous qualities of *The Little Clay Cart.* Under the leader "Dublin Comes to Intellectual Grand Street," Gilbert W. Gabriel, in a long notice in the *New York Telegram,* speculated on a meeting of ethnicities that seems to patronize both: "If it seems faintly whimsical to you to have an Irish genius entering via Grand Street, be comforted by the fact that *Exiles* is to do with a double triangle, which was, after all, the Star of David." His final verdict was "tedious": "We yawned as much over portions of it as others all around us yawned." In contrast, George Jean Nathan, in a review essay of mostly uptown shows, found in this downtown one "an interesting sex drama" rendered tedious by "an Irish vagueness—in many cases it is described as mysticism" not to be found in "fine poets like Synge" who link their work more directly to their people. Joseph Wood Krutch seemed to realize that the reputation of James Joyce rather than the reputation of *Exiles* was the attraction to the producers. "To any-one capable of sufficient interest in abstractions it will prove an absorbing play in its own right," he wrote in the *Nation*, where he so frequently praised and defended the Neighborhood Playhouse. "But [it is] as a study in the mental history of both the author and his age that it will be found most significant." He found the interest in total psychological honesty prone to naive errors that "the truly wise man—the author, let us say, of *The Little Clay Cart*—would never make."[59]

Three days after the opening of *Exiles*, a further test of the playhouse mission was resolved. Eugene O'Neill's *Desire Under the Elms* had moved in the previous fall from the Greenwich Village Theatre uptown to the Earl Carroll Theatre on Broadway. The Neighborhood Playhouse was not alone in envying the profits of its long run in a large house. In *The Little Clay Cart*, the company had a good candidate for such a restaging and evidently during the winter of 1925 debated again the merits of such a move, which had succeeded in 1916 with a recast *The Queen's Enemies* on a revised Dunsany-Shaw program and had failed in 1922 with a scarcely altered production of *The Madras House*. The debate was brought to a close at a morning meeting on February 23, 1925, summarized by Helen Arthur in a letter to Lillian Wald. On Wald's copy someone has written "Evidence against the Proposal." Those present were Alice Beer, Irene, Agnes Morgan, and Helen. As Helen recorded the event, "We went into a very thorough discussion of taking *The Little Clay Cart* uptown, and it is the unanimous recommendation of the staff that there were too many problems in connection with it to make it advisable at this particular time." The major problem was casting and design resources, which were already overextended by two planned Festival Dancers performances. Closed to make room for *Exiles, The Little Clay Cart* was already nearly two weeks out of production: some of the leads had taken roles in the Joyce play and some of the rest had found other projects. Of the codirec-tors, Irene would not underestimate the difficulty of trying to recreate in a new production the stylized movement and authentic music of the old one. Agnes Morgan, moreover, was "the only person that it was possible to release for such an undertaking," and that, apparently, was not enough leadership. Given the directors present at the meeting, the final conclusion must have come from the newly assertive Irene.

It would have been in the professional interests of Agnes and Helen to produce uptown, and at this time they did secure some future basis for that because it was "unanimously agreed that a wise thing to do would be to find enough people interested in forming a group that would care to reset uptown any Playhouse productions which seemed to have enough drawing power to be remunerative." After the close of the Neighborhood Playhouse in 1927, Agnes and Helen would continue to work roughly in this vein with their Actors-Managers Company, though after 1927 they would be trading on the Neighborhood Playhouse reputation rather than financially supporting its repertory. Lillian Wald was already convinced of the superiority of playhouse goals and settlement mission to professional theatrical ones, and she did not accept Helen's offer of another meeting "should your opinions differ."[60] Alice was not copied on the letter. The outcome, however, was perfectly compatible with the speech she had given the company nearly one year before, at the staff meeting that included Thomas Dickinson, in which she spoke at length on how the Neighborhood Playhouse had "differences from other theatres," including, in the present context, the producers of Eugene O'Neill, and on how the Neighborhood Playhouse company "recognizes the necessity of not comparing ourselves with other groups as our functions were quite different."

The season ended with Irene's two productions of the Festival Dancers, which had the positive effect of bringing the designer Donald Oenslager into the company, and the Sheridan comedy *The Critic*, which replaced the promised new play and had the unproductive effect of bringing Whitford Kane back into the company. Helen Arthur and Agnes Morgan had complete control of the next edition of the *Grand Street Follies*. The annual spoof had become the most remunerative dimension of the playhouse activities, and, in 1925, as in the previous year, the opening in June was extended into the fall season. The program was credited to Agnes, and the dances to Albert Carroll. It included an expansion of the previous year's *Hamlet* sketch that established Carroll as Barrymore playing Hamlet as his and the *Follies* trademark. A woodcut of the set design, which satirized the gigantic Broadway dimensions of the Barrymore set by littering the 466 Grand Street stage with ladders, became a logo for the playhouse. The production did not lack for topical satires of the New York theater world: the O'Neill popularity uptown appeared as "They Knew What They Wanted Under the Elms" and Sidney Howard's Broadway hit *What Price Glory?* appeared as "What Price Morning Glories?" The contemporary popularity of ethnic reconciliations appeared in operatic form as *"L'Irlandesa Rosa Dell' Abie,"* or *Abie's Irish Rose,* "with an all-star

22. Agnes Morgan as "Mrs. Scandal" in "The Wild Duck of the Eighteenth Century" in *The Grand Street Follies* of 1925.

23. Albert Carroll dressed as "Pavlowa" for "L'Irlandesa Rosa Dell'Abie" in *The Grand Street Follies* of 1925.

cast in honor of the consolidation of The Irish Free State and Palestine." However, for all the wit, the third edition of the *Follies* lacked the original inspiration for the parodic enterprise: satire of Neighborhood Playhouse productions. The season of *The Little Clay Cart* and James Joyce's *Exiles* did not lack ripe targets for exaggeration and subjects for self-critique. But from this edition on, the Neighborhood Playhouse enjoyed immunity, and the satire instead focused entirely on its competitors.

The previous edition, in 1924, had promised a "third act" for the Neighborhood Playhouse that would have "higher aspirations and brighter hopes." By pleading immunity, the 1925 edition of the *Follies* lacked that confidence and began to resemble the many other follies at the time in New York designed to fill seats during the slow summer season. The Neighborhood Playhouse satire of platitudes in *Abie's Irish Rose* substituted for attention to the Jewish-Irish identity issues evident in the repertory's infatuation with playwrights such as Yeats, Shaw, Dunsany, and Joyce in apparent obliviousness or denial of the context of the Lower East Side, the role of settlement houses, or the potential of cultural activism. In the 1925 edition, however, the real third act was announced. Without detailing the next season's offerings, the program announced that the season would begin "with one of the most acclaimed plays of the continental stage." It would not be the kind of continental fare suggested by John Galsworthy or Arnold Bennett. Instead, it would be S. Ansky's *The Dybbuk*, derived from a Moscow Art Theatre production, representing "the mystical legend which this Russian-Jewish writer has made to live again [about] the spirit (the dybbuk) of a young man which after his death possesses the body of the girl he has loved." The announcement promised onstage "the picturesque background of a religious sect called the Chassidem" and music by an "eminent Hebrew composer."[61] The third and final act of "higher aspirations and brighter hopes" would thus find its inspiration in its locality and so its final identity as the Neighborhood Playhouse.

6

1925-1926

The Dybbuk *and the Repertory Model*

In August 1925, on board the *Olympic,* returning to New York from South-ampton, England, and on course toward the design for the fall *Dybbuk* production, Aline Bernstein met Thomas Wolfe. He had not yet even begun *Look Homeward, Angel,* the novel published in 1929 that would es-tablish his reputation as a novelist. In the summer of 1925 he considered himself a playwright. On graduation from the University of North Caro-lina in Chapel Hill, close to his roots in Asheville, he had moved in 1920 to the Harvard Graduate School, where he completed a M.A. in English in 1922. He remained in Cambridge, Massachusetts, an additional year to attend the "47 Workshop" of George Pierce Baker. Its objective of training students for professional careers in theater was less successful in Wolfe's case than in Agnes Morgan's. Relocated to New York in 1923, Wolfe never satisfied the Theatre Guild with rewrites of his play manuscript "Wel-come to Our City," and by 1924 was supporting himself by teaching at New York University. When they met at the end of summer 1925, he was booked in third class and Aline was in first. Suzanne Stutman edited their correspondence and introduced their meeting as follows:

> It was shortly before his twenty-fifth birthday, and she, at forty-four, was literally old enough to be his mother. For both, love was almost instantaneous and became the overriding passion of a lifetime. On the surface, the relationship between the lovers seemed a series of contradic-tions. She was a Jew, he, a Christian; she was a successful stage and costume designer for the Neighborhood Playhouse, at the pinnacle of

her career, while he was unsuccessful in the theater; she was a north-
erner, from the sophisticated city, while he was from the provincial
South; she was firmly rooted in reality, while Wolfe consistently fought
against losing himself within the violent landscapes of his imagination.

One of the earliest notes she wrote to him was about her disappointment
that he missed her "stage debut" in the chorus of beggars in the *Dybbuk*.[1]

At this point in time, Bernstein's career in theater design was ascend-
ing the same arc from amateur to professional pursued by the playhouse.
Daughter to parents Joseph, a professional actor, and Rebecca, as a child
she had lived on tour and in theater boarding houses. Her parents had
both passed away by 1897, when she became the ward of her aunt Rachel
Goldsmith, who objected to a stage career and steered her to fine arts,
especially portrait painting, which she studied in New York with Robert
Henri. In 1902, she married Wall Street broker Theodore Bernstein, with
whom, by 1906, she had two children, the second of which, Edla, would
also become involved in the productions of the Neighborhood Playhouse. The first woman to become a member of the Brotherhood of Painters, Decorators, and Paperhangers of the American Federation of Labor,
or the stage designer's union in New York, she began her career as a
volunteer at the Henry Street Settlement, first for the dramatic club, and
then for the nascent Neighborhood Playhouse. Fifteen years after *The
Dybbuk,* and after she had developed a Broadway career in productions
of the dramas of Lillian Hellman and a Hollywood one with RKO, she
wrote that "I was fortunate enough to begin my work at the Neighborhood Playhouse, one of the three art theatres that came into being in New
York at about the same time. The other two were the Washington Square
Players (now the Theatre Guild) and the Provincetown Theatre [*sic*].
Those theatres created their own audiences and set a standard of acting,
designing, and playwrighting (*sic*) that Broadway has followed, and the
profession of scene designer as it exists today started in those three
organizations."[2]

Her first credit for the Neighborhood Playhouse had been *The Queen's
Enemies* in 1916; her reputation escalated significantly because of the design of *The Little Clay Cart* in fall 1924, when she was simultaneously

doing costumes for Max Reinhardt's production of *The Miracle;* in fall 1925, she was working on *The Dybbuk* simultaneously with an uptown modern-dress *Hamlet* that included a motor car on stage and the killing of Polonius with a revolver. Nicholas Fox Weber, in his book *Patron Saints* about new art emerging in the 1920s and after, echoes Stutman on the contrasts in the match of Bernstein and Wolfe. On the *Olympic*

> a Harvard friend of his had introduced him to two ladies who were traveling first class. Mrs. Bernstein was one of them; the other was Mina Kirstein. Wolfe was poor and unworldly, Mrs. Bernstein a beautifully dressed woman. . . . Mrs. Bernstein moved easily in an echelon of New York life that could make a pivotal difference to the struggling writer; the Neighborhood Playhouse was just in the process of considering Wolfe's play *Welcome to Our City.* Wolfe was then twenty-four years old, Mrs. Bernstein forty-three; he was six and a half feet tall, she diminutive. In spite of—or because of—some of these differences, they developed a great liaison.[3]

Wolfe's play was actually under consideration at the Theatre Guild, and it was ultimately rejected by Lawrence Langner because the same sprawling inclusiveness that characterized Wolfe's novels made his plays unproducible. But the notion of a liaison of contrasting forces is true of the Bernstein-Wolfe relation, both intellectual and physical, and also the whole context of *The Dybbuk,* a dramatization of a miraculous reconciliation of contrasting Talmudic and Hassidic traditions that on opening linked uptown and downtown New York City and also the neighborhood and the playhouse on Grand Street.

Among the many contrasting polarities that Aline Bernstein managed to bridge was the different company goals represented by Helen Arthur and Agnes Morgan, who favored uptown transfers and high-end, remunerative professional settings, and those of Alice and Irene, whose ideal remained the quixotic one of a fully realized festival achievement on the order of *Salut au Monde* or *The Little Clay Cart* by enlightened amateurism. The return to that ideal in the new season of 1925 in the elaborate staging of text, music, and dance in *The Dybbuk* entailed considerable risk. Wolfe, however poor and unworldly, was not without opinions, and his account in the novel *The Web and the Rock* of the narrator's visit to "Esther Jack" at the "Community Guild" represents some of the anti–Neighborhood Playhouse venom building ten years after the founding of it, the Washington Square Players, and the Provincetown Players, and the resentment of them as complacent establishment from a new group of ardent bohemians:

> he had come here in a spirit truculently prepared, and the words and phrases he had heard flicked him rawly like a whip. They angered him because he had always thought of the theatre as a place of enchantment, a place where one might forget himself in magic. So, at any rate, it had been with him in his childhood, when "going to see the show" had been a miraculous experience. But now all of this seemed to have been lost. Everything these people did and said strove to defeat the magic and the illusion of the theatre. It seemed to him that instead of going to the theatre to watch people act, they went to act themselves, to see one another and be seen, to gather together in the lobbies before the show and between the acts, exhibiting themselves and making sophisticated and knowing remarks about the play, the acting, the scenery, and the lights.

The "knowing remark" that particularly rankled was "a rather good O'Neill."

Bernstein brought Wolfe to one of the fall performances of *The Grand Street Follies* of 1925. In fictionalized form, Wolfe noted the parody of O'Neill ("They Knew What They Wanted Under the Elms"), "a satire of Hamlet of a famous actor" with Bernstein's clutter of ladders in parody of the height of Barrymore's stage on Broadway, and Albert Carroll's cross-gender roles, "apparently a great favorite of the audience, a pet-of-fashion." Wolfe's narrator focused on the Lewisohn faction of the directors. Monk Webber, the narrator of *The Web and the Rock,* meets Esther Jack in a theater lobby crowded with celebrities: "As they were entering the door, she also introduced him to a meager, emaciated little woman with a big nose and a drawn and tormented-looking face. This was Sylvia Meyerson, the director of the theatre, a woman of great wealth, whose benefactions were largely responsible for its existence."[4] The objects of Wolfe's greatest resentment in the novel were imitations of O'Neill psycho-drama, patronizing reception of them, and burlesque as satire of others without self-critique. In the actual playhouse, however, these were less the product of a benefactress "Sylvia Meyerson" than of the professional ambitions of Helen Arthur and Agnes Morgan. The Lewisohn producing ideal, of dynamic festival, in fact, was much closer to Wolfe's own ideal of "the magic and the illusion of the theatre."

In fall 1925, Alice Lewisohn was forty-two years old, nearly the halfway point of a life that would end at eighty-nine. Throughout her life, the projects she funded came from enthusiasm rather than torment, and this was true of the season opener of 1925. In the chapter of her memoir called "*The Dybbuk* in Embryo," she describes her discovery of the text in a Henry Alsberg translation: "At the time, I merely knew of the existence of Chassidism as a mystical sect of Judaism which developed in the eighteenth century." She was attracted to the text not because of personal heritage or because of representation of the Lower East Side neighbors of the playhouse but because of what she took to be a powerful resolution of conflict—such as the smug and the artistic spheres that Wolfe detected in the lobby of 466—expressed in the form of festival in song and dance that was fundamental and specific to the Neighborhood Playhouse. In her memoir, she describes Hassidism as "a protest against dogmatic ritualism, in which the rabbinical law dominated." In this protest, "The Chassid expresses, in contrast, his relation to God through mystical enthusiasm or ecstasy." The performance potential for a paradigm of enthusiasm and passion erupting from a stoical and pedantic academicism were clear to her from her first reading, and she listed pairs of antitheses that could be designed and staged, such as light and dark, static and dynamic, human and extraterrestrial. For her, "the conflict between two worlds is suggested throughout the play, reaching a climax in the trial of the Dybbuk, that is, the soul of one who has died and returned to inhabit—in this case—the body of the beloved."[5] The possession of the body of Leah the bride by the spirit of the deceased young scholar Channon would climax and resolve the performance.

However universal *The Dybbuk* could be conceived in most generalized terms, it could not on the Lower East Side be considered as remote from the local audience as a work by a John Galsworthy or an Arnold

Bennett. It had unmistakably Jewish content at a time when ghetto images onstage were not common, at least for uptown audiences. The story of *The Dybbuk,* however, also had within it an action about rebellion and youth that could serve as corrective to the smugness and complacency attributed to the wealthy and secure by angry young artists like Thomas Wolfe. In publicity notes for the *Evening World* that were prepared during the performance run, this dual nature of Jewishness and youth were the qualities the Neighborhood Playhouse used to define its success. Starting on the most generalized of levels, the press release explained that

> of all the battles that have been staged on various parts of the earth's surface, there is probably none more curious than that which raged in Russia during the latter part of the past century. The Revolt of the Children, it might have been called, for it was nothing less than an intellectual uprising of the younger generation against the fanatical tyranny of the male parent. Among the Jews the struggle was particularly fierce because the tyranny was greater. The oppression, the endless routine, the drudgery and staleness of life in the schools was matched by the overpowering religious life at home, so that between these millstones the youths were compelled to throw over the ancient traditions which bound them to their parents and seek freedom and happiness in the new education that was struggling to make itself felt throughout Russia.[6]

The relevance of such a parable when performed in New York was quite evident to Jews and non-Jews in the middle of the 1920s and helped explain the extraordinary reception of the play.

Ansky's play *The Dybbuk* had become well known at least in theater circles since its production Moscow in 1922 by the Habima Theatre,[7] which had been founded there in 1918 as a studio theater devoted exclusively to Hebrew productions and revival of the Hebrew language. The reputation of the company rose when its work was endorsed by Stanislavsky, who sent Yevgeni Vakhtangov from the Moscow Art Theatre to the Habima to direct *The Dybbuk.* While reading the play in Europe, Alice had been urged by cable from the Neighborhood Playhouse to visit Moscow and its original director. For Alice, however, "the idea did not appeal": "I felt that the playhouse would have to grow out of our own experience and that the Russian method, however brilliant, might somehow inhibit our spontaneous approach." However, when she returned to New York in 1925, spontaneity was fortuitously aided by experience when Alice met David Vardi:

> The day I arrived in New York I met Mr. Vardi, a tiny man expertly groomed, suggesting in no way the ravages of the recent revolution through which he had lived. At the first interview, although he knew practically no English, his mobile face and expressive gestures revealed far more than any kind of discussion or lecture. We sensed without words the point of view of the Habima organization and its definite departure from the Moscow Art Theatre methods. Mr. Vardi's sympathy and imaginative gesticulation showed an Hebraic background vital to the production of The Dybbuk.[8]

Vardi was born in the Ukraine. He became a teacher of Hebrew, traveled to Palestine, and there enrolled as a student of Hebrew at the University of Jaffa. While there he also became interested in theater and especially street theater. According to program notes gathered at the playhouse, his first street sketch, performed in Palestine, was called "A Greenhorn in America." He returned to Russia in 1920, toured the countryside as "diseur and character improviser," and then, in Moscow, his performance skills and Hebrew language skills earned him a small role in the first performance of The Dybbuk at Habima. After traveling in Europe, he arrived in New York in 1924, heard about the Neighborhood Playhouse plans for a production, and volunteered. When the production opened, the director credit was "David Vardi in association with Alice Lewisohn."[9]

For Alice, Vardi was essential to the production because the new world "spontaneous approach" needed some grounding in old world Jewish culture, and Vardi "could reveal contrasting attitudes between the Kabala and Talmud."[10] The multiple cultural contexts and contrasts of the production required considerable annotation: the uptown audience was familiar with Moscow Art Theatre but not the Hassidic history, and the Lower East Side immigrants from Russia could hardly be expected to identify with Stanislavsky or contemporary experimental theater. For cultural background, the Neighborhood Playhouse program as well as the published version of the text relied heavily on Chaim Zhitlowsky, a popular writer and lecturer who, until his death in New York in 1948, happily reminisced when asked on his childhood with Ansky. Zhitlowsky material provided biographical background on Ansky, born Rappaport in 1859, and "his childhood entirely submerged in orthodox Jewish culture and religion." In rebellion against the family setting, Ansky became a laborer in the salt mines of Eastern Russia and then a writer and ethnographer interested in the interrelation of issues in the class struggle and in ethnic identity. In 1892 he traveled to France to study under the philosopher P. Ladrow and remained for a period isolated from specifically Jewish issues. The isolation ended during the Dreyfus Affair in France of the 1890s. According to Zhitlowsky:

> In the beginning of the twentieth century (after Ladrow's death), [Ansky] came to Berne, Switzerland, in order to take a closer part in the Russian Social Revolutionary movement, which had its centre in that city. Under the influence of the Jewish-National and Jewish Revolutionary movements, which were actively carried on in the Russian colony in Berne, and also under the influence of the Zionists and other Jewish groups, he became more of a nationalist. Probably, too, he was influenced by his intimate friend of childhood days, the writer of these lines.

Ansky also became an ardent collector of Jewish folklore when "none of the Jewish intelligentsia had ever dreamed of such a wonderful mass of material dealing with the spiritual life of the Jewish people." Among the results of his study was *The Dybbuk,* which Zhitlowsky translated as "Between Two Worlds." For the program, Zhitlowsky also quoted a previously published Ansky letter on the play:

> The play is, of course, a realistic one about mystic people. The only part of it which is not realistic is the *Meshulakh,* whom I have purposely portrayed in mystic terms. I introduced him on the advice of Stanislavsky, and in bringing him in, I have emphasized the central idea of the drama. Throughout the play there is a constant conflict between individualism

and collectivism—Channon and Leah struggle to attain personal happiness. On the other hand, the Rabbi thinks of them . . . [as members of] the House of Jacob. . . . Who of them is right? To [the messenger] both Channon and Leah—and also the Rabbi—are right, and furthermore are justified in their struggle.[11]

In the Neighborhood Playhouse production, the role of the messenger was taken by the house lead actor, Ian Maclaren.

In pursuing its own spontaneous approach, the Neighborhood Playhouse did not obscure its history or even its own contemporary competition. Its publicity notes for the *Evening World* reported an apocryphal story that in Russia Ansky had brought the play to the charismatic Yiddish actor Jacob Adler, later a Broadway star in New York, and then refused it to him when Adler "insisted on incorporating in it songs and dancing!"[12] The songs and dancing were probably in the more operatic style of the young Adler, and not the music and dance associated with the festival spirit at the Neighborhood Playhouse. There had been a production of *The Dybbuk* in New York at the Yiddish Theatre in 1921. In its program, the Neighborhood Playhouse also publicized the previous history of *The Dybbuk* and the Habima Theatre, with its staging in Moscow, "up a narrow stair case to a small hall with a seating capacity of about 150, lined with a dozen unpainted benches, curiously reminiscent of a prayerhouse in the Ghetto." That stood in contrast to the staging a reader of the program would see, in a lavishly appointed Georgian theater in a ghetto. While the published version of the Henry Alsberg translation used in the production included a lengthy "Note on Chassidism" by Chaim Zhitlowsky, the program included only a very brief "Note on the Production" intended to communicate the Neighborhood Playhouse's less academic and more romantic conception of the Hassidim for its dramatic purposes in its location: "Chassidism, a mystical interpretation of Judaism, was founded by Ba'al Shem Tob about the middle of the eighteenth century. It developed as a reaction against rabbinical asceticism through ecstatic song, movement, and feasting as a preparation for communion with God." The focus on dynamism differed from the prayer-centered approach of the Habima, but it had a justification in Ansky's own the conception of the messenger as "the central idea of the drama." The Neighborhood Playhouse program notes of 1925 explain that the meshulach or messenger plays a picturesque and human role in the village life of the Jewish communities of Southern Russia and Poland. He is the link between the tear-stained Ghetto walls and the outside world. With him and his staff and pack travel all the romance, the imagery and poetry of the troubadour combined with the mystery of the unknown."[13] The conception is also evocative of the institutional role the Neighborhood Playhouse sought as a link between the Lower East Side and the outside world through the romance of professional theater and the practical skills it offered to students in the assimilationist framework of the settlement.

The text for the production was a translation by Henry G. Alsberg and Winifred Katzin "from the Original Yiddish," rather than the Hebrew text of the Habima; as published in book form in 1926 it included material from Zhitlowsky and an introduction by the newspaper reviewer Gilbert W. Gabriel that was specific to the Neighborhood Playhouse production. The text was divided into four acts: the first two in Brainitz, in what is now the Ukraine, both inside and outside a synagogue near the home of Sender, father of the bride, and the second two in the nearby larger town of Miropol and in the home of Rabbi Azrael, who will adjudicate a dispute on wedding arrangements. The performance opens on Aline Bernstein's design for a darkened, fairly open stage and the chanting in the synagogue of three batlonim, who are described in the text as professional prayer men. The batlonim debate theological issues until the Messenger dismisses their argument with the observation that "only the heat of a too intense desire can cause the vessel to burst when the spark breaks into a flame."[14] Only the young student Channon responds to this liberating thought, and he and the Messenger remain fixed in each other's sight "with equal intensity" (33). Channon is the student who would replace the Talmud of "chains" with the Kabala that "tears your soul away from the earth and lifts you to the realms of the highest heights" (46). Leah, who is engaged to be married to another young man, visits the synagogue with her father, Sender. Channon, on seeing her, falls into an ecstatic trance. At the close of act 1, Sender and others erupt into a wedding dance and then, at curtain, discover Channon to be dead.

The second act opens with a wild dance in the Brainitz town square, where a corps of women beggars are served food by Sender as part of the wedding ritual and then return the favor in dance. The Messenger has been warning that "there are vagrant souls which, finding neither rest nor harbor, pass into the bodies of the living, in the form of Dybbuk, until they have attained purity," and, at the end of the act, Leah, previously celebrating with the beggar women, is now possessed. She speaks for the first time in the voice of Channon, who inhabits her: "I have come back—to my destined bride. I will leave her no more" (92).

In the second half of the play, action moves to Miropol where Rabbi Azrael will attempt to resolve the case brought to him by Sender. The rabbi has his own crisis of confidence because the Talmud and its authority seem overwhelmed by Channon's intellectual adventurousness. His first attempt at direct exorcism fails, and as a second attempt the rabbi plans a formal trial by rabbinical court to prove or disprove the charge that it is Sender who has in fact betrayed law and personal promise and so incurred the spiritual intervention. The spirit of Sender's deceased childhood friend Nissen is summoned; he remains invisible and inaudi-

24. The possession of Leah in *The Dybbuk* in 1925.

ble, but characters on stage, including the rabbi, respond to his testimony. From beyond the grave, Nissen confirms the story that, in their youth, Sender had pledged his child to marriage with Nissen's if they produced a son and a daughter. Nissen's son was Channon, whose possession of Leah fulfills the pledge so is just. The rabbi sentences Sender to give his wealth to the poor and to perform annual memorials for Nissen and his son. Having delivered just retribution, the rabbi again attempts direct exorcism: "I, Azrael ben Hadassah, do for the last time command you to depart out of the body of the maiden Leah." The exorcism, to a chorus of Shofer horns, succeeds, the Dybbuk calls for his own Kaddish, or funeral prayers, and Leah speaks again in her own voice. Her bridegroom is summoned, and wedding music and dance begins. But, in a final, spectacular stage effect combining sound and light and movement, Leah chooses Channon over the bridegroom by stepping outside a circle inscribed by the rabbi. By doing so Leah directly contradicts Talmudic authority. She chants, "a great light flows about me . . . predestined bridegroom, I am united to you forever, now we soar upward together higher and high," and the *coup de théâtre* created the soaring effect. The Messenger comments "blessed be a righteous judge" on this liberating outcome, and a chorus chants to the closing curtain:

> Why, from highest height,
> To deepest death below,
> Has the soul fallen?
> Within itself, the Fall
> Contains the Resurrection. (145)

The company had realized early on that the task of producing the play with full festival values would be difficult. Alice reported that rehearsals were scheduled for ten weeks rather than eight, but in the archive full rehearsal schedules exist from September 22, which would put the rehearsal period closer to twelve weeks. Alice considered even ten weeks a "lavish" payroll expenditure. One casting difficulty not anticipated in New York was finding a suitably "Jewish" cast, without stereotypical signs, who also had festival ideals potential. "Those first weeks of the

25. The repossession of Leah at the conclusion of *The Dybbuk* in 1925.

prospective casting seemed the most difficult part of the production," Alice wrote later. "The actors who considered themselves qualified, Jewish actors of Broadway proved themselves least suited because their whole approach and emphasis was upon obvious values, and they had no relation to mystical feeling." Eventually auditions were suspended and Albert Carroll was cast as Channon. Even after rehearsals had begun, the production lacked a Leah, and Alice walked through the part for rehearsal purposes. Finally, a newcomer to the house was cast: Mary Ellis, who would later build a substantial theater record in New York before choosing early retirement and life in Britain. The role of Rabbi Azreal was played by Edgar Kent, whose usual repertory was small parts in Shakespeare and Shaw. Despite original intentions to be truly "lavish" and cast the production with professionals, most of the rest of the parts were filled from within the company and included amateurs. The choruses were especially important to the desired effect, and their ranks were led by performers from the dance company such as Blanche Talmud and also by directors Irene Lewisohn and Aline Bernstein. After casting Ellis, Alice wrote that "my task was to lavish the intensity of undivided responsibility upon the production."[15] The degree of ensemble participation was extremely high and higher than originally intended.

The earliest production notes blocked out a first act that would slowly introduce the audience to a foreign culture: the effects sought were "peace and satisfaction—easy and smooth." The messenger in the first act was to be an omen, a "Secret Service," "a sense that something is about to happen." Aline Bernstein's set and costume notes for the opening planned the three quarreling batlonim to be slightly surreal in stark lighting and cleared stage emphasizing angular effects: "Here the same crooked, mysterious grotesque line exaggerated. Should have almost sculptural quality."[16] But very early in rehearsal the direction found a focus in the dance of the beggars that opens the second act in the lapse between Channon's death and his rebirth as the Dybbuk that possesses Leah. The unedited notes plan a dance scene in which "the beggars are an army of Channon to kidnap Leah . . . mysterious power. Leah happy when dancing with beggars—ecstasy. Leah becomes exhausted by their violence."[17] The corps of beggars also became a focus in Bernstein's planning of costume design. For Blanche Talmud as "Rivke, the pale one" of the beggars, Bernstein planned, "Character, paralysed left side. Long tightly-fitted dress, long sleeves, painted dark red, fading into ivory white on left side. Rag around neck and overhead streaked with white. Slipper for left foot is yellow, for right green." Another beggar role was filled by Vera Allen, who had filled small roles in the company since *The Critic* in 1925 and who, after the success of *The Dybbuk,* went on to a celebrated career in theater including a special Tony Award in 1948 for Distinguished Wing Volunteer Worker Through the War and After. For her beggar, Bernstein planned "purplish-black full skirt. Jacket, black, full sleeve, shawl over head and arms to give effect of wings." The chorus required twenty-five wig and beard sets from Zanuder Brothers Hair Goods and Sundries for a total rental fee of $273.50, or more than the weekly salary of the lead actor.[18]

Protracted rehearsal was required for a dynamic beggar dance to portray simultaneously grudging gratitude for a rich man's charity and also liberating and subversive ecstasy with the "sin that is about to happen." The dance was credited to Irene, and, in Alice's account, "in rehearsal the beggars fought among themselves, fumbled, growled, suffered, grabbed, and gobbled food, at first politely and decorously, then with growing abandon, until at last their beggarhood seemed to take to itself supernatural attributes and ultimately the grotesque stature of fiends let loose by the disembodied Channon to capture his promised bride."[19] The effort was evidently successful, for one month after opening the *New York Times Magazine* ran a feature that delighted in the idea of women like Irene and Aline struggling to become truly grubby:

> The beggars in *The Dybbuk* who are so convincing on the stage were put through a whole course of simulated begging from getting up in the morning to wrapping up in realistic rags in a less exposed corner for a night's rest. To gain convincing realism, the Neighborhood Playhouse company, made up of persons of mixed nationality and miscellaneous religions, was relentlessly drilled by a Chassidic Jew who knew exactly how Chassidic Jews should behave. When things seemed to slow he tore his hair and cried *"Plus d'extase, plus d'extase!"*—"more ecstasy, more ecstasy!"—until he got them all wound up in the truly terrifying pitch at which you find them in the theatre.

The result, for the *Times,* was "the highest point of acting and of production, the most faultless performance, taken all together, which the Neighborhood Playhouse, with all its highly creditable record, has yet managed."[20]

The rehearsal period of *The Dybbuk* was not without its problems. On September 20, Alice received a telegram from Paris that read, "Impossible ascertain whether score sent. Investigating. Meyerovitch." Chronic discontent over salary issues continued. Many were discussed at an "Executive Staff Meeting" on November 6, 1925. The first agenda item was "problems with regard to engagements and salary adjustments." The problem lay in continuing *The Grand Street Follies* into the fall season for the purpose of raising revenue and allowing a longer rehearsal period for the first full production of the season. Because it was the most prioritized production, the company of *The Dybbuk* had higher salaries in rehearsal than the company filling the house with paying audiences in full production. The resolution at the meeting was "Instruction to Miss Arthur as to the salaries of *The Dybbuk* cast. In view of the problems arising from the long rehearsals, the probability is that the members of the *Follies* cast will not be willing to play for the same salary they are getting now." A further cause of unrest was conflicts between a hierarchical, professional company salary structure and both Lower East Side and bohemian ideals of equality. Maclaren's weekly salary of $200, which he probably considered a sacrifice against his other professional options, was the highest in the production. Blanche Talmud's of $37.50 was among the lowest of the "professional" actors, and her responsibilities included uncredited choreography and some direction of the dance company corps. In addition, there were maintenance problems: the sole meeting agenda item under "problems connected with the house" was "What of the painting and when shall it begin?" No resolution was made. Then there was the agenda of "problems connected with *The Dybbuk*":

Is it safe now to announce the opening as December 15?

If the Dybbuk is a great success and can move uptown, shall we invite Doris Keane to play at the Neighborhood with outside actors?

If the Dybbuk is only a partial success and runs at the Neighborhood about 8 weeks, then a ballet or the Salut seems good as a following bill.

If the Dybbuk is a failure and runs from 4 to 6 weeks, a new play should be gotten ready using the permanent company.[21]

No decisions appear to have been made on these options, and decisions of this sort do not appear to have been within what Alice considered within "my task . . . to lavish the intensity of undivided responsibility upon the production." Keane was a fading Broadway star whose last vehicle, *Starlight*, had been a stage biography of Sarah Bernhardt. A revival of *Salut au Monde* had been announced to subscribers as a late spring production. Even on the opening night of *The Dybbuk*, the program offered to subscribers it and "another," as yet unnamed play, so nothing had been "gotten ready using the permanent company." The company plan, as such, even after the executive staff meeting, remained to launch

The Dybbuk at the most ambitious production level and attend to contingencies afterwards.

The Dybbuk did, in fact, open on December 15. It was a great success, but that did not necessarily mean that the production would move uptown. As Alice recalled: "The next morning the unanimous praise of the critics created a situation for which we were once again unprepared. From early morning till late at night, the box-office telephone never ceased ringing. Members of the playing company were besieged by private calls with pleading requests for seats. Under this avalanche of public interest the Playhouse staggered a bit at first, and then proceeded quietly on its way."[22] The reception was different in kind from the simple rave reviews that ensure demand for tickets. The printed notices consistently went beyond the usual compliments to favorably compare this opening by the Neighborhood Playhouse to the entire New York season, uptown and down. Gilbert Gabriel in the *New York Times* insisted that while the Neighborhood Playhouse was already known as "that postern gate to some of the most interesting experiments New York has known in recent years," *The Dybbuk*, "in the acting and atmosphere they brought to it, could cover the poor silly bones of this autumn of theatrical famine with a garment of true grandeur." Alexander Woollcott, then with the *World*, wrote that "no production in the endless, shuffling parade of plays that have passed this reviewing stand since the season began can compare in moving and memorable beauty with *The Dybbuk*. . . . no production sponsored uptown by the Theatre Guild, by Arthur Hopkins, and the rest has [had] so much courage, so much imagination, so much tranquil wisdom, so much loving care."[23] In particular, the production values were considered so high that they quickly inspired reassessments of the company with *The Dybbuk* as culmination of its history, as in H. L. Brock's piece "East Side, Too, Has 'Synthetic Theatre'" for the *Times:* "they began as amateurs, chiefly armed with an aspiration. Indeed, the original aspiration was not so much to improve the theatre as to use the theatre as an instrument to brighten the lives of people seemingly condemned to a drab existence by economic urban conditions." Brock found *The Dybbuk* the realization of ten years' institutional work in which Alice, Irene, Agnes Morgan, and Helen Arthur drew from the neighborhood, "absorbed that vitality, and directed it."[24]

The Dybbuk also prompted personal responses that far exceeded in volume and praise the usual polite congratulatory notes. Winthrop Ames of the Little Theatre cited the beggars and wrote of "the Dybuk" that "I think I've never seen, here or abroad, anything finer than that second act. Thank you." A reviewer for the *Springfield Republican* broke the convention of distance from producers and wrote a fan letter to Helen Arthur in which he called "the Dibbuk" "the weirdest, most spiritual and most interesting play of the season." The poet Witter Bynner, always intent on fraudulent infatuations with exotic cultures, wrote that "*The Dybbuk* makes of old superstition a new reality; so that the auditor is inclined to wonder if he may himself be possessed by some spirit not his own. And the Neighbourhood Players [*sic*] infuse the drama with a vigor and beauty that lend their performance an outshining distinction." The popular novelist Fannie Hurst wrote to Lillian Wald that "the whole history and yearnings and torments and ecstasies of a race seemed crammed into those two and a half hours."

The correspondence also included a great deal of entrepreneurial interest. The president of the American Play Company, a major New York producing agency at the time, appears to have recognized the conflict between downtown theater and New York commerce, and he had his own international solution to it:

> I cannot tell you what an extraordinary effect the performance of *The Dybbuk* had on me last Wednesday night. I don't blame you for discouraging any commercial activities in connection with it uptown. It would seem a sacrilege.
>
> Do you think it possible for me to negotiate for its use in London under very fine conditions?

The correspondence included support for two likely outcomes of the great success. For Enid Johnson, executive secretary of the New York Civic Club, the next step was clear: "I had the extreme pleasure of seeing *The Dybbuk* at the time of the Civic Club benefit, and I am writing to urge that you give a larger audience an opportunity of seeing this wonderful play by moving up to an uptown theater after the run at the Neighborhood

Playhouse is ended. I realize this is different from your policy, which I appreciate very much. But I feel that so beautiful a production should not have so short a life." While her letter recommended moving uptown, just as much correspondence urged an extended performance schedule downtown. For a Neighborhood Playhouse fan named Eleanor Gilbert, the audience downtown was the priority need: "For the sake of the thousands who have not yet seen the play I hope there's no truth in the rumor that it is to close at the end of a few weeks. I think its withdrawal would deprive the community of one of the finest things that has ever happened in the American theatre."

Alice responded to Johnson's letter on the Neighborhood Playhouse policy against transfers uptown: "Thank you for your suggestion about moving uptown. We have considered the matter deeply but as yet we are not converted to the idea of moving away from 'our home' which gives *The Dybbuk* part of its atmosphere and background."[25] She used similar language in many return notes. However, the issue was not moot, the idea had its converts, and the "policy" had never been publicly established. The dilemma evolving since the transfers of *The Queen's Enemies* and *Madras House* had been whether transfer abandoned community or whether transfer was a commitment to community because of the revenue it produced for reinvestment. More recently, the debate was revived in advance of *Exiles*. The minutes of an "Advisory Committee" meeting on February 2, 1925, which happened to be James Joyce's birthday, record that "Mrs. Morgenthau moved that if *Exiles* proves to be a success it be taken uptown. Miss Wald pointed out that from past experience this had not been successful, but it was thought that the situation uptown and the growth of the Playhouse's popularity might make it possible now." Alice was absent in Europe, but Irene suggested revival uptown of *Salut,* an idea which was more compatible with the firm festival ideal. Ultimately, neither was relocated for Broadway revenue, and instead the decision was made to seek resources from major donors such as Mrs. Straight, Mrs. Felix Warburg, and the Carnegie Foundation, "which is interested in the little theatre movement."

A subsequent meeting, on March 6, was devoted to formalizing the "Advisory Committee" itself. The names that were considered—Louis

Shipman, editor of *Life;* Stark Young; Mrs. Straight; Mrs. Cornelia Sullivan—suggest the dual functions of the committee, to advise and also to fund, the latter especially in collaboration with women in the "Lady Bountiful" role originally assumed by Alice and Irene alone. Formally, however, the second function was nearly hidden behind others: "they needed new members for the Advisory Committee 1. for advice; 2. for putting the Playhouse in touch with other groups of people whom they had not touched; 3. to help determine the repertory and policy for the coming year from the viewpoint of the audience and to help with ways and means of relieving the financial burdens." Either unable to define formally the philanthropic role of the committee, or unwilling in Irene's presence and Alice's absence to invite new competitors into the playhouse, the committee in spring 1925 left aside the candidacy of Louise Shipman and Stark Young, assigned the playhouse directors to invite five female benefactors, and added five male benefactors because "Mrs. Morgenthau and Miss Lewisohn thought that there was a need of a stronger masculine element and that the committee should represent the audience and its point of view." All new members would be considered temporary, and "if the members worked out successfully, then they should be asked permanently for next season."[26] Action on the advisory committee never became decisive, and the membership never came to represent the broader governance required for sustainability beyond original benefactors.

On December 21, 1925, six days after the opening of *The Dybbuk* to great acclaim, the advisory committee met again to discuss how to "capitalize" on its success. *The Dybbuk,* that dramatization of resolutions of conflicts, evidently failed to unite members of the company in a common vision. Alice and Irene were present, as were Aline Bernstein, Agnes Morgan, and Helen Arthur, and the "masculine element" was represented by two new members. Minutes were signed for the first time by Alice McCoy as "Executive Secretary." All agreed on the issue: moving uptown promised the benefit of greater revenue and "the danger of losing our identity." The dimensions of "identity" discussed included artistic control, the value of bringing an audience down to Grand Street, "the atmosphere which our environment contributes" to productions, and the cost to downtown attendance of a precedent that might tempt the audience to wait for uptown and more convenient revivals. The benefits were on the order of up to a 33 percent profit margin, allowing for opening costs, weekly costs, and percentage to the house. Alice spoke about the possibility of uptown revivals leading a new audience to become new subscribers to 466 Grand Street. Irene stated that the company was at a decision point: the endowment was not supporting the current year, including the higher production costs of *The Dybbuk,* and her language seemed to suggest that the Lewisohns would not supplement it. Irene's comments were paraphrased as "If the experiment is not a success now, after a 10-year trial period, it would be better to use up the principal and let the thing die." In her view, uptown visibility might help attract underwriters and so sustain "the experiment." The new male element, Mr. Alger and Mr. Holstein, spoke against deficit budgeting and for outside producing investors as a fiscal plan that was superior to endowment. Otto Kahn and John D. Rockefeller were mentioned as potential angels. Without a motion and without a vote, the advisory committee appeared to settle with the greatest reluctance on transfer uptown at the risk of eroding the identity.[27]

In January, the company produced a five-page plan for uptown productions of a Neighborhood Playhouse repertoire, including *Grand Street Follies,* with some special conditions for an initial transfer of *The Dybbuk* alone. Oversight would be provided by an unpaid sponsoring committee of five, "four outside persons and one representative of the Neighborhood Playhouse." In the margin of the typescript, someone, perhaps Helen Arthur, wrote "great disaster for committee." The agreement was initialed by Alice and hand delivered to Lillian Wald. Wald replied within twenty-four hours:

> January 14, 1926
>> Dear Alirene:
>> I am sorry to say that the reading of the proposed alternatives for action on the up-town production of the Neighborhood Playhouse successes leaves me with no clearer conception of what should be done. It looks to me very much like an impasse.

To her mind, uptown transfer under the control of "outside persons" eliminated the Neighborhood Playhouse identity that accounted for the success. At the same time, uptown transfer under the control of the Neighborhood Playhouse seemed beyond its resources. "If Alice Lewisohn cannot undertake that task," she wrote to "Alirene," "who could take the responsibility in her place?" She concluded that "if there is nothing more to suggest than is outlined in the letter, there seems to be nothing to do but to go on with the Neighborhood Playhouse productions and to secure additional money to maintain it on its present artistic and educational plane."[28] Lillian Wald spoke without consulting the "masculine element" and apparently without much interest in the advisory committee. She clearly chose the Neighborhood Playhouse identity over potential revenue, and she linked its mission to the original principles of artistic and educational functions. She was certainly not naive about financing nonprofits or soliciting underwriters. But she saw no profit in visibility in a substitute locale and every advantage in neighborhood identity. She mentioned no new sources for "additional money," and the frosty reference to Alice Lewisohn may have been intended to remind the readers of the letter who the original backers of "the experiment" were, who the sponsoring organization that gave them the opportunity to do so was, and so where the responsibility for sustainability lay. She did not see the Neighborhood Playhouse as a start-up whose expenses would be transferred to some other source or as a commodity to be traded. No doubt she had her competing needs and other plans for any solicitation to benefactors such as Rockefeller or Kahn. While she opened her letter by writing that "it looks to me very much like an impasse," Lillian Wald rapidly resolved that impasse and the indecision of the advisory committee.

The production of *The Dybbuk* continued its run as originally scheduled through March on Grand Street. There was no immediate, absolute rift between Wald and "Alirene." Before the end of December, *Better Times*, a magazine published by the United Neighborhood Houses as "New York's Welfare Magazine," asked Wald for nominees for medals for "distinguished social service." Among her nominees, and the only ones associated with the arts, were Alice and Irene "for their remarkable demonstration in the establishment and maintenance on a lofty, noncommercial plane of taste and education of a unique theater which has as its basic purpose the democratizing of culture in this field and development of talent in the neighborhood."[29] For her part, Alice continued to attempt to resolve the conflicting priorities of the playhouse and the neighborhood. On February 11, 1926, on the occasion of the eleventh anniversary of her own company, she addressed the Moscow Art Theatre during a visit to New York, greeted them "on behalf of the Neighborhood Playhouse family," praised their well-known accomplishments, and insisted on "a still closer personal tie and relationship, for there has been throughout the years an unconscious bond linking our vision, stimulating our belief."[30]

Meanwhile, in January, O'Neill's *The Great God Brown* had opened downtown at the Greenwich Village Theatre. In its combination of psychological realism and stylized representation of identity with masks, it was no less challenging than the exoticism and dance vocabulary of *The Dybbuk,* and perhaps the Greenwich Village interest in psychology was equivalent to some audiences to the exoticism of the Lower East Side context of orthodox and Hassidic Jewishness. In March, *The Great God Brown* did relocate from its original community to Broadway for a long and profitable run for eight months at two theaters. However, even though the production involved longtime associates of Provincetown Playhouse such as Kenneth Macgowan, it had been produced independently. The three most significant noncommercial companies, Provincetown, Theatre Guild, and Neighborhood Playhouse, did unite for an exhibit at the Greenwich Village Theater during the O'Neill performances there.

At about the same time, Helen Arthur was working to correct the notion that the oft-cited "endowment" of the Neighborhood Playhouse constituted in itself wealth and security. She wrote to Alexander Woollcott that "ever since the Sunday issue of *The World* of December 27 in which you spoke so sympathetically of *The Dybbuk* and the Playhouse, I have been wanting to write to tell you something more of our background":

May I take this opportunity of explaining that the subsidy of the Playhouse is in no sense an endowment? A yearly income provides, you might say, merely a home to shelter the experiments in production that have been slowly crystallizing during these ten years. This income guarantees only certain functional necessities. The major portion required to maintain the Playhouse productions is dependent upon subscribers, the more general audiences, and largely upon those who participate in the organization and testify through their service a belief in a non-commercial standard in salary as well as in production.[31]

She wanted journalism to recruit subscribers and not to suggest that the company was fully funded; in that she was following Irene's new insistence that the Lewisohn funding, an estimated annual contribution rather than a large restricted fund wholly controlled by the playhouse, was intended as and functioned as seed funding for experimentation. That conception of the Lewisohn support had evolved from the earliest years when fellow funders were not welcome by the principal benefactors.

In the spring of 1926, lacking consensus for uptown transfer, and loathe to forego the steady box office of a success like *The Dybbuk*, the Neighborhood Playhouse launched a new institutional organization, "the repertory model," and they chose to launch it as an innovation rather necessity or financial cutback. The model was not truly innovative, though it was more common in Britain than the United States. The repertory plan was to produce more than one play at one time and to stage them on a revolving performance schedule. The idea was to diversify company artistic work and to encourage more frequent audience return to the same theater. The practical limitation, in terms of both company personnel and space, was development of new productions during a running production that might be extended or shortened. The financial liability lay in new productions that failed and left the house empty or became a success on the order of *The Dybbuk* and threatened instead to monopolize the house and block successor productions. In Alice's recollection years later, "one possible way to salvage the immediate situation was to test repertory and in this way to reduce the number of new productions."[32] In this later analysis, she allowed that it was ironical that a company founded on the ideal of experiment would resort to repetition. The company announced the change in a press release:

Beginning March 23, The Neighborhood Playhouse will become a repertory theatre . . . The Neighborhood Playhouse believes the time has come
when its permanent company, trained through long association together
in many and varied experiments in both lyric and dramatic forms, is
prepared for the important step into repertory. The Playhouse is the oldest experimental theatre in America, and it is fitting that it should be the
first professional organization of the present day to realize in New York
City the ideal of the repertory company.[33]

The reorganization was presented as decisive in pursuit of innovation
and as compromise with persistent conflicts and limitations. It was not
alone, and many other companies were simultaneously pursuing the
same "innovation."

The new initiative would begin with the opening of a new program,
Three Lyric Dramas, which the company members had developed over a
longer than usual rehearsal period of twelve weeks while continuing as
cast members in *The Dybbuk.* The trio of one-acts emphasized exoticism:
the pieces were a dumb show with marionettes, "A Burmese Pwe"; an
operetta staging of Haydn's "The Apothecary"; and a Chinese dance
drama, "Kuan Yin." The three-part program allowed a greater number
of directors to assume smaller tasks: direction was divided among Alice
and Irene; scoring among three different musicians; and costuming
among Aline Bernstein, longtime company member Esther Peck, and
newcomer Ernest de Weerth. The results were good and the reception
reminiscent of *The Dybbuk.* Brooks Atkinson commended the "organization and performance . . . acting with dancing . . . costumery and setting"
in a program in which "acting and producing begin to reach a high plane
in Grand Street. One feels that the essential elements of the theatrical art
have been molded into symmetrical form at this remote playhouse. In
this respect they surpass all other local enterprises."[34] The two programs
complemented each other and when running in repertory—*The Dybbuk*
midweek and *Three Lyric Dramas* weekends—represented collectively a
distinctive organizational identity.

The announcement of the new repertory organization was linked by
the press with similar plans at the Theatre Guild. The Guild had an-

nounced in spring that it would shift to a repertory production schedule the following fall. In order to do so, it had to build a company, one asset the Neighborhood Playhouse already had in place. For its "permanent repertory company," the Guild recruited Alfred Lunt, Lynn Fontaine, and other well-known performers, and it planned a school for student actors who would simultaneously fill out casts. As reported in the *New York Times* in February, in the Guild model: "the advantage to the actor is clear. . . . With the company already under contract, no time will be lost in casting. The actor can read and study long before rehearsals begin. The actor himself will be a delicate, sensitive instrument, ready to act the part, not chosen to fit the part, and play himself, and it is expected that a play will receive more understanding, fuller performances, than from actors to, in some measure, act themselves."[35]

Their publicity material did not explain what would prevent Lunt and Fontaine from playing themselves. The *Times* quoted approvingly the Neighborhood Playhouse emphasis instead on experiment and did not challenge its claim to being the oldest experimental theater in the United States or the first with a repertory model in New York. The latter claim could be weighed against nineteenth-century American theater history as well as against visitors to New York such as Granville Barker's company or the Moscow Art Theatre and emerging companies such as Eva La Gallienne's Civic Repertory Company.

Some of the differences between the two models in development can be seen in Lawrence Langner's account of the Guild's "Alternating Repertory System" in his history of the company. He called his system "modified repertory," "which was a compromise between repertory as understood by the Moscow Art Theatre, for example, and our own system of long runs." As launched in fall 1926, the Guild operated two theaters with two productions in each. Actors alternated not just between plays but between theaters. The benefits of the model were that performers would accept small roles in alternation with leading ones, thus enhancing depth of cast and box office appeal of noncommercial plays.

In Langner's account, the Alternating Repertory System accounted for the "golden age" of the Theatre Guild as measured by the critical and artistic success of the "permanent repertory company" in fourteen productions from 1926 to 1928: "I lived in a seventh heaven of delight." However, he acknowledged difficulties within the company, especially with scene designers and the newly organized labor force of carpenters: the first resisted the design limitation to adaptable flats, and the second demanded overtime for redressing a stage several times in a week. Langner made other commitments necessary for a company with a subscription list he claimed topped 23,000 (Neighborhood Playhouse's was at best 10,000) and profitable national tours of successful plays with even more modest sets for portability and substitute casts. Ultimately, he acknowledged that "two forces, the pro-Play and the pro-Acting Company, were in constant opposition because we lacked the unity of purpose to keep both forces working together."[36]

By contrast, the Neighborhood Playhouse model was recognized as a different kind of "delight" based on its audience and its locality rather than on its actors and nomadic movements between different theaters. Of the two, H. L. Brock, in a feature in the *New York Times Magazine,* found the Neighborhood Playhouse to be the more promising and more like the model of the Moscow Art Theatre, which was visiting New York that winter. He pointed to MAT's model of a company capable of revolving productions because "Nemirovitch Dantchenko's theatre also serves a more or less permanent public and the frequent change of bill is necessary." By virtue of being in Manhattan, even lower Manhattan, the Neighborhood Playhouse had a much larger audience, and it could have sent *The Dybbuk* uptown or kept it running at 466 Grand Street for the limousine trade. Lillian Wald's objection to transfer uptown was based on loss of Neighborhood Playhouse identity, and the repertory schedule for the kind of audience built in Moscow and praised by Brock was a further acknowledgment and commitment by the playhouse to the local, neighborhood audience. Like Brock, Brooks Atkinson praised the Neighborhood Playhouse for superior organization and commitment to both company, rather than stars, and community, rather than commerce. In March 1926, Atkinson in praise of Neighborhood Playhouse was also prescient of the difficulties that would be encountered by the Guild: "For the organization of the Neighborhood Playhouse company has enjoyed for some time the advantages of unity and intimate association under a definite scheme of dramatic development. More than any other major institutions in the city, the various actors, directors, and designers have worked toward a common ideal in Grand Street. To the average playgoer a Neighborhood Playhouse production carries a distinct connotation." The Grand Street theater seems to have cultivated the powerful *New York Times* more successfully than larger performing arts organizations. In March, the *Times* also published an editorial on the new repertory model and what benefits it would bring to the "intelligent playgoer." In May, it ran a long feature, "One Day in Grand Street," that stressed the synergy of design, shop, and company under one roof; the interchange of professional, semiprofessional, and student members of the company; and, above all, the interaction of company with neighborhood, including the "excitable and voluble mothers" of Grand Street: "Where, for instance, on Broadway would the baby carriage parade with the throngs of mothers in attendance be drawn up in front of a theatre to greet the players on their way to rehearsal?"[37]

The ensemble conception underlying the Neighborhood Playhouse ties to both festival and settlement ideals was significantly renewed by its new repertory model. In May, several weeks after running *The Dybbuk* and *Three Lyric Dramas* in repertory, Lillian Wald was solicited by *Theatre Magazine* for an article. The article never seems to have been written, but in the course of considering it Wald asked Alice Lewisohn for a definition of "experimental theatre." The reply, through Alice McCoy, ranked, in order of priority, acting, production, playwriting, and "establishing a critical audience interested in the processes and unfoldment of new tendencies in the theatre." Underlying all was the priority of "bringing into closer relationship the art of the dramatist, decorator, actor, poet and musician" in order to achieve "dynamic expression through the theatre."[38] These were also the priorities of an illustrated pamphlet called *The Repertory Idea* that was presumably prepared by the Neighborhood Playhouse in the summer of 1926 and published during the 1926–27 season. Its history was told in relation to "The Permanent Company" ("as removed from the old fashioned star system as Grand Street is from Broadway"), such as Ian Maclaren and Albert Carroll; then the semiprofessional company, such as Lily Lubell and Blanche Talmud who had moved up from the student Festival Dancers groups; and the current students, "not only from the neighborhood but from all parts of the city." The pamphlet promised that the repertory idea would mean revival of successes such as *Salut au Monde,* and it also promised that new work would continue to build the "critical audience" Alice described to Wald. On "The Audience," *The Repertory Idea* pledged to "place far more value in the knowledge that our audiences—at every performance—are composed of persons who know us and are sympathetic to our work and who bring to the theatre that intelligently critical attitude which in itself calls forth the highest response from the actors."[39] Nothing in the pamphlet suggested that the season it described—1926–27—would be the last of the Neighborhood Playhouse.

The ambition of the plan was extraordinarily high, and the level of performance extremely difficult to maintain. The first true repertory rotation of work in May 1926, which ordinarily would have rotated out the oldest production, instead closed *Three Lyric Dramas,* opened *The Romantic Young Lady,* maintained *The Dybbuk* with a second cast, and put *The Grand Street Follies* of 1926 into rehearsal. *The Romantic Young Lady* was a romance translated by Granville Barker and his wife about a young lady whose love for a novelist survives complications and becomes requited. It was an atmospheric piece rather like *Three Lyric Dramas* and a genre that had been a regular part of the company programming at least since *A Sunny Morning* in 1917. The "critical audience" recruited by the playhouse learned from a program note by Granville Barker that "While there may be much to say, there is really very little to explain about the plays of Martinez Sierra, for they have in the first place the supreme dramatic virtue of explaining themselves."[40] The focus of the production, which was the first to be directed by Agnes Morgan in the entire 1925–26 season, was to continue to produce performance in ensemble harmony of set and costume, which were both by Aline Bernstein, with movement and speech. In this it appears to have been successful. Joseph Wood Krutch wrote in the *Nation:*

> In connection with this performance I cannot but remark, as I have remarked several times before, both upon the variety which the programs

at the Neighborhood Playhouse offer and upon the skill with which the tone or mood of each work is almost invariably caught, whether the piece require the exquisite fantasy of "The Little Clay Cart," the grim seriousness of "Exiles," or the half-mocking, half-melting romanticism of the present piece. This act of creative interpretation, an art which depends quite as much upon the sensitive direction of the whole as upon individual performances, is not one which calls attention to itself. Its essential characteristic is to be so obviously *right* as to seem inevitable, and it is its absence rather than its presence which is most readily perceived.[41]

One less ambitious and less successful means to duplicate the mood of *The Dybbuk* was moving Mary Ellis and Ian Maclaren over to the other play, with the spectral quality of Leah enhancing the role of the young lady and the world-weary, experienced Messenger looking rather old for her young novelist lover. The *The Romantic Young Lady* appears to have matched in performative levels the quality of *The Dybbuk,* but it lacked an equally powerful text. Of that, Neighborhood Playhouse stalwart Brooks Atkinson wrote, "in the program this bit of nonsense according to an old pattern is described as 'gentle,' which is the polite way of saying slight, inconsequential, or more brutally—dull."[42] A new limit of the repertory idea may have been the priorities of performance that Alice, in her definition of "experimental theater" for Lillian Wald, placed in order of importance as acting, production, and playwriting. Having developed over the twelve years at 466 the kind of vivid inevitableness described by Krutch, the repertory productions now needed to recover the consequentiality of *The Dybbuk* on the Lower East Side.

The end of the season that had begun on such a high note was the "fourth edition" of *The Grand Street Follies,* and this, too, despite the high recognition of the series throughout the theater world of New York, was greeted with disappointment. The 1926 version introduced a "theme" of the North Pole as continuity through the sketches, but the effect seemed to most contrived and antithetical to the spontaneity underlying previous successful *Follies.* In the press, Bernstein's designs were compared to the many other revues in New York at end of season to the effect that *The*

Grand Street Follies were now less distinct from others such as *George White's Scandals* uptown and too meagerly funded to attempt spectacle and pageant on that scale. The satires closest to the Neighborhood Playhouse's own productions remained favorites: in 1926 these included an old cleaning woman, Mrs. Feitelbaum, who periodically returned to the stage as if by accident to explain to the audience that *The Dybbuk* was exaggerated and not to be believed. The major number of the second half was *Uncle Tom's Cabin*, performed in "A Constructivist Setting—an Example of the Sympathetic Elastic Theatre," a parody of the Neighborhood Playhouse's and the rest of the city's infatuation with the Moscow Art Theatre. In it, constructivist stage platforms, which Atkinson called "meaningless junk in the modernistic spirit,"[43] allowed choruses of slaves and angels in the most contemporary stage style to sing over Tom, Topsy, and others in their most melodramatic and archaic plight.

More generally, extending a trend set the year before, the satire of 1926 was directed more often at other theater companies, stars, and fashions in a manner that suggested Broadway envy. The Theatre Guild, as "The Gilt," was represented briefly, but the most elaborate sketches paro-

26. The constructivist set for *Uncle Tom's Cabin* in *The Grand Street Follies* of 1925.

died the season's Broadway hits such as George Kelly's *Craig's Wife*, which had won the Pulitzer Prize for theater (in the *Follies* "for purity"). *The Shanghai Gesture*, about a young Chinese woman entering the gambling world, was transferred to Texas and staged as a movie. Impersonators also chose uptown targets, especially Dorothy Sands parodying Beatrice Lillie in her revue. Then the objects of satire became national politics, especially the Teapot Dome Scandals, which duplicated the focus of the Guild's *Garrick Gaieties*. The review by John Anderson of the *New York Post* reflected most. The *Grand Street Follies* "is usually the blowing off of steam pent up all winter in the artistic but jovial bosoms of its sponsors," he explained. "Usually they rush forth to unrestrained hilarity, poking fun at themselves and other practitioners in the theatre. . . . [But] Miss Morgan, who wrote the previous *Follies*, has tried this time to take in too much territory—to spoof the Florida land boom, the rehabilitation of the North Pole and the current theatre all with one and the same joke."[44] The challenge that *The Grand Street Follies* of 1926 seemed to represent rather than meet was whether the uniquely high production values that had become associated with the company required Broadway scale more than experimental aspiration. By moving across "too much territory," this *Follies* also represented the dilemma of whether the content of a neighborhood playhouse and the interest of the critical audience it hoped to develop should be focused and local or broad and cosmopolitan. The satire was unsuccessful with a faithful audience already prone to delight in the singular "experimental" perspective required for effective satire.

The *Grand Street Follies* in 1926 ended the first repertory season. As in the previous year, the *Follies* played through the summer and into the fall. In summer 1926, a free bus service from Times Square was inaugurated, and its expense must have been required by less than robust ticket sales. The 1925 edition ran through November; in 1926 the *Follies* closed in October. The penultimate 1925–26 season had seen the company's greatest success in its most expensive production, *The Dybbuk*. Otherwise, with only *Three Lyric Dramas* and *The Romantic Young Lady* as original productions, it was the thinnest season to date. The theater, in production and rehearsals all week in the repertory style, also had fewer celebrity visitors,

27. Helen Arthur and Sadie Sussman in a skit from *The Grand Street Follies* of 1926.

lecture series, loans of the stage to community groups, or rentals to other noncommercial productions. The Neighborhood Playhouse had won the title of "first" repertory theater from the Guild, and it had been energized by the self-assessment required to position the new organization as both institutionally innovative and artistically sound, but the immediate re-sults of coping with *Dybbuk* success were disappointing. 1926–27 would offer the opportunity to plan a full season that combined original produc-tions with revivals that defined company distinction.

The season also had a significant distinction of its own by bringing *The Dybbuk* to New York and beyond. In 1926, the Habima Players of

Moscow, their way having been prepared by the Neighborhood Playhouse, came to New York on tour. In 1926 there were also other productions of *The Dybbuk* at the Bayes Theatre in New York City, in Chicago, in Philadelphia, and in Newark, New Jersey. The Neighborhood Playhouse's own revival would open in December 1926, almost exactly one year after its premiere. The record certainly documents the artistic success of the production. It is less explicit on the social dimension of that success, on the theater's creation of an audience community both Jewish and Gentile and uptown and downtown, and on the relation of the theater function to the mission of the Henry Street Settlement.

In retrospect, the introduction of an English-language version of a Yiddish tale and performance of it to a largely patrician audience can seem patronizing or worse. In 2000, in his introduction to *The Dybbuk and the Yiddish Imagination,* Joachim Neugroschel described the dangers of such an enterprise, which was his own: "By translating Ansky into English, a non-Jewish language, we assimilate the author into a Gentile world. Translation tends to be more curatorial, adaptation more transformative. Both are imperialistic in that they wrench a text from another culture, a foreign context, and shove it into its new home. We take from the 'other,' giving little in return."[45] In its time, however, the Neighborhood Playhouse production, which was intended to be adaptive rather than curatorial, would have been proud of being termed "transformative." Toward the end of its first-year run in June 1926, the *New Yorker,* in its second year in the contemporary format with cartoons, printed one by Peter Arno with the caption "One of the neighbors drops in at the Neighborhood Playhouse."[46] The drawing showed an old man in Hassidic dress in the lobby, surrounded by top-hatted and bejeweled visitors to the neighborhood, who all glare disapprovingly at him. Two ushers appear confused, and it is not clear if the "neighbor" should be seated in the house. Arno's point in 1926 was the hypocrisy of the audience for *The Dybbuk* who preferred their Hassids on stage or out of sight. The cartoon documents the degree of importance of the transformation that the playhouse, and the Lewisohns in particular, hoped to effect with the play properly subtitled "Between Two Worlds." Attending to issues surrounding the transformation of being "shoved" into a new home was among the ideals of the Neighborhood Playhouse and underlay its links with the Henry Street Settlement. In their time, assimilation was not assumed to be imperialistic.

Neugroschel's translation was also the basis for Tony Kushner's "adaptation" *A Dybbuk,* which was produced at the Public Theater in New York City in 1997. Kushner's ending puts the emphasis on loss rather than release when Leah and Channon are united spiritually. In a speech not included in the Neighborhood Playhouse text, Rabbi Azriel (Neugroschel/Kushner spelling) makes a final lament that "though His love become only abrasion, derision, excoriation, tell him, I cling. We cling. He made us, He can never shake us off." In an afterward to the published text of Kushner's version, Harold Bloom properly calls its focus a post-Holocaust performance of "the dying of normative tradition."[47] In 1925, however, Alice Lewisohn saw the text just as clearly as "a protest against dogmatic ritualism" and performance of a liberating "mystical enthusiasm or ecstasy."[48] In a context not yet altered by the Holocaust, Alice put her emphasis, as performed in the context of a Jewish population in a new home, on rebirth and opportunity. The highest artistic success of the Neighborhood Playhouse was also its most incisive communication on social transformation, and its assimilation of a Yiddish tale into a Gentile theater world was consistent with the broader social goals of its settlement setting.

7

꧁꧂

1926-1927

The Close of "The Unworldly Little Theater"

The thirteenth season of the Neighborhood Playhouse, 1926–27, would be its last under the auspices of the company formed in 1915 in association with the Henry Street Settlement. The final production would be an exit *Grand Street Follies,* the fifth edition, which opened a month after the closing was announced. The season would open two new productions, *The Lion Tamer,* directed by Agnes Morgan and designed by Aline Bernstein, and *Pinwheel,* directed by Alice and Irene Lewisohn and designed by a new name to the playhouse that would later equal Bernstein's in influence, Donald Oenslager. The season schedule included revivals of *The Little Clay Cart* and *The Dybbuk* in repertory with the new productions and a "lyric triple bill" mostly directed and designed by Irene and Aline Bernstein. The last had the encouraging sign of collaboration across the two conflicting contingents within the company directorship, or, in Bernstein's phrase, "the N.P.H. Women."

Bernstein's letters to Thomas Wolfe are incidentally an interesting record of the conflicting personalities at the playhouse. In the fall of 1926, her love letters to him are very chatty about the playhouse, although his responses are neither love letters nor chatty on any subject. Bernstein liked to report items such as "This one Helen Arthur told me today— gentlemen prefer blonds, but blondes are not so particular." He liked to sign off with phrases such as "Semper infidelis." In September she wrote to him sailing back to Europe:

> I got my work through this week, bolstered up largely by Agnes. It [*Lion Tamer*] is very poor and every one is disappointed . . . I had a rather bad

time with Alice & Irene when I returned and have refused to do the next new production. They accused me most unjustly of pushing my own department last year, meaning of course in their round about way, my own work, and covering myself with undue glory. I was feeling down and out and sore at life in general, so I lay about me with a cudgel and we all went home with broken heads, more or less. Helen & Agnes took my side vociferously.

Later in the same month, Bernstein wrote to Wolfe: "You know, about the Lewisohns and their attitude toward me, I think they are perfectly sincere, in their own way. Helen seems to think that they were distressed in a measure at the amount of publicity I had last year, a sort of personal publicity that no one else seemed to get, and that I really did not deserve any more than any of the others." At the outset of the thirteenth season, and on the considerable success of *The Dybbuk,* the longtime collaborators weighed personal ambitions against N.P.H. goals and personal styles against the collective one. The issues would be addressed at a higher, formal level in public statements on repertory ideals. They also resided at the lower levels recorded by Bernstein for Wolfe, whose personal turbulence was on a grander scale. "Any way," she wrote him at the beginning of the final season, "they are getting over it, and behaving somewhat like human beings. They had better."[1]

In pre-publicity for the opening production of the season, Helen Arthur published in the *New York Times* a very candid summary of the challenges her and other noncommercial theaters faced in mounting repertory seasons. In "Repertory and Its Difficulties," she asked, "What makes it all so difficult?" She devoted most of her space to the difficulties of maintaining a permanent company for multiple productions: "the demands of repertory are such that your actors must be able—and willing—to play together in a variety of roles." In reference to the Neighborhood Playhouse midyear plans, which were the revival of *The Little Clay Cart* to be joined in repertory by the new production, *Pinwheel,* she confessed that "we must, therefore, be mentally casting *Pinwheel* while we are actually casting *The Little Clay Cart* and we must select the outside players in the former with a view to their fitness for the latter." The challenge under the circumstances was to protect high performance values from compromise, and even if that challenge was met there was a further, higher one to allow for "the processes of experiment, of trial, of elimination." Almost as a coda, she listed a number of other difficulties including attracting playwrights to noncommercial theater, the cost of advertising, the expense and regulation of "backstage operatives" newly unionized, and, inevitably, lack of endowment: "A real repertory theatre serves the arts of the theatre as a great museum serves the arts of painting and sculpture, and, like a museum, such a theatre needs endowment." In reference to the well-known Neighborhood Playhouse support (not in endowment but in annual expenditures) of the Lewisohns, Arthur proposed that the necessary endowment "need not come from a few individuals only. It can come and ultimately it must come, from the enthusiastic support of that vitally concerned public, whose great interest in the arts of the theatre such a playhouse honestly serves."[2]

In addition to personal conflicts and organizational difficulties, in its final season the Neighborhood Playhouse was also situated in the midst of a longer trend to reorient the settlement movement, which both directly and indirectly influenced Lillian Wald and the Henry Street Settlement. Albert Kennedy, head of the National Federation of Settlements since 1922, and an elder statesman of the movement who had served with Robert Woods at Boston's South End House in 1906, found his emphasis on settlements with arts increasingly under challenge from social activists. In 1925, in a correspondence that mentioned and was copied to Lillian Wald, Charles Cooper, then member-at-large of the federation's board, wrote to Kennedy to contrast "two tendencies" evident in the movement: "development of the settlement as an experimental, educational institution with a special emphasis on arts and craft" and, in opposition, the effort for the settlement "to reoccupy its old field as a liberalizing influence in all aspects of life."[3] Cooper was one of Kennedy's most diplomatic critics. Paul Kellogg, then editor of *Survey Graphic* and later the heir to settlement leadership, publicly challenged Kennedy a little later by declaring that without greater emphasis on "civic functions" the settlements were "likely to become more like abbeys and monasteries than like missionary posts."[4] The *Graphic* had praised the Neighborhood

Playhouse in 1925 because it defined itself "as a social force, as an educational institution, and as a vehicle for artistic creation," in that order of priority.[5] Had the journal revisited the playhouse in the fall of 1926 it could have inferred, on the basis of Arthur's piece on repertory in the *Times*, that the priorities had been reversed. The Neighborhood Playhouse was becoming more artistic and less activist when the settlement movement began to prioritize "civic functions," including the original emphasis on health care and housing.

Lillian Wald's work for the National Federation for Settlements included leadership on 1926 committees to investigate settlement action relevant to the social effects of prohibition, and, in early 1927, or the midpoint of the playhouse's final season, on increasing professionalism in the settlement movement. The first was a good example of the kind of effects of poverty on life that Cooper, Kellogg, and others thought should prevail over cultural education. The second was a matter on which the Neighborhood Playhouse, because it had instituted a professional, permanent company, had departed from settlement ideals. Helen Morton, for the federation, had asked Wald to study "why so many of the younger generation insist upon 'paid jobs.'" Rather ambiguously, Wald replied, "Sincerity, intelligence and a social feeling to people is as necessary for the volunteers as for the professionals. Some of the best workers we have ever had, and some of the excellent workers we now have, are unpaid." Whatever the case in the Henry Street Settlement, in the theater professionalism had replaced amateur ideals. In a comparative study of theaters operated at the same time by Hull House in Chicago, Karamu House in Cleveland, and Henry Street Settlement in lower Manhattan, Melanie N. Blood describes the opening of the Neighborhood Playhouse as intentionally distant, on Grand Street, from Henry Street and how that distance grew greater over time:

> Wald's early praise of the theatre demonstrates her interest in using the theatre to represent the settlement neighborhood, but when the interest of the producing staff shifted to more general artistic experimentation and an exploration of folk traditions of diverse cultures, Wald did not have the same power as [Jane] Addams [at Hull House] to shape Play-

house policy. The Producing Staff controlled all artistic decisions, and since the majority of the annual budget came from the Lewisohns and ticket sales, Wald does not seem to have interfered.[6]

Wald, of course, was a member of the producing staff, and none of the other members were immune to her influence. She does not seem to have interfered, but it is likely that her enthusiasm for the Neighborhood Playhouse waned as its emphasis centered on the artistic growth of a permanent company more than on the neighborhood audience and as the settlement movement, in which all her work was integrated, shifted its goals from artistic to civic. In Helen Arthur's "Repertory and Its Difficulties," artistic difficulties dominate and the audience is mentioned only as potential benefactors. However, even as an independent entity within the Henry Street Settlement, the Neighborhood Playhouse had a long history with the settlement and relied on its link with the settlement as a fundamental aspect of its identity. In its final season, "the N.P.H. Women," along with personal conflicts, were also divided by contrasting idealisms: neighborhood priorities above all, represented by Lillian Wald; playhouse priorities above all, represented by Morgan and Arthur; with Alice and Irene positioned in between and holding the decisive power of finance.

The widening gaps between the producing directors in the 1926–27 season can be seen in incidental correspondence over tickets. At the beginning of the year, on September 24, Wald wrote, through a scheduler and a typist ("AEG:IS"), to "Dear Miss Lewisohn," which was a salutation very remote from the "Alirene" of the opening years. The letter, addressed to Alice, said, "Miss Wald will be very glad to go to the Little Theatre Dinner with you on Sunday afternoon." The Little Theatre Dinner was apparently a benefit which may or not have included performance of all or part of the theater's current offering, *Two Girls Wanted*, a comedy about female camaraderie by Gladys B. Unger. The letter found its way to Irene, who typed her own response and sent information on the classes at the playhouse: "so that if a millionaire who happens to sit next to you insists on your explaining the education program of The Neighborhood Playhouse, you will have just the right set of facts on which to proceed." The personal, organizational, and even institutional ambience for collaborative fund-raising continued to decline through the season. Two nights before the opening of the *Lyric Triple Bill* in April, which was the ending of the producing record of the playhouse except for the final *Grand Street Follies,* Helen Arthur wrote to Wald about her usual complimentary tickets. "This is the hideous thing that now confronts us, due to the fact that we have already mailed out to newspaper critics your three seats," she wrote to the founder of the Henry Street Settlement and founding sponsor of the Neighborhood Playhouse since the early days in Clinton Hall. "If I give you three of the four seats in the second row, to all intents and purposes that wastes one very good ticket [because] we cannot use it for a newspaper person. . . . The situation with regard to tickets for this opening has been peculiarly aggravated by the fact that Miss Lewisohn wished to invite certain music people for the opening." That Miss Lewisohn would be Irene, who directed the program and sought the "music people."[7]

The 1926–27 season opened in October with not just the Neighborhood Playhouse and the Theatre Guild starting repertory seasons, but also with the debut of the Civic Repertory led by Eva Le Gallienne on Fourteenth Street. Competitiveness was evident. Aline Bernstein attended an opening party of the Theatre Guild's *Juarez and Maximilian,* with Alfred Lunt as an Austrian adventurer in republican Mexico. "It was a mighty dull play in the acting, but I imagine [it] would read pretty well," she wrote to Wolfe. "I bought a copy in the lobby, and left it on my seat." Her own set, constructed on Grand Street, for *The Lion Tamer* was to open in four nights when she wrote to Wolfe, "[Lee] Simonson's scenery [for *Juarez and Maximilian*] is very handsome, but they tell me it cost thousands to build and is almost impossible to handle." It was also in pre-Holocaust rhetoric that she, a New York Jew, wrote about the heavily Jewish Guild, to Wolfe, the writer whose fictionalized portraits of the Neighborhood Playhouse and others were hostile: "It was a regular Guild first night, all the Jews in the world. You would have made a lovely pogrom, you could have cut all their throats and seen the dollars trickle out."[8] Her feelings about Simonson's set, at least, were widely shared, although her own set was not immune to the same criticism for being an intrusive spectacle.

The final season's first new play opening on October 7 was *The Lion*

Tamer, a translation of *Le Dompteur* by Alfred Savoir in which an enlightened reformer hopes to punish a circus performer for cruelty to animals and ends, in a special sound and light finale, being fed himself to the lions. It would have some subsequent lives, especially in London and Berlin productions. At the time, in New York, Savoir was known to audiences for *The Grand Duchess and the Waiter*, a Paris importation first produced on Broadway by Charles Frohman. *The Lion Tamer* was directed by Agnes Morgan and plainly represented, in the repertory, the Morgan-Arthur direction rather than the Lewisohn one or the Wald one. "It plays more interestingly than it reads, but I think our company is unequal to playing it," Bernstein wrote to Wolfe. "Not a bit of excitement and sicklied o're with the pale cast of Cambridge," in reference to Cambridge, Massachusetts, and George Pierce Baker's 47 Workshop at Harvard in Morgan's time there. "Thank god this is the last dress rehearsal tonight, I don't want to sit through it again and watch how like a wig Dorothy [Sands's] wig looks." On opening night, she reported to Wolfe: "I should say it was far from being a triumph. The second act, which I had painted on the inside of the first turned out quite well, it is funny and not too ugly. I was frightfully nervous, but you should have seen Savoir, he was nearly as nervous as you would have been. He didn't come down until it was half over, and then paced back and forth in the lobby until Alice Lewisohn hauled him in for part of the last act."[9]

In a new phenomenon for the playhouse, used to unanimous critical verdicts, *The Lion Tamer* introduced mixed critical reception. For Brooks Atkinson, who compared it as equally unsuccessful as *Juarez and Maximilian*, *The Lion Tamer* was a disappointing opening season choice "just as everybody was lying back in the fatuous belief that intellectual symbolism had been driven out of the theater." He located the failure in the playwright: "From the playgoer's point of view, M. Savoir's symbolism robs his skit of its inherent merriment as a joust between an idealist and a stupid brute." From the playgoer's point of view, he seemed to imply, the choice of text made the realization of festival ideals so essential to the Neighborhood Playhouse nearly impossible. However, Joseph Wood Krutch, who praised the text for "conception of the struggle, eternal and inconclusive, between the logical idealist and the brutal master of things as they are," found the production to be something of an apotheosis for the company. "Those who have followed the development of the company at the Neighborhood need hardly be told that the play is one which they are peculiarly fitted to perform." For Krutch, however, the fitness was entirely in acting: "Nowhere else in America, I think, has the tradition which insists that acting depends, not upon the exploitation of personality but upon the conscious control of the voice and body, been so consistently followed."[10] Atkinson's disappointment was in the totality of production style and Krutch's satisfaction was in acting technique, which are reasonable approximations of the decisions the company faced on future directions and playhouse identity.

In its repertory season, the company presented along with *The Lion Tamer* revivals of its two most recent celebrated successes: *The Little Clay Cart* and *The Dybbuk*. Both seem to have lived off reputation. Irene was dissatisfied enough with Agnes Morgan's direction of *Cart* that on November 2, two nights before opening, she issued the previously quoted memo to the cast "to add one or two general suggestions to those Miss Morgan made last night." The suggestions were that the revival rehearsals were "lacking at the present time" and required "more concentrated intensity." The lack was exoticism: "I am convinced that unless we are all equally saturated with the Rajput feeling and an understanding of the Hindu point of view and philosophy, we are apt to impose a Western quality that will lift *The Little Clay Cart* out of its sphere."[11] On reopening, Bernstein, whose design it was, would go no further in report to Wolfe than that "it went pretty well." She added that afterwards "we all went to Irene's for the usual frigid supper."[12] *The Lion Tamer* had closed by the time *The Dybbuk* opened in December. That allowed Ian Maclaren to move as lead from the first to the second, which may have helped compensate for the absence of Mary Ellis as Leah. However, the repertory reached full rotation at two rather than three plays and with concurrent revivals rather than revival in rotation with new production. The opening of *The Dybbuk*, in the theater historian Gerald Bordman's words, "perhaps not coincidentally,"[13] was three nights after the Habima from Moscow opened on Broadway with their Hebrew version. Later in the season, in his annual roundup, Joseph Wood Krutch did comment that there had not been "any production equal in poetic richness to *The Dybbuk*,"[14] but it wasn't clear whether he was referring to *The Dybbuk* of 1926 or of 1925.

Alice's memoir recalls what must have been a difficult winter in a chapter strangely titled "The Pace Quickens." On *The Little Clay Cart*, she recalled that "the directors were at a loss to know why the exquisite lyric quality of the original production could not be recaptured," which suggests that Irene's concerns were justified. Of the second revival, she wrote that "in the same way, the dynamic verve of the original production of *The Dybbuk* would soon be missing in its revival." In retrospect, she attributed the lukewarm reception of the revival to a peculiarly American fascination with novelty, not to the quality of performance. "Because of this tremendous eagerness for the new, the experimental and inventive here and now," she wrote, "the past with its traditions, positive and negative, has naturally little appeal."[15] Her purpose then, nearly thirty years after the closing, appears to be to justify the final major opening, Francis Edward Faragoh's *Pinwheel*, which was a constructivist critique of impersonal, chaotic, and valueless contemporary urban culture. But *Pinwheel*, with a major set designed by Donald Oenslager very early in his career, must have been in production months before *The Little Clay Cart* and *The Dybbuk* disappointed in revival. With direction by Alice instead of Agnes Morgan, and set by Oenslager rather than Bernstein, *Pinwheel* seems to have been planned as the latter half of a compromised, shared-custody season. It continued the final season trend of diminishing returns by getting a worse reception than *The Lion Tamer*, *The Little Clay Cart*, or *The Dybbuk*, and closing after four performances. When Faragoh published the script in book form later in the same year, he inserted a "Note" stating that "the text of *Pinwheel*, as published in this volume, is the author's original version and does not embody the changes made by the Neighborhood Playhouse in the course of production."[16]

Faragoh was Hungarian-born, educated in New York at City College and Columbia, and a working newspaperman who wrote short stories earning publication in *O. Henry Prize Stories*. *Pinwheel*, in 1927, was his first professionally produced play; two years later he would begin a film career with screenwriting credits that, in 1931 alone, included *Little Caesar* and *Frankenstein*. His attempt in *Pinwheel* was to capture the energy of the city and to posit a humanized space in it. The opening stage direction of the published text reads, "This is New York. Not a single street, not a definite, identifiable section of the city, but a crosscut, a focusing, the tangible essence of the metropolis." It opens with a crowd scene on the subway, isolates the principal characters "The Jane" and "The Guy," follows them through encounters in places like Coney Island and a billiard hall with character types like "The Fast Lady" and "Sugar Daddy," and closes with their revelation of the value of individual identity at night in a Bronx park. To design this, Alice brought in Oenslager, who was then, at the age of twenty-five, involved in the founding of the Yale University departments of drama and design. He had designed for the playhouse once before, for Irene's *Lyric Double Bill* in 1925, and he would have a remarkably prolific and distinguished career in New York theater, work in conjunction with the Neighborhood Playhouse School of Theater after the playhouse closed at 466 Grand, and leave a special collections archive at Yale.

To stage Faragoh's dynamic and chaotic metropolis, Oenslager constructed multiple platforms, with overlapping scenes to cacophonic music with characters in overstylized and so depersonalized costume and makeup. The effect was successful: of the two Neighborhood Playhouse stalwart reviewers, Atkinson wrote that "perhaps for the first time, the 'constructivist' stage setting, as the academicians classify it, has been made serviceable," and Krutch wrote that "at the Neighborhood Playhouse modernism now runs riot." Both, however, also felt that the effect enabled no content. For Krutch, "one does not feel that the elaborateness of the means is justified by the result. . . . Here is a technique of expression more striking than any of the things which it has to express."[17] But no other Neighborhood Playhouse production had closed so quickly, and since the revivals were also less than warmly received, the playhouse in its repertory season was left entirely dark for most of February and all of March. In memoir, Alice asked, "Was the reception due to what was, at that time, a bizarre treatment? Or had *Pinwheel* as a pioneer attempt to dramatize the forces of Manhattan not come through convincingly?" She did not allow for the likelihood that the failure was not because of pioneering experiment, which had always succeeded at 466 in the past. Nor did she admit that the production embraced a style without content, or that it was in fact a style the playhouse had successfully satirized in its own constructivist *Uncle Tom's Cabin*. *Salut au Monde, Little Clay Cart*, and *The Dybbuk* all used novel materials and pioneering stage effect to dramatize progressivist ideals in the context of ethnic and racial identity. *Pinwheel*, like *The Lion Tamer*, chose allegory and deracination, and *Pinwheel*, in particular, and in sharpest contrast with *Salut au Monde*, chose to lament urban anonymity and sterility instead of activating a cultural agenda against those qualities. The performance of *Pinwheel* could have been staged by the Theatre Guild, which Krutch specifically mentioned, and had no relationship with Grand Street or the Neighborhood Playhouse history on it. When, in the context of personal, organizational, and settlement culture conflicts, the playhouse needed on stage a statement of affirmation, it could not produce one, and so, Alice wrote years later, when "the landslide of interest for the earlier Playhouse productions had dwindled to the barest attendance at *Pinwheel* . . . we were forced once again to reconsider the problem of our direction."[18]

No reconsideration is evident in the short term. The season proceeded to the customary April opening of a lyric bill. In 1927 the program was a dance to compositions of Charles Griffes, a commedia dell'arte performance in an historic style by the dramatic company, and a large cast, three-part "Dance Romance" to a Bartok gypsy suite, *Ritornell*. Irene choreographed the first and the last and directed all three. Bernstein designed the first two and Esther Peck the third. The company was fully deployed, but the fourteen-piece Neighborhood Playhouse Ensemble orchestra players were not members of the company. In addition, the program listed many new names identified as consultants and advisors and experts in areas such as "suggesting authentic Hungarian traditions and customs." The introduction of the program in the penultimate "Neighborhood Playbill" was elegiac, particularly in the presentation of the past record without reference to any future except to the next *Grand Street Follies*. The program recounted the history of the lyric dramas from *Jephtha's Daughter* in 1915 and included one from every season, including an Agnes Morgan production without the Lewisohns in the sabbatical year of 1922–23. The historic list commentary celebrated the playhouse because it "experimented with this art form" and because gave "lyric drama its rightful place in the theatre" and because "study and work in this form are invaluable training for the modern actor." The centrality of the art form was not generally linked to students or to arts education or to audiences, but only to "training for the modern actor." The program also introduced the Griffes compositions as "among the earliest" of the composer who died in 1920, introduced the commedia with a text from *Studies of the Eighteen Century*, and *Ritornell*, a form based on repetition, as a revival of a performance first staged by the Cincinnati Orchestra two years earlier.[19] In a restatement of "the problem" in her memoir, Alice wrote in reference to the lyric bill that "the problem that we could not solve was to draw individuality out of a form stamped by a conventionalized tradition."[20] In terms of the season, "the problem" was repetition and derivation, of being unable to renew sources in Neighborhood Playhouse style. The longer pattern was being unable to match the internal and external exhilaration of *Jephtha's Daughter* or *Salut au Monde*. Alice did not indicate any problem regarding audience. However, the same playbill introduced the bus service from Times Square to Grand Street and to elevated and subway links. As correction to the "barest attendance" Alice mentioned in reference to *Pinwheel*, the new service was not a particularly interactive address to the dilemma of the neighborhood relations to the playhouse.

When the Neighborhood Playhouse at 466 Grand Street opened in 1915 with *Jephtha's Daughter*, the first of the lyric dramas listed in the program of 1927, Lillian Wald had welcomed the audience with the words, "It pleases me to think that what will seem best to-night has been woven out of the traditions of our neighborhood, and that the music and the dance and the color are part of the dower brought to New York by the stranger."[21] Even if Bartok could be justified on the basis of folk exoticism, the lyric drama of historic commedia and early Griffes was programming quite distant from the founding principles. Another indication of the evolution of mission from founding to closing can be seen in an undated document drawn up as a plan for the 1926–27 season. In 1915, Irene had told the New York *World Magazine* that the core belief of the new organization was "that every one should have a share in the world's treasures of imagination and poetry, and in return contribute something to the interpretation of human experiences."[22] In the fall of 1926 the planning document was based on "The Idea" that "now, to meet the demands of our newly organized repertoire, where dramatic, plastic and lyric productions follow in quick succession, it is even more essential than before to have a company technically well-equipped in these various branches" and, hence, "the personnel of this company, as planned for the season of 1926–27, will be divided into three groups." The first of these groups was, as before, the permanent company of professional players. The second and the third groups, Group B and Group C, would be "Associate Players" and "a semi professional group." The latter two would follow a five-week, 3 to 6 P.M. training schedule for eight weeks in areas such as technique, dance, choral singing, and pantomime. "Those especially selected by the directors"[23] would additionally be given private sessions of 30 minutes per week. For this, Groups B and C would pay a fee of $70.00 per week. The plan includes no reference to the amateurs so fundamental to founding plans. The students paying for membership in the Neighborhood Playhouse certainly benefitted from the instruction. The instruction staff included Bird Larsen, an important advocate of dance in public education; Maria Ouspenskaya, the associate of Richard Boleslavsky who would later open her own school of acting; and Howard Barlow, the composer and conductor who brought symphonic music to the Columbia Broadcasting System. This organization anticipates the Neighborhood Playhouse School of Acting, which evolved after closing of the playhouse as founded and continues to provide instruction in performing arts today. However, the professional and semiprofessional model without amateur counterpart and the unlikelihood that this system would capture and exploit "the dower brought to New York by the stranger" must have disappointed Lillian Wald and become at least a factor in the gradual separation of the Neighborhood Playhouse from the Henry Street Settlement. "The Idea" constructed in fall 1926 was based entirely on the needs of the repertory season and not at all on the needs and interests of the complex of constituencies found in a neighborhood playhouse.

The *Lyric Triple Bill* opened on April 5, 1927, and it would run on weekends through May 1. The fifth edition of *The Grand Street Follies* would open on May 19. However, it was on April 10, less than a week after the *Lyric Triple Bill* opening, that the Neighborhood Playhouse formally announced its closing. The front-page coverage in the *New York Times* for the most part reiterated the press release. The reasons stated were "location, size, and endowment," and each of these was related to the repertory project. On the reason of location, the statement attributed to Alice stated, "Deeply as we deplore this step, we are forced to realize that economically and from the working angle, and in view of our geography and the psychology of an audience, our present system is not conducive to the further development of creative expression." There was no comment and no discussion and so no response to the point that the "audience" referred to, which was challenged by the geography of the Lower East Side, had become the sole audience. Nor was it asked whether location, if it limited reception of creative expression, actually prevented creation of it. On the reason concerning size, the statement located the difficulty in the 1920 production of Galsworthy's *The Mob,* which "drew its audience from all parts of the city, and the financial returns could have been far greater had the capacity been larger or the theater more centrally located." The lack of box office capacity led to the third reason, the endowment, and the *Times* relied on its own sources to claim that the Lewisohns had provided an "annual endowment" of $45,000, and so in twelve seasons, assuming no contribution in the sabbatical season, $540,000, without calibration of any changes of overhead between 1915 and 1927 and without any calculation at all of the pre–Grand Street years at Clinton Hall and other sites. The overall point, for the playhouse and for the newspaper, as quoted earlier, was: "In announcing the decision to close the present theatre, the Misses Irene and Alice Lewisohn, who have sponsored the enterprise from the beginning, said that it was a step dictated by its success and the necessity for expansion. Problems of 'location, size and endowment,' they declare, had caused them to realize that their playhouse 'had come to the end of its present method.'" In closing, the story listed *The Dybbuk, The Little Clay Cart,* and bringing Lord Dunsany to the American stage as the Neighborhood Playhouse's greatest successes.[24]

The participants had no such clarity about the reasons for closing then or later. It must have been soon after the announcement that Irene composed the untitled, undated typescript that stated that "in 1927 when we closed the doors of the building in Grand Street we announced that having completed a certain phase in the development of our idea we felt it necessary to pause and contemplate the next step." Her "certain phase" echoed "its present method" in the statement delivered to the *Times* by Alice, and for all the pretense about pauses and beginning again, as in 1922–23, everything that followed the spring of 1927, under whatever name, including "Neighborhood Playhouse," and in whatever location, including Grand Street, would be distinctly different from the program at 466 from 1915 to 1927. In retrospect, Alice ridiculed her own statement on closing as "how coldly obvious beside the depth of emotion stirred" and acknowledged the real message as "The Neighborhood Playhouse as it had existed was dissolved."[25] Alice and Irene several times in this context referred to "the idea," which seems to refer to festival ideals and seems to have ceased at this point to be their personal project. Interestingly, Alice, in her statement to the press on closing, stated that "we stand in the position of being forced by the pressure of economic needs and the hazards of competition either to adopt methods of expedience or to step aside for a time and find a new adjustment."[26] The issue of expedience was also the focus of Lillian Wald's explanation much later in *Windows on Henry Street*. "When it was realized that the pressure of the expedient would gradually compel a departure from the more formal point of view," she wrote, in a passage where "the more formal point of view" seems analogous to "the idea," "the closing of the Neighborhood Playhouse was inevitable."[27] The coded language seems to indicate a noble pact to end the project if the necessary means and policy implementing it became inferior to it.

If Alice and Irene, publicly and privately, found "the idea" difficult to articulate, their principal journalist defenders did not. Between the announcement of closing and the opening of the "last new" edition of the *Grand Street Follies*, Joseph Wood Krutch published the first of several memorial notices on "the idea" on Grand Street. In invidious comparison with other repertory companies and recent parallel companies such as Provincetown Playhouse, Krutch formulated his idea: "Though it has never made any pretense of calling itself a national or civic theater, it has, nevertheless, come nearer to being that than have any other more ambitiously named enterprises. No other was actually so firmly rooted in a community and no other showed so great a capacity for steady and healthy growth."[28] In a long feature article, Brooks Atkinson also located the value of the idea firmly in the neighborhood dimension of the playhouse: "After theatregoers had come to regard the Neighborhood as one of the most vital forces in local drama, the Grand Street location seemed stubbornly incongruous. As a matter of fact, it kept the enterprise in harmony with its principles. It was always more akin to settlement work than to competitive play-producing." Atkinson, too, included his invidious comparison with "other organizations [that] have achieved a more spectacular success" while "everyone will agree that the unaffected spirit of the Neighborhood has not been matched elsewhere."[29]

Both testimonials unintentionally adverted to the more complex problem confronted by the playhouse directors. Krutch suggests that there is a kind of healthy growth that would remain distinct from that of other more ambitious enterprises. The playhouse directors had failed to find such a rosy organizational state. Although they persisted through several company models, they failed to find an indicator of ambition or measure of success other than growth, especially into the professional repertory theater that overextended their resources. Atkinson similarly imagined a status of enterprise harmony that could remain noncompetitive. The playhouse failed to find that state and, without it, found instead the lure of transfers uptown, increasingly professional company structure, and what Atkinson called "competitive play-producing." When saying that the closing "was a step dictated not by the failure of the theatre, but by its success," as the *New York Times* paraphrased it, Alice and Irene may have meant that they had succeeded in establishing a civic and community theater of artistic and commercial ambition without succeeding in finding a model of sustainability without growth and market competitiveness. Having reached that limit, and having with Wald a pact to end the project if the means become inferior to it, the only successful action could be to close the Neighborhood Playhouse.

Even before the *Lyric Triple Bill* closed, and before the Krutch and Atkinson pieces on the company closing, announcements had appeared in print that the 1927 *Grand Street Follies,* after its opening at 466 Grand Street, "may be moved to a theatre uptown either by the players themselves or by another management."[30] The final *Follies* were constructed around that prospective audience and not a satirical valedictory to the playhouse's past season. The first edition in 1922 had burlesqued the Neighborhood Playhouse in parodic restaging of its *Madras House* and *Salut au Monde.* The final edition in 1927 satirized celebrity, but not the playhouse's own. The largest numbers were "Stars with Stripes," a sketch in which stage luminaries do time in a maximum security prison for crimes against good taste; "Hurray for Us!," a Gilbert and Sullivan–style satire of Washington politicians; and "The School for Rivals," a satire on the recent trend for benefactors to take the stage themselves in celebrity pseudo-staging of Restoration comedies. In shorter sketches, company regulars took their own star turns, with Albert Carroll's appearances proceeding from Mrs. Fiske to Ethel Barrymore and concluding with his annual appearance as John Barrymore playing *Hamlet.*

The printed program for the *Follies* did self-critique the company history, and the results were wholly self-congratulatory. For the printed program, Joseph Wood Krutch contributed a "Vale" that again compared the company favorably to the Washington Square Players and the Provincetown Players, located its originality in its "origin in a community center" and in the festive "stage creations" that derived from extensive ensemble work. The only other contribution was from Alice, who promised an "interpretation" of the Neighborhood Playhouse, reasoned that its history was to indicate principles through productions only, and hazily concluded that it was in "dimly perceived, inchoate, half-visioned ideas and aspirations that the Neighborhood Playhouse has often attempted to voice in a desire to make tangible the intangible threads suggested but unexpressed."[31] In retrospect, in her memoir, she was less inchoate and deadly accurate about "the serio-comic fate" of *The Grand Street Follies:* "Unless a revue can maintain its individual character there is danger that it will become identified with the very standards and attitudes it is lampooning . . . . in the natural course of its growth [it] can either remain free to evolve its unique character, or else bit by bit it begins to compete with

28. Lily Lubell as an incarcerated Gloria Swanson in
"Stars with Stripes" from *The Grand Street Follies* of 1927.

its own achievement and, through imitation, to lose the original thrust of
the idea."[32]

The doors to the Neighborhood Playhouse, the building at 466 and
the program, closed on May 29, 1927, with a "Finale" rendition of "Many
Old Friends" with the entire company, onstage and offstage personnel,
longtime members and new students, on stage wearing some of the most
familiar costumes from past productions. Albert Carroll, as John Barrymore playing Hamlet, read a last will and testament and bequeathed gifts

29. Aline Bernstein as an industrious prisoner in "Stars with Stripes" from *The Grand Street Follies* of 1927.

to members of the company, members of the press, and faithful members of the audience. In the next few months, members of the company were very visible in New York theater but in activities far in kind from the original idea. While *Follies* was still playing downtown, the transfer uptown to the Little Theatre was announced, along with the news that the Lewisohns were paying company bonuses based on length of service and staking the new group a full future year in salary. The announcement also stated that the new "executive personnel" would be Agnes Morgan, Helen Arthur, Aline Bernstein, and Thornton Delehanty, a newcomer to the group who would become best-known as a film reviewer and was perhaps immediately intended as a kind of dramaturg. The announcement also stated that the new business plan was "on a cooperative basis," and that the "entire production" of Grand Street Follies would be "revised" for the new run.[33] Eventually, the new company became known as Actors-Managers: "It is thought that this name best expresses the plan of operation under which the company existed during the run of the *Grand Street Follies* and through which future productions will be made, that is, a scheme whereby the actors will share in the executive and financial control and which therefore makes them managers as well as actors." The full festival ideal of performance had devolved to acting technique. That was not unusual in theater culture of the time, but it was unusual as a culmination to a more ambitious and multidimensional theater enterprise.

The Neighborhood Playhouse ancestry was both the opportunity and the burden of the new company. Its first production in fall 1927 was Dunsany's play *If*, also at the Little Theatre. E. W. Osborn of the *Evening World* complained that "they can't fool us by a little shift like changing a name. They call themselves the Actor Managers. So they may be on paper. But as a matter of fact they are the same old Neighborhood Players." The same old ethos was not immediately successful in a new location and in the midst of a newer set of theatrical fashions and expectations than prevailed when the Neighborhood Playhouse first did *A Night at an Inn* in 1916. For the *New Yorker*, which was then defining its sardonic style, "To get excited about Dunsany now would be as timely as to start buying bound volumes of *The Yellow Book*," which was the journal launched in 1894 and somewhat unfairly associated with Oscar Wilde. For the *New Yorker*, Dunsany was "the god of Art Theatre of yesteryear, [and] he is still the god of the Art Theatre of yesteryear." For all the good will brought to the Actor-Managers by their history, they could not succeed without an original idea. Burton Davis in the *Telegram* reported that "half the critics attended the proceedings in Forty-fourth [Street] out of respect for the past achievements of this brave little band that used to be missionaries in Grand Street. They went away, I fear, not to praise Lord Dunsany, but to bury him."[34] The Actor-Managers attempted to produce on Broadway every year, then every other year, until most of the participants, including

Agnes Morgan, took advantage of opportunities offered by the Federal Theater Project. *The Grand Street Follies* were revived in spring of 1928 and 1929 and, under other auspices, even later, with programs derived entirely from the foibles of Broadway fare of that season. There was no Neighborhood Playhouse to focus the satire on self-critique, and there was no distinct audience to come to Grand Street to treat the burlesque as a celebration of a subscription season.

The other Neighborhood Playhouse directors, once known as Alirene, also gravitated uptown, but to music more than drama. Their conception was to extend the record of lyric programs and festival ensembles. The first production was announced in the press on January 15, 1928, for a May opening to mark the first anniversary of the closing of 466 Grand Street. The press was informed that "the early experiments out of which the Neighborhood Playhouse grew concerned the combination of choral movement, speech and songs and were termed festivals," and that the new "Orchestral Dramas" would reclaim this original inspiration. "These performances, however, will be given, not at the theater on Grand Street, but in a larger uptown theater."[35] Three days after the press announcement, Alice and Irene sent a typed postcard to "My dear Miss Wald" saying, "Before the announcement is made through the daily papers, we would like you who have shown your interest in the Neighborhood Playhouse idea by subscribing through its various seasons to know that we will make our next production in May of this year at an uptown theatre." The card was signed "Cordially yours, Alice and Irene Lewisohn."[36] The Wald archive has no response to the invitation.

The first of the orchestral dramas opened at the Metropolitan Opera House for three consecutive nights beginning May 4, 1928. The program was Ernest Bloch's *Israel*, two Debussy nocturnes, and two dances by Borodin, all performed by the Cleveland Symphony Orchestra. Irene was credited as director and choreographer of all three, Aline Bernstein designed the third, and Alice went without a performance credit. In some circles it was received in the spirit of experiment: in *Theatre Arts Monthly*, for example, regular contributor Helen Ingersoll wrote that Alice and Irene "had the courage to push at a door heavily barred by tradition, but one which, opening wider and wider, will lead far into a new experience." For her, the task was not for dance to embellish music or for music to decorate dance but for some new integration of aesthetic expression to emerge, and the performance was promising. She attributed the mixed, at best, reception as evidence of the alternate prejudices of dance or music critics. As example, she quoted the *New York Telegraph:* "You may be thinking—but what of the music? And here we come to the question, what of the MUSIC? Was it a symphony concert, or was it a pantomime, accompanied by music?"[37]

A similar program was created in May 1929, also at the Metropolitan Opera House. In 1930, a program not tied to the anniversary of the closing of the playhouse was produced in New York and in Cleveland, and in 1931 the venues became New York and Washington, D.C. "The Idea" had become diffuse when removed from neighborhood and then further so when unmoored even to the city; the "Neighborhood Playhouse" title was still used, but its reference was unclear.

Alice and Irene continued to be involved in children's productions at 466 Grand Street. But in 1928 they liquidated their gift to the Henry Street Settlement. The terms were that the Henry Street Settlement would pay the Neighborhood Playhouse $50,000 for its properties on Grand Street and Pitt Street. The strategy appears to have included trying to bankroll a Neighborhood Playhouse descendant, such as the school, and to give Henry Street at least an option to match. In June 1928, Irene wrote to "Dear Miss Wald" that "we will wait, of course, before taking any steps to dispose of the Playhouse, hoping for favorable action on the part of the directors." She signed the note "Affectionately yours, Irene," and someone, perhaps Wald, wrote on the original copy, "Keep with the Data."[38] In 1930, there was an announcement in the press under the headline "Lewisohn Sisters Plan New Theatre" that Alice and Irene were planning, for the fifteenth anniversary of the opening at 466, a new company organized around road tours. Nothing appears to have come of those plans. In 1935, as a twentieth anniversary of the founding, a production of Lorca's *Bitter Oleander* was directed by Irene at the Lyceum Theatre on Broadway. Brooks Atkinson reported that "this is the twentieth anniversary of the founding of the unworldly little theatre in Grand Street where the drama was once served unselfishly and well. . . . But, alas, it is twenty years since the Neighborhood Playhouse was founded and seven or eight years since it ceased its high-minded activities on the East Side. The magic has gone."[39]

The longest lasting and most influential legacy of the original company was the Neighborhood Playhouse School of the Theater, which was founded in 1928. The driving force behind it was Rita Morgenthau, long-time supporter of the Henry Street Settlement and volunteer in countless roles including board member at the theater since the pageant of 1913. She had prepared a report at that time called "The Henry Street Settlement, 1893 to 1913," which formed a plan for theater as an instrument of social action without ambitions of professional production or uptown celebration. Thus she was able to extend from pageant to school without the complications represented by the professional playhouse enterprise. After the playhouse closed, she also appears to have been energized by divorce from her husband Maxmillian, and in the year of the divorce, 1928, she founded the school with Irene. According to the *New York Times* obituary for Morgenthau in 1964, "many well-known artists, among them Martha Graham, Paul Morrison, and Sanford Meisner, taught the slum youngsters who flocked to the school."[40] Meisner joined the school in 1935, and afterwards it began its shift from social assimilation toward professional achievement through conservatory training, at which it continues to excel. Morgenthau remained a presence in the school for thirty-five years, published educational materials, and became the first vocational counselor in the New York City public school system.

The school drew one part of the playhouse directors, and the Actor-Managers the other. Helen Arthur, whose involvement with the Henry Street Settlement preceded Morgenthau's, brought to the new initiative the financial skills to match Agnes Morgan's performance ones. As Actor-Managers became less active, she built a practice producing artists on tour, such as Mrs. Patrick Campbell and Ruth Draper. Then, with Morgan, through 1939, she produced summer stock at the Casino Theatre in Newport, Rhode Island. In that year, at the age of sixty, she became ill, and Doris Fox Benardete, who was involved with all participants, gives a dismaying account of the outcome. According to Benardete, "an appeal was made to Irene Lewisohn for pecuniary assistance; but Miss Lewisohn said her money was all tied up at the time and she could not contribute anything to Miss Arthur's comfort."[41] No other report confirms that. The extended appeal, supervised by Aline Bernstein, who contributed a third of her annual income, could not offset the Morgan-Arthurs' financial need, which consumed their vacation home in Westchester and other property. Nor was the appeal fast enough. The plan was to send Arthur to California for care by a friend, but she died in New York City before the end of 1939. After Arthur's death, Agnes Morgan, who had joined Alice and Irene as a volunteer with the Neighborhood Players before the building at 466 opened, joined the Paper Mill Playhouse in Milburn, New Jersey. There she produced and directed with the founder, Frank Carrington, for thirty-two years until, in 1972, she visited a sister in California and chose to stay there. She died in California at the age of ninety-six, the last surviving director of the Neighborhood Playhouse.

Aline Bernstein, of course, had even greater professional and artistic success after the Neighborhood Playhouse. Her affair with Thomas Wolfe ended in 1930, and it became a source for a collection of stories, *Three Blue Suits,* and a novel, *The Journey Down,* by Bernstein. They were published in the 1930s, and that decade was her most prolific in roles as stage and/or costume designer. Among the most conspicuous successes were productions with Eva La Gallienne, Philip Barry, Lunt and Fontainne and the Theatre Guild, and three collaborations with Lillian Hellman: *The Children's Hour* (1934), *Days to Come* (1936), and *The Little Foxes* (1939). In the mid-1930s she also traveled to Hollywood and designed for the RKO spectaculars *She* and *The Last Days of Pompeii.* In 1937, with Irene and also Lee Simonson, Bernstein became a founder of the Museum of Costume Art, which opened in a loft on West Forty-sixth Street with collections from the Neighborhood Playhouse and the Theatre Guild storage. In 1946, the museum was adopted by the Metropolitan Museum as part of its Diamond Jubilee and became the foundation for the current Costume Institute there. In 1949, at age seventy, Bernstein received a Tony Award for the Broadway production of Marc Blitzstein's opera, *Regina,* from Hellman's *The Little Foxes.* She continued to work through the design of *The World of Sholom Aleichem* in 1953 and died in New York City two years later.

In addition to working with Rita Morgenthau on the school and Aline Bernstein on the costume museum, Irene continued to collect causes in the later years of her life, including the Spanish Child Welfare Association, American Theatre Group Stage Door Canteen, and a club for merchant seamen. She died in New York City in 1944 of cancer, at the age of fifty-one, and, according to Benardete, "the night before the funeral, full of the same excitement and tension they used to feel before opening nights, the faithful Festival Dancers and Neighborhood Players draped her coffin with a blanket of bright spring flowers and set it in the centre of the stage" at 466 Grand Street.[42] In addition to obituary notices, the *New York Times* ran a news story headlined "400 at Rites Here for Irene Lewisohn." At the April service, it reported, "the entire stage of the theatre was banked with red and pink roses, also sprays of dogwood blossoms and other spring-flowering shrubs."[43] The attendance by prominent figures from the New York City worlds of politics, philanthropy, and arts was widely reported. Lillian Wald, who had continued her well-known career as leader of the Henry Street Settlement until retirement in 1933, had died in Connecticut in 1940. At the time of Irene's death, Alice was in Europe under wartime travel constraints. The memorial notices for Irene in the *Times* included ones by the boards of the Henry Street Settlement, the Neighborhood Playhouse School, and the Museum of Costume Art. The distribution of her legacy bequests of $540,000 was also widely reported: to the school, the museum, the Henry Street Settlement, the Vocational Service, the American Friends Service Committee, the Indian Defense Fund, the Federation of Jewish Philanthropies, the Palestine University, and a host of individuals, including Alice.

When she wrote her memoir in 1959, Alice ended her preface with the words, "To you, Irene, what can I say. Your presence, creative impulse, energetic spirit lives in every memory."[44] In the 1930s, Alice had divorced from Herbert Crowley and moved to Zurich to become part of the C. K. Jung "Circle" there. Writing in the 1940s from secondhand accounts, Benardete reported that "she has become, if possible, more ethereal than ever. Someone recently put her case this way: in the old days she used to eat a pea; now a leaf of lettuce will do." For Benardete, "of the four directors it was she [Alice] who adhered most conscientiously and most scrupulously to the goal of the Neighborhood Playhouse. Her complete retirement long ago at the height of her productivity proves with what genuine selflessness and devotion she pursued her dream."[45] She died in Zurich in 1972, when Agnes Morgan was retiring to California and the legacy of the Neighborhood Playhouse was largely forgotten. There was no obituary in the *Times* and no news story on a memorial service. The Neighborhood Playhouse School alone printed a newspaper memorial, under the name Crowley, with the sentiment that "her unselfish interests and generous support of esthetic and cultural pursuits in all areas will be sorely missed."[46]

Doris Fox Benardete perhaps understandably takes a romantic view of the closing of the company, one that equates Alice's retirement from Henry Street to Switzerland with selflessness much as the Neighborhood Playhouse's concluding press release equated closing with success. The final revival season of *The Dybbuk* had in fact proven the failure of the repertory model, which was a system the Neighborhood Playhouse adopted with many contemporaries and called "innovation." The system has since been proven economically untenable,[47] and even at the time of its adoption, the company was joining the midstream of theater practice in New York and not adhering to the singular conditions of Grand Street. The history of the Neighborhood Playhouse is a history of the tension between individual mission and professional practice, and adoption of the repertory method relinquished Alice's vow, recorded secondhand at a meeting in the month before the opening of *The Little Clay Cart*, that the playhouse "had to present its differences to other theatres and that she assumed that all were agreed on certain fundamental ideas and that we recognized the necessity of not comparing ourselves with other groups as our functions were quite different."[48] Lack of confidence in a singular mission was one of the reasons why the Neighborhood Playhouse close was caused by failure, not success.

The company's successes, however, were considerable. For Kenneth Macgowan, a competitor writing soon after the closing, the Neighborhood Playhouse pursuit in performance of festival ideals was unique and an exhilarating departure from the concentration elsewhere at the time on textual performances and playwriting. He located its success in integrated performance, in, "if we consider the theater, as we should, a union of all the arts, and remember the mingling of music, movement, dance, pantomime, and speech in *Salut au Monde.*" In addition, he found "playwrighting" "a rather masculine field" and the success of the Neighborhood Playhouse as "our one thoroughly feminist theater."[49] The company was feminist in overall organization and not merely in presentation of plays with feminist content. One of the weaknesses of the organization was persistent internal rivalries and, ultimately, divergent ideals among the company directors. This too, was balanced by the considerable success of a kind itemized by Melanie Nelda Blood: "Bernstein was attracted as a philanthropist and became a great designer. [Helen] Tamiris and [Anna] Sokolow, children of poor Jewish immigrants, found artistic education and empowerment toward self expression in the emerging field of modern dance."[50] The list of people who developed skills at the Neighborhood Playhouse could go on much longer, and the accomplishments of these women extended beyond personal achievement to institutional change in public education in New York. In some cases, the philanthropists of the Neighborhood Playhouse may have been confused about the roles that distinguish benefactors from beneficiaries, but they established more empowered philanthropic roles than permitted by the culture of "Lady Bountiful" they inherited. The net outcome of the philanthropic commitments of a group of very different women was without question positive and of significant effect both within and beyond the walls at 466 Grand Street. Because the influence of the Neighborhood Playhouse extended into other educational institutions, the company also represented the civic roles of theater, the opportunities of theater tied to locality, and the broadest influence of settlement ideals of education.

"Why did the Neighborhood Playhouse stop?" Irene asked soon after it did. It stopped because of mission confusion, internal rivalries, poor financial planning, and an unsustainable philanthropic model for a noncommercial theater. In addition to internal problems, there were adversarial external trends in the theater industry and in settlement-organized social services. All these, of course, are administrative problems rather than artistic ones. The success of the Neighborhood Playhouse was on the stage and not behind it. The project is represented best by its beginning, before professional envy, personal conflicts, and exhaustion of resources. That was Lincoln's birthday, February 12, 1915, when Lillian Wald told an audience of mainly observant Jews about the gifts immigrants brought to the United States and then that audience saw a feminist revision of *Jephtha's Daughter* in a brief and rare moment of ideal unison between artists, audiences, and administrators.

Notes

❦

Bibliography

❦

Index

Notes

Introduction: The Life of the Neighborhood Playhouse

1. Joseph Wood Krutch, "Vale," *Neighborhood Playbill*, no. 6 (1926–27): 2.

2. Quoted in Margaret M. Knapp, "Theatrical Parody in the Twentieth-Century American Theatre: *The Grand Street Follies*," *Educational Theatre Journal* 27, no. 3 (October 1975): 359.

3. "Endowed Theatre Is to Close," *New York Times*, 11 April 1927, 1.

4. Krutch, "Vale," 4; J. Brooks Atkinson, "Last of the Neighborhood Frolics," *New York Times*, 20 May 1927, 22; Atkinson, "End of an Era," *New York Times*, 29 May 1927, sec. 8, p. 1.

5. Leon Whipple, "Entre Acte on Grand Street," *Survey Graphic* (July 1927); rpt. in *The Neighborhood Playhouse: Notes from Various Talks Given by Irene Lewisohn and Reprints from Newspaper and Magazine Comments* (privately printed, n.d.). Neighborhood Playhouse Gift, Billy Rose Theatre Collection, New York Public Library, mwez n.c. 2335, #9. Hereafter referred to as the "Billy Rose Theatre Collection."

6. Program, *The Neighborhood Playhouse* (New York: Neighborhood Playhouse, 1915), 1.

7. Lillian Wald, *The House on Henry Street* (New York: Henry Holt, 1915), 187; Lillian Wald, *Windows on Henry Street* (Boston: Little, Brown, 1939), 170.

8. "Speech Made by Professor George Pierce Baker at the Neighborhood Playhouse, February 11th," typescript, Lillian Wald Papers, Rare Book and Manuscript Collection, Columbia University, box 61, reel 74. Hereafter referred to as "Wald Papers."

9. Lillian Wald to George Pierce Baker, 13 February 1925, Wald Papers, box 61, reel 74.

10. Thomas Wolfe, *The Web and the Rock* (New York: Sun Dial Press, 1940), 321.

11. Suzanne Stutman, ed., *My Other Loveliness: Letters of Thomas Wolfe and Aline Bernstein* (Chapel Hill: University of North Carolina Press, 1983), 62.

12. Doris Fox Benardete, "The Neighborhood Playhouse in Grand Street," Ph.D. diss., New York University, 1949, 606.

13. *The Rogers and Hart Songbook* (New York: Simon and Schuster, 1951), 19.

14. Untitled typescript, Billy Rose Theatre Collection, mwez n.c. 10,290.

15. "The Neighborhood Playhouse," *Nation*, 18 May 1927, 548.

16. Kenneth Macgowan, *Footlights Across America: Toward a National Theater* (New York: Harcourt Brace, 1929), 48.

1. The Henry Street Settlement and Its Playhouse

1. Leonard Lewisohn to Lillian Wald, 24 and 30 January 1902, Wald Papers, box 14, reel 12.

2. Adolph Lewisohn to Lillian Wald, 2 June 1920, Wald Papers, reel 66.

3. Kathleen D. McCarthy, *Noblesse Oblige: Charity and Cultural Philanthropy in Chicago, 1849–1929* (Chicago: University of Chicago Press, 1982), 99.

4. Stephen Birmingham, *"Our Crowd": The Great Jewish Families of New York* (1967; rpt. Syracuse: Syracuse University Press, 1996), 290–91, 292–93.

5. Alice Lewisohn Crowley, *The Neighborhood Playhouse: Leaves from a Theatre Scrapbook* (New York: Theatre Arts Books, 1959), xix, 3.

6. Ibid., 4, 5, 7.

7. Robert A. Woods and Albert J. Kennedy, *Handbook of Settlements* (1911; rpt. New York: Arno Press, 1970), 206.

8. Wald, *The House on Henry Street*, 2, 169, 310, 271.

9. Christopher Lasch, ed., *The Social Thought of Jane Addams* (Indianapolis, IN: Bobbs-Merrill, 1965), xiv.

10. Clare Coss, ed., *Lillian D. Wald: Progressive Activist* (New York: Feminist Press, 1989), 72, 88.

11. Irving Howe, *World of Our Fathers: The Journey of the East European Jews to America and the Life They Found and Made* (New York: Harcourt Brace Jovanovich, 1976), 93.

12. Wald, *Windows on Henry Street*, 165.

13. Alice Lewisohn to Lillian Wald, n.d., Wald Papers, box 14, reel 12.

14. Benardete, "The Neighborhood Playhouse in Grand Street," 105.

15. Birmingham, *"Our Crowd,"* 271.

16. Alice Lewisohn to Lillian Wald, n.d., Wald Papers, box 14, reel 12.

17. Clipping quoted in Benardete, "The Neighborhood Playhouse in Grand Street," 8.

18. "A Short Stage Career," *New York Daily Tribune*, 15 November 1906, 8.

19. Benardete, "The Neighborhood Playhouse in Grand Street," 106.

20. Robert A. Woods quoted in Michael B. Katz, *In the Shadow of the Poorhouse: A Social History of Welfare in America* (New York: Basic Books, 1986), 158.

21. Quoted in R. L. Duffus, *Lillian Wald: Neighbor and Crusader* (New York: Macmillan, 1938), 174.

22. Sinclair Lewis, *Ann Vickers* (New York: P. F. Collier, 1933), 236, 237.

23. Ibid., 239.

24. Arthur C. Holden, *The Settlement Idea: A Vision of Social Justice* (New York: Macmillian, 1922), 38, 39.

25. Thorstein Veblen, *The Theory of the Leisure Class* (1899; Harmondsworth: Penguin, 1979), 340, 341.

26. Lewis, *Ann Vickers*, 239.

27. Crowley, *The Neighborhood Playhouse*, xix.

28. There is an excellent chronology of Neighborhood Playhouse productions, including "Pre 1915," in Melanie Nelda Blood, "The Neighborhood Playhouse 1915–1927: A History and Analysis," Ph.D. diss. Northwestern University, 1994.

29. Coss, *Lillian D. Wald*, 10.

30. Benardete, "The Neighborhood Playhouse in Grand Street," 196.

31. Crowley, *The Neighborhood Playhouse*, 30.

32. Ibid., 32.

33. John Galsworthy, *Plays: The Silver Box, Joy, Strife* (New York: G. P. Putnam's Sons, 1909), 9, 15.

34. *The Settlement Journal* (April–May 1913), clipping, Billy Rose Theatre Collection, mwez + 10,288.

35. Typescript program, Billy Rose Theatre Collection, mwez x n.c. 10,290.

36. American Pageant Association brochure, Billy Rose Theatre Collection, mwez + 10,287, 2 of 2.

37. Script for 1913 pageant, Billy Rose Theatre Collection, mwez + 10,287, 1 of 2. Information about the pageant that follows comes from materials archived with the script.

38. Clippings, script for 1913 pageant, Billy Rose Theatre Collection, New York Public Library, mwez + 10,287, 2 of 2.

39. Typescript "Report on 1913 Pageant," script for 1913 pageant, Billy Rose Theatre Collection, mwez + 10,287, 1 of 2.

2. 1915–1916: Opening the Little Theater of Art and Activism

1. Crowley, *The Neighborhood Playhouse*, 38–39.

2. Benardete, "The Neighborhood Playhouse in Grand Street," 61, 60.

3. Susan Glaspell, *The Road to the Temple* (1927; rpt. New York: Frederick Stokes, 1941), 249; Yiddish newspaper reviews quoted in translation in Benardete, "The Neighborhood Playhouse in Grand Street," 117 and 118.

4. "The Neighborhood Playhouse: Four Hundred and Sixty-Six Grand Street," pamphlet, n.d., Billy Rose Theatre Collection, mwez n.c. 9678.

5. Cost of the Neighborhood Playhouse, Benardete, "The Neighborhood Playhouse in Grand Street," 60; Henry Street Settlement 1916 budget in Howe, *World of Our Fathers*, 94.

6. Wald, *Windows on Henry Street*, 166.

7. Crowley, *The Neighborhood Playhouse*, 35.

8. Ibid., 39; Benardete, "The Neighborhood Playhouse in Grand Street," 60–61.

9. John J. Klaber, "Planning the Moving Picture Theatre," *Architectural Record* 38 (October 1915), quoted in Benardete, "The Neighborhood Playhouse in Grand Street," 62.

10. Crowley, *The Neighborhood Playhouse*, 35.

11. Alexander Woollcott, "Second Thoughts on First Nights," *New York Times*, 3 December 1916, sec. 2, p. 6.

12. Benardete, "The Neighborhood Playhouse in Grand Street," 69.

13. Percy MacKaye, *The Playhouse and the Play: And Other Addresses Concerning the Theatre and Democracy in America* (1909; rpt. New York: Greenwood Press, 1968), 9.

14. "Mr. Belasco's Quarrel with the Experimental Theaters," *Current Opinion*, March 1917, 184.

15. *The Rodgers and Hart Songbook* (New York: Simon and Schuster, 1951), 17–18.

16. Crowley, *The Neighborhood Playhouse*, 40.

17. "Miss Lillian D. Wald Speaks at the Neighborhood Playhouse," *Settlement Journal* 10, no. 4 (March–April 1915): 3.

18. "Community Theatre Opens," *New York Times*, 12 February 1915, 9.

19. Here and below, quotes from the script of *Jephtha's Daughter*, Billy Rose Theatre Collection, mwez n.c. 10,271, folder 1 of 2.

20. "Community Theatre Opens," 9.

21. "Jephtha's Daughter," *Settlement Journal* 10, no. 4 (March–April 1915): 5–6.

22. Quoted in translation in Benardete, "The Neighborhood Playhouse in Grand Street," 117.

23. Wald, *The House on Henry Street*, 270–71.

24. Crowley, *The Neighborhood Playhouse*, 40–41.

25. Benardete, "The Neighborhood Playhouse in Grand Street," 150–51.

26. Walter Prichard Eaton, *The Theatre Guild: The First Ten Years* (1929; rpt. Freeport, NY: Books for Library Press, 1970), 23, 20.

27. Sheldon Cheney, *The Art Theater* (New York: Knopf, 1925), 66.

28. "The Neighborhood Playhouse: A Gift to the East Side," *World* Sunday magazine insert, 14 March 1915, 4.

29. Whitford Kane, *Are We All Met?* (London: Elkin Mathews and Marrot, 1931), 175, 176.

30. "Ellen Terry at the Neighborhood Playhouse," 150 copies printed by the Neighborhood Playhouse, August 1915.

31. Kane, *Are We All Met?* 185.

32. Edward Maisel, *Charles T. Griffes: The Life of an American Composer* (New York: Knopf, 1984), 173.

33. "The Neighborhood's Year," *New York Times*, 10 October 1915, sec. 6, p. 7.

34. Quoted in Benardete, "The Neighborhood Playhouse in Grand Street," 161.

35. Notes for the first "Neighborhood Playhouse Committee" meetings are found in the Wald Papers, box 62, reel 75.

36. Quoted in Duffus, *Lillian Wald*, 152.

37. "See America's Hope in Unpreparedness," *New York Times,* 7 April 1916, clipping, Wald Papers, reel 102.

38. Wald Papers, reel 102.

39. Clarke A. Chambers, *Seedtime of Reform: American Social Service and Social Action 1918–1933* (Minneapolis: University of Minnesota Press, 1963), 127.

40. Robert A. Woods and Albert J. Kennedy, *The Settlement Horizon* (1922; rpt. New Brunswick, NJ: Transaction Publishers, 1990), 157, 151.

41. Lynde Denig, "The Most Talked of Playlet of the Year," *Vanity Fair,* May 1916, clipping, Billy Rose Theatre Collection; "New Dunsany Play Has Its Premiere," *New York Times,* 24 April 1916, 11.

42. Harold Brighouse, *The Price of Coal* typescript, New York Public Library NCOF + p.v. 316, annotated "Prod. Neighborhood Playhouse, N. Y., 1915–16 Season."

43. Sholom Asch, "With the Current," translated by Jacob Robbins, typescript, New York Public Library NCOF +, bookplate "From the Library of Alice and Irene Lewisohn."

44. Lord Dunsany (Edward John Moreton Drax Plunkett), "A Night at an Inn," typescript, Billy Rose Theatre Collection, NCOF + p.v. 251, bookplate "From the Library of Alice and Irene Lewisohn."

45. Clayton Hamilton, "The Neighborhood Playhouse and a Birthday," *New York Times,* 2 October 1935, sec. 8, p. 1.

3. 1916–1920: Art, Militarism, Movies, and Mission

1. The various drafts of the "Statement Aug. 1916" are scattered in at least three files of the Neighborhood Playhouse archive in the Billy Rose Theatre Collection, mwez + 10,288; mwez 10,290, folder 1; and mwez + n.c. 10,292.

2. "Shaw and Dunsany in Grand Street," *New York Times,* 15 November 1916, 9.

3. Crowley, *The Neighborhood Playhouse,* 66.

4. Michael Holroyd, *Bernard Shaw,* vol. 2 (New York: Random House, 1989), 273.

5. "Neighborhood Playhouse," *The Theatre* (New York), January 1917, 21.

6. "Shaw and Dunsany in Grand Street," 9.

7. Crowley, *The Neighborhood Playhouse,* 68.

8. R. F. Foster, *W. B. Yeats: A Life,* vol. 1 (New York: Oxford University Press, 1997), 403.

9. "Portmanteau Theatre," *The Theatre* (New York) January 1917, 21.

10. *The Queen's Enemies,* in Lord Dunsany, *Plays of Gods and Men* (Boston: John W. Luce, 1917), 140, 168.

11. Clayton Hamilton, "The Plays of Lord Dunsany," *The Bookman,* January 1917, 478.

12. "Up from Grand Street," *New York Times,* 19 December 1916, 9.

13. Crowley, *The Neighborhood Playhouse,* 68.

14. Ibid., 17.

15. Helen McAfee, "Lord Dunsany and Modern Theatre," *The Drama* 7 (October 1917): 484.

16. Glaspell, *The Road to the Temple*, 262, 241, 263.

17. Arthur and Barbara Gelb, *O'Neill: Life with Monte Cristo* (New York: Applause Books, 2000), 575, 583.

18. Crowley, *The Neighborhood Playhouse*, 102.

19. Letter to the editor, *New York Times*, 20 November 1916, 12.

20. Program, *Kairn of Koridwen*, Billy Rose Theatre Collection.

21. Maisel, *Charles T. Griffes*, 188.

22. Linda J. Tomko, *Dancing Class: Gender, Ethnicity, and Social Divides in American Dance 1890–1920* (Bloomington: Indiana University Press, 1999), 85–86, 118–19.

23. Miles Malleson, *Black 'Ell*, in *The Masses*, February 1917, 13.

24. Angelina Weld Grimké, *Rachel: A Race Play in Three Acts*, program, Billy Rose Theatre Collection, mwez x n.c. 25,334.

25. Crowley, *The Neighborhood Playhouse*, 62.

26. Wald Papers, reel 102.

27. Crystal Eastman to Lillian Wald, 10 October 1917, Wald Papers, reel 102.

28. Wald Papers, reel 40.

29. Crowley, *The Neighborhood Playhouse*, 47.

30. "The Neighborhood Playhouse," typescript, Billy Rose Theatre Collection, mwez 10,290; "Report of the Neighborhood Playhouse for the Directors of the Henry Street Settlement," Billy Rose Theatre Collection, mwez + n.c. 10,289.

31. Wald Papers, reel 102.

32. Benardete, "The Neighborhood Playhouse in Grand Street," 313.

33. Wald Papers, reel 102.

34. Crowley, *The Neighborhood Playhouse*, 27–28.

35. Wald Papers, reel 102.

36. Crowley, *The Neighborhood Playhouse*, 75.

37. Wald Papers, reel 102.

38. Benardete, "The Neighborhood Playhouse in Grand Street," 244.

39. Crowley, *The Neighborhood Playhouse*, 87–88.

40. Ibid., 86; "Tamura" typescript, Billy Rose Theatre Collection, mwez + n.c. 10,318.

41. Maisel, *Charles T. Griffes*, 231.

42. W. B. Yeats, "Certain Noble Plays of Japan," *Essays and Introductions* (New York: Collier Books, 1961), 221, 223.

43. Wald Papers, reel 102.

44. Ibid.

45. *Guibour: A Miracle Play of Our Lady*, Neighborhood Playhouse Plays No. 11 (New York: Sunwise Turn, 1919), 13, 49.

46. Robert Edmond Jones, *The Dramatic Imagination: Reflections and Speculations on the Art of the Theatre* (New York: Theatre Arts Books, 1969), 40.

47. ''A Chapter of My Gospel of Patriotism, by Yvette Guilbert.'' Billy Rose Theatre Collection, mwez + n.c. 10,262.

48. Program, *Guibour*, January 24, 1918, the Neighborhood Playhouse, Billy Rose Theatre Collection, mwez + n.c. 10,262.

49. John Corbin, ''Drama,'' *New York Times*, 14 April 1919, 11.

50. Helen Arthur to Lillian Wald, 11 August 1918, Wald Papers, box 61, reel 74.

51. ''Lectures at the Neighborhood Playhouse,'' *Theatre Arts Magazine*, April 1919, 135–36.

52. Lillian Wald to Alice and Irene Lewisohn, 17 November 1919 and 22 November 1919, Wald Papers, box 62, reel 75.

53. ''Lionizing a Lord in Grand Street,'' *New York Times Magazine*, 26 October 1919, 6.

54. Quoted in Benardete, ''The Neighborhood Playhouse in Grand Street,'' 290.

55. Crowley, *The Neighborhood Playhouse*, 71, 72.

56. ''Shaw and Dunsany in Grand Street.''

57. Benardete, ''The Neighborhood Playhouse in Grand Street,'' 249.

58. A short list of good examples would include Noel Ignatiev, *How the Irish Became White* (New York: Routledge, 1995) and the work of Diane Negra, such as ''Consuming Ireland: Lucky Charms Cereal, Irish Spring Soap, and 1-800-Shamrock,'' *Cultural Studies* 15, no. 1 (2001): 76–97. In reference to theater in New York City, see John P. Harrington, *The Irish Play on the New York Stage* (Lexington: University Press of Kentucky, 1997).

59. Helen McAfee, ''Lord Dunsany and Modern Theatre,'' 484.

60. Louise Bryant, ''The Poets' Revolution,'' *The Masses*, July 1916, 29.

61. Benardete, ''The Neighborhood Playhouse in Grand Street,'' 253.

62. Wald Papers, box 62, reel 75.

4. 1920–1922: New Plans, *Salut au Monde,* and *The Grand Street Follies*

1. Crowley, *The Neighborhood Playhouse*, 105.

2. John Galsworthy, *The Mob: A Play in Four Acts* (New York: Charles Scribner's Sons, 1914), 72.

3. Alexander Woollcott, review of *The Mob*, *New York Times*, 11 October 1920, 23.

4. Crowley, *The Neighborhood Playhouse*, 105.

5. Benardete, ''The Neighborhood Playhouse on Grand Street,'' 317.

6. Glaspell, *The Road to the Temple*, 262–63.

7. Helen Arthur, untitled manuscript hand dated 10/31/22, Wald Papers, box 62, reel 74.

8. Crowley, *The Neighborhood Playhouse*, 49.

9. Benardete, ''The Neighborhood Playhouse in Grand Street,'' 314.

10. Crowley, *The Neighborhood Playhouse*, 105, 107–8.

11. Irene Lewisohn, notes, Billy Rose Theatre Collection, mwez x n.c. 10,290.

12. Galsworthy, *The Mob*, 11.

13. "The New Season," *Theatre Arts Magazine* 5 (January 1921): 9.

14. Review of *The Mob, New York Dramatic Mirror,* 16 October 1920, 683.

15. Wald, *Windows on Henry Street,* 168–69.

16. Thomas H. Dickinson, "Theatre Arts Chronicle," *Theatre Arts Magazine* 4 (October 1920): 344–45.

17. Review of *Dark Rosaleen, Theatre Magazine* (June 1919): 341.

18. Billy Rose Theatre Collection, mwez x n.c. 10,290.

19. Crowley, *The Neighborhood Playhouse,* 111–12.

20. Norman Hapgood, "The Barker Season," *Harper's Weekly,* 30 January 1915, 99.

21. Review of *Harliquinade, Theatre Magazine* (August 1921): 98.

22. "Audience Goes on Trip to Fairyland," *New York World,* 11 May 1921, clippings in Billy Rose Theatre Collection.

23. "Harliquinade Amusing," *New York Times,* 11 May 1921; review of *Harliquinade, New York Post,* 11 May 1921; review of *Harliquinade, New York Dramatic Mirror,* 25 June 1921; clippings in Billy Rose Theatre Collection.

24. Crowley, *The Neighborhood Playhouse,* 113.

25. Billy Rose Theatre Collection, mwez + n.c. 10,292.

26. Benardete, "The Neighborhood Playhouse in Grand Street," 372.

27. Ibid., 367–68.

28. Billy Rose Theatre Collection, mwez + n.c. 10,292.

29. Benardete, "The Neighborhood Playhouse in Grand Street," 380–85.

30. *The Purpose and the New Plans of the Neighborhood Playhouse,* brochure, Billy Rose Theatre Collection, mwez + n.c. 10,288.

31. Harley Granville Barker, *The Madras House: A Comedy in Four Acts* (Boston: Little, Brown, 1920), 75, 86, 94, 104.

32. Crowley, *The Neighborhood Playhouse,* 115, 114.

33. Kenneth MacGowan, "The Neighborhood Playhouse and 'The Madras House,'" *Boston Globe,* 6 November 1921; clipping, Billy Rose Theatre Collection.

34. Billy Rose Theatre Collection, mwez + n.c. 10,292.

35. *Greenwich Villager,* 17 December 1921; clipping, Billy Rose Theatre Collection, mwez + n.c. 9663.

36. *Theatre Arts Magazine* (January 1922): 23, 20.

37. *Life,* 9 January 1922, clipping, Billy Rose Theatre Collection, mwex x n.c. 9664.

38. Oliver M. Sayler, "The Neighborhood Playhouse," *Theatre Arts Magazine* (January 1922): 15, 16.

39. "'The S. S. Tenacity' Moves," *Metropolitan Guide,* 2 February 1922, clipping, Billy Rose Theatre Collection, mwex x n.c. 9664.

40. Laurence Langner, *GBS and the Lunatic: Reminiscences* (New York: Atheneum, 1963), 46.

41. Arthur and Barbara Gelb, *O'Neill* (New York: Harper and Brothers, 1962), 496, 497.

42. *The First Man*, clippings, Billy Rose Theatre Collection.

43. Oliver M. Sayler, *Our American Theatre* (New York: Brentano's, 1923), 84.

44. Maisel, *Charles T. Griffes*, 268, 269, 288, 319, 344–45.

45. Billy Rose Theatre Collection, mwez + n.c. 10,292.

46. Walt Whitman, "Salut au Monde!" *Leaves of Grass* (New York: Modern Library, n.d), 108.

47. Billy Rose Theatre Collection, mwez + n.c. 10,292.

48. Review of *Salut au Monde, Brooklyn Eagle,* 2 May 1922; clippings, *Salut au Monde,* Billy Rose Theatre Collection.

49. Wald, *Windows on Henry Street*, 171.

50. Benardete, "The Neighborhood Playhouse in Grand Street," 423, 421.

51. Wald Papers, box 61, reel 74.

52. *Grand Street Follies*, clippings, Billy Rose Theatre Collection.

53. "New 'Follies' Is Prodigal," *New York Times*, 6 June 1922, 27.

54. "Greenwich Village Gets Its Follies," *New York Times*, 16 July 1919, 14.

55. "Theatrical Notes," *New York Times*, 8 June 1922, 24.

56. Joseph Wood Krutch, review of *The Grand Street Follies, Nation*, 15 May 1929, 594.

57. Crowley, *The Neighborhood Playhouse*, 119.

58. Benardete, "The Neighborhood Playhouse in Grand Street," 474.

59. Billy Rose Theatre Collection, mwez + n.c. 10,292.

60. "The Neighborhood to Close for Year," *New York Times,* 27 June 1922, 16.

61. Wald Papers, box 61, reel 74.

62. Billy Rose Theatre Collection, mwez + n.c. 10,292 and mwez + n.c. 9663.

5. 1922–1925: The Lessons of the East and *The Little Clay Cart*

1. Alice Goldfarb Marquis, *Art Lessons* (New York: Basic Books, 1995), 77.

2. McCarthy, *Noblesse Oblige*, 106, 110.

3. William J. Baumol and William G. Bowen, *Performing Arts: The Economic Dilemma* (New York: Twentieth Century Fund, 1966), 55.

4. W. J. Baumol and W. G. Bowen, "On the Performing Arts: The Anatomy of their Economic Problems," in Mark Blaug, ed., *The Economics of the Arts* (London: Martin Robinson, 1976), 222, 221.

5. Jack Poggi, *Theater in America: The Impact of Economic Forces 1870–1967* (Ithaca, NY: Cornell University Press, 1968), 99, 104. A few more references that are more recent but not as focused on theater companies include James Heilbrun and Charles M. Gray, *The Economics of Art and Culture* (Cambridge: Cambridge University Press, 1993); M. J. Wyszomiaski and P. Clubb, *The Cost of Culture: Patterns and Prospects of Private Arts Patronage* (Washington, DC: American Council for the Arts, 1989); and C. David Throsby, *Economics and Culture* (Cambridge: Cambridge University Press, 2001).

6. Poggi, *Theater in America*, 115, 128.

7. "Dramatic Work Increases," *Henry News*, 17 March 1923, 17.

8. Helen Arthur to Lillian Wald, 31 October 1922, Wald Papers, box 61, reel 74.

9. "Miss Lewisohn's Itinerary 1922–23," Wald Papers, box 62, reel 75.

10. Crowley, *The Neighborhood Playhouse*, 134.

11. Alice and Irene Lewisohn, "The Little Theatre in Egypt," *Atlantic Monthly*, July 1924, 93, 95, 100, 97.

12. Drafts of "Statement Aug. 1916," Billy Rose Theatre Collection, mwez + 10,288; mwez 10,290, folder 1; and mwez + n.c. 10,292.

13. Undated ms., Billy Rose Theatre Collection, mwez + n.c. 10,289.

14. A. L. Fovitzky, *Moscow Art Theatre and Its Distinguishing Characteristics* (New York: A. Chernoff, 1922), 8.

15. Program, "American Laboratory Theatre 1924–1925," Billy Rose Theatre Collection, mwez x 1496 #6.

16. "Moscow in Grand Street," *New York Times*, 21 October 1923, sec. 10, p. 2.

17. Miss Aline MacMahon. Oral Memoir. 1978. William E. Wiener Oral History Library of the American Jewish Committee, New York Public Library, Jewish Division, box 359, no. 1.

18. Typescript, "My Dear Subscriber," 1923, Wald Papers, box 61, reel 74.

19. Program, *The Player Queen* and *The Shewing-up of Blanco Posnet*, Billy Rose Theatre Collection.

20. Quoted in Robert Welch, *The Abbey Theatre 1899–1999: Form and Pressure* (Oxford: Oxford University Press, 1999), 77.

21. "Act Shaw and Yeats," *New York Times*, 17 October 1923, 14.

22. Robert Gilbert Welsh, review of *The Player Queen* and *The Shewing-up of Blanco Posnet*, *New York Herald*, 18 October 1923; clippings, *The Player Queen*, Billy Rose Theatre Collection.

23. Crowley, *The Neighborhood Playhouse*, 168, 170, 171.

24. Also quoted in chapter 2: MacKaye, *The Playhouse and the Play*, 9.

25. Gerald Bordman, *American Theatre: A Chronicle of Comedy and Drama 1914–1930* (New York: Oxford University Press, 1995), 123.

26. Carl Van Doren, "Mountain Comedy," *Nation*, 16 January 1924, 69.

27. Crowley, *The Neighborhood Playhouse*, 175.

28. Macgowan, *Footlights Across America*, 51.

29. Thomas H. Dickinson to Alice and Irene Lewisohn, 17 January 1924, Wald Papers, reel 75.

30. "Neighborhood Playhouse Minutes," 19 January 1924, Wald Papers, box 61, reel 74.

31. Thomas H. Dickinson, "Ten Years of the Neighborhood Playhouse," *American Review* 2 (March–April 1924): 134, 135, 136, 138.

32. Benardete, "The Neighborhood Playhouse in Grand Street," 461.

33. *An Arab Fantasia* script, scrapbook, Billy Rose Theatre Collection, mwez + n.c. 10,233.

34. "The Festival Dancers," *New York Times,* 7 March 1924, 18.

35. Paul Rosenfeld, "Griffes on Grand Street," *Modern Music* (November–December 1940), quoted in Benardete, "The Neighborhood Playhouse in Grand Street," 463; Irene Lewisohn, "Essence of the Mohammedan East," *New York Times,* 13 April 1924, sec. 4, p. 7.

36. "Meeting of the Production Groups and Staff, March 30, 1924," Wald Papers, box 61, reel 74.

37. Thomas H. Dickinson, *The Insurgent Theatre* (1919; rpt. New York: B. W. Huebsch, 1927), 165–66, 163–64, 170.

38. Undated slip attached to "The Neighborhood Playhouse Organization" typescript, Billy Rose Theatre Collection, mwez + n.c. 10,289.

39. Telegram carbon, Thomas Dickinson to Alice Lewisohn, 18 June 1924, Billy Rose Theatre Collection, mwez + n.c. 10,290.

40. Programs (spring and fall), *The Grand Street Follies 1924,* Billy Rose Theatre Collection; review of *Grand Street Follies, New York Times,* 27 May 1924, clippings, Billy Rose Theatre Collection.

41. "A Condensed Statement of the Program of The Neighborhood Playhouse for the Season 1924–25," undated typescript, Billy Rose Theatre Collection, mwez + n.c. 10,290.

42. Program, *The Little Clay Cart,* Billy Rose Theatre Collection. Additional information from Revilo Pendleton Oliver, *The Little Clay Cart: A Drama in Ten Acts Attributed to King Sûdraka* (Urbana: University of Illinois Press, 1938) and Arvind Sharma, ed., *The Little Clay Cart* (Albany: State University of New York Press, 1994).

43. Billy Rose Theatre Collection, mwez + n.c. 10,280.

44. Carole Klein, *Aline* (New York: Harper and Row, 1979), 88–89.

45. Stark Young, review of "The Little Clay Cart," *New York Times,* 6 December 1924; rpt. *Immortal Shadows: A Book of Dramatic Criticism* (New York: Scribner's, 1948), 53.

46. Promptbook. *The Little Clay Cart,* New York, 1924. New York Public Library NCOF+ (Sudraka. [Little Clay Cart]).

47. Benardete, "The Neighborhood Playhouse in Grand Street," 479.

48. Billy Rose Theatre Collection, mwez + n.c. 10,253A.

49. Review of *The Little Clay Cart, New York World,* 6 January 1924, clippings, Billy Rose Theatre Collection; Basanta Koomar Roy, review of *The Little Clay Cart, Theatre Arts Monthly* (February 1925): 85, 87; review of *The Little Clay Cart, Brooklyn Times,* 6 December 1924, clippings, Billy Rose Theatre Collection; Arthur W. Ryder to Helen Arthur, November 14, 1924 and December 27, 1924, and Rabindranath Tagore to Irene Lewisohn January 4, 1925, Billy Rose Theatre Collection, mwez 10,290.

50. Irene Lewisohn to "Mr. Macy," 10 December 1924, Wald Papers, reel 75.

51. "Alice Lewisohn a London Bride," *New York Times,* 16 December 1924, 25.

52. "Speech Made by Professor George Pierce Baker," typescript, and Lillian Wald to George Pierce Baker, 13 February 1925, Wald Papers, box 61, reel 74.

53. "Another Anniversary," *New York Times,* 15 February 1925, sec. 8, p. 1.

54. "Accounts Receivable as of Dec. 31, 1924," Wald Papers, box 62, reel 75.

55. Alice Lewisohn to "Comrades Dear," 20 February 1925, Wald Papers, box 62, reel 75.

56. The litigation and the reception of *Exiles* in New York in 1925 are discussed in a different context in John P. Harrington, *The Irish Play on the New York Stage* (Lexington: University Press of Kentucky, 1997), 75–97.

57. Richard Ellmann, *James Joyce* (New York: Oxford University Press, 1954), 414.

58. Crowley, *The Neighborhood Playhouse,* 197.

59. Gilbert W. Gabriel, "The Joyce *Exiles,*" *New York Telegram,* 20 February 1925, clippings, Billy Rose Theatre Collection. George Jean Nathan, "The Theatre," *American Mercury,* April 1925, 501. Joseph Wood Krutch, "Figures of the Dawn," *Nation,* 11 March 1925, 272.

60. Helen Arthur to "Miss Wald," 23 February 1925, Wald Papers, box 61, reel 74.

61. Program, *The Grand Street Follies* (1925), Billy Rose Theatre Collection.

6. 1925–1926: *The Dybbuk* and the Repertory Model

1. Stutman, ed., *My Other Loveliness,* 4, 41.

2. Aline Bernstein, "In Production," *Atlantic Monthly,* September 1940, 324.

3. Nicholas Fox Weber, *Patron Saints: Five Rebels Who Opened America to New Art, 1928–1943* (New Haven: Yale University Press, 1992), 99.

4. Wolfe, *The Web and the Rock,* 328, 329.

5. Crowley, *The Neighborhood Playhouse,* 199, 200.

6. "Publicity Notes for *Evening World,*" n.d., Billy Rose Theatre Collection, mwez + n.c. 10,259.

7. "Habima" was the spelling used by the Neighborhood Playhouse in 1925; "Habimah" is now more common. Similarly, contemporary pronunciation of "dybbuk" tends to favor equal emphasis on the two syllables, while at the playhouse in 1925 "DYB-buk" was used in performance. Contemporary spelling of "Hassidic" and variations are used except in quotations.

8. Crowley, *The Neighborhood Playhouse,* 208.

9. "Publicity Notes on David Vardi," n.d., Billy Rose Theatre Collection, mwez + n.c. 10,259.

10. Crowley, *The Neighborhood Playhouse,* 209.

11. Program, *The Dybbuk* (1925). Billy Rose Theatre Collection, mwez + n.c. 7333, p. 2, 6.

12. "Publicity Notes for *Evening World,*" n.d., Billy Rose Theatre Collection, mwez + n.c. 10,259.

13. Program, *The Dybbuk* (1925). Billy Rose Theatre Collection, mwez + n.c. 7333, p. 10, 3.

14. S. Ansky, *The Dybbuk: A Play in Four Acts,* trans. Henry G. Alsberg and Winifred Katzin (New York: Liveright, 1926), 32. Subsequent page references to this edition are provided parenthetically in the text.

15. Crowley, *The Neighborhood Playhouse,* 211–12.

16. Costume notes, Billy Rose Theatre Collection, mwez + n.c. 10,257.

17. Production notes, Billy Rose Theatre Collection, mwez + n.c. 10,259.

18. Costume notes, Billy Rose Theatre Collection, mwez + n.c. 10,257.

19. Crowley, *The Neighborhood Playhouse,* 213.

20. "The East Side's Theatre," *New York Times Magazine,* 31 January 1926, clippings, costume notes, Billy Rose Theatre Collection.

21. Billy Rose Theatre Collection, mwez + n.c. 10,259.

22. Crowley, *The Neighborhood Playhouse,* 216.

23. *The Dybbuk,* clippings, Billy Rose Theatre Collection.

24. H. L. Brock, "East Side, Too, Has 'Synthetic Theatre,'" *New York Times,* 31 January 1926, sec. 4, p. 13.

25. Letters to Neighborhood Playhouse, Billy Rose Theatre Collection, mwez + n.c. 10,290 and mwez + n.c. 10,256.

26. Neighborhood Playhouse Advisory Committee meeting notes, Wald Papers, box 62, reel 75.

27. Ibid., 21 December 1925.

28. "A Plan for Moving Productions of the Neighborhood Playhouse" and 14 January 1926 letter from Lillian Wald to "Alirene," Wald Papers, box 62, reel 75.

29. Letters, Robert Forest to Lillian Wald, 28 December 1925, and Lillian Wald to Robert Forest, 4 January 1925, Wald Papers, reel 112.

30. "Miss Alice Lewisohn's Speech to Mr. Nemirovitch-Dantchenko and His Company," ts., Billy Rose Theatre Collection, mwez + n.c. 10,253A.

31. "Letter to Alex Woollcott re: Dybbuk," n.d., Billy Rose Theatre Collection, mwez + n.c. 10,251.

32. Crowley, *The Neighborhood Playhouse,* 219.

33. "Draft Press Release," typescript, Billy Rose Theatre Collection, mwez + n.c. 10,290.

34. Brooks Atkinson, "Three Lyric Dramas in Grand Street," *New York Times,* 17 March 1926, 28.

35. "Two Theatres Adopt Repertory Policy," *New York Times,* 27 February 1926, 12.

36. Lawrence Langner, *The Magic Curtain* (New York: E. P. Dutton, 1951), 214, 218.

37. H. L. Brock, "Two Theatres Aspire to Repertory," *New York Times,* 21 March 1926, 26; Brooks Atkinson, "Even Drama Grows," *New York Times,* 28 March 1926, sec. 8, p. 1; "Repertory Plays and Acting," *New York Times,* 1 March 1926, 18; "One Day in Grand St.," *New York Times,* 2 May 1926, sec. 10, p. 2.

38. Alice McCoy to Lillian Wald, 14 May 1926, Wald Papers, box 61, reel 74.

39. *The Repertory Idea* (New York: Neighborhood Playhouse, 1927), n.p.

40. Program, *The Romantic Young Lady* (1926), Billy Rose Theatre Collection, n.p.

41. Joseph Wood Krutch, "Señorita Nora," *Nation*, 19 May 1926, 561.

42. Brooks Atkinson, "Light Comedy for the Spring," *New York Times*, 5 May 1926, 24.

43. Brooks Atkinson, "Frivolity in Grand Street," *New York Times*, 16 June 1926, 23.

44. John Anderson, "Grand Street Follies," *New York Post*, 16 June 1926, 12.

45. Joachim Neugroschel, ed., *The Dybbuk and the Yiddish Imagination* (Syracuse: Syracuse University Press, 2000), xii.

46. Peter Arno, cartoon, *New Yorker*, 5 June 1926, 19.

47. Tony Kushner, *A Dybbuk*, trans. Joachim Neugroschel (New York: Theatre Communications Group, 1998), 110.

48. Crowley, *The Neighborhood Playhouse*, 199.

7. 1926–1927: The Close of "The Unworldly Little Theater"

1. Stutman, ed., *My Other Loveliness*, 47, 48, 61, 81.

2. Helen Arthur, "Repertory and Its Difficulties," *New York Times*, 3 October 1926, sec. 8, p. 2.

3. Charles C. Cooper to Albert J. Kennedy, 2 July 1925, Wald Papers, reel 109, p. 1.

4. Quoted in Chambers, *Seedtime of Reform*, 128.

5. Maida Castelhun Darnton, "A Playhouse of Wide Interests," *Survey Graphic* 51 (1 March 1924): 561; quoted in Clarke A. Chambers, *Paul U. Kellogg and the Survey: Voices for Social Welfare and Social Justice* (Minneapolis: University of Minnesota Press, 1971), 107.

6. Melanie N. Blood, "Theatre in Settlement Houses: Hull-House Players, Neighborhood Playhouse, and Karamu Theatre," *Theatre Studies* 16 (June 1996): 56.

7. Lillian Wald to Alice Lewisohn, 24 September 1926, and Irene Lewisohn to Lillian Wald, 28 September 1926, Wald Papers, reel 75; Helen Arthur to Lillian Wald, 3 April 1927, Wald Papers, box 61, reel 74.

8. Stutman, ed., *My Other Loveliness*, 92.

9. Ibid., 93–94.

10. J. Brooks Atkinson, "Good and Evil," *New York Times*, 17 October 1926, sec. 10, pp. 1, 2; Joseph Wood Krutch, "The Lion Tamer," *Nation*, 20 October 1926, 408, 409.

11. Irene Lewisohn "To The Company," ts., 2 November 1926, Billy Rose Theatre Collection, mwez + n.c. 10,253A.

12. Stutman, ed., *My Other Loveliness*, 114.

13. Bordman, *American Theater*, 305.

14. Joseph Wood Krutch, "Summary," *Nation*, 22 June 1927, 702.

15. Crowley, *The Neighborhood Playhouse*, 226, 227.

16. Francis Edward Faragoh, *Pinwheel* (New York: John Day, 1927), n.p.

17. J. Brooks Atkinson, "Not a Motion Picture," *New York Times,* 4 February 1927, 16; Joseph Wood Krutch, "Fireworks," *Nation,* 23 February 1927, 216.

18. Crowley, *The Neighborhood Playhouse,* 231, 234.

19. Program, *A Bill of Lyric Drama* (1927), Billy Rose Theatre Collection.

20. Crowley, *The Neighborhood Playhouse,* 235.

21. "Miss Lillian D. Wald Speaks," 3.

22. "The Neighborhood Playhouse: A Gift to the East Side," 4.

23. "The Idea" Planning Document, ts., n.d., Wald Papers, box 61, reel 74.

24. "Endowed Theatre Is to Close," 1, 18.

25. Crowley, *The Neighborhood Playhouse,* 237.

26. "Endowed Theatre Is to Close," 1.

27. Wald, *Windows on Henry Street,* 170.

28. Joseph Wood Krutch, "The Neighborhood Playhouse," *Nation,* 18 May 1927, 548.

29. Atkinson, "End of an Era," 1.

30. "Grand Street Follies," *New York Times,* 25 April 1927, 20.

31. Program, *The Grand Street Follies* (1927), Billy Rose Theatre Collection, 1, 2, 4, 5.

32. Crowley, *The Neighborhood Playhouse,* 120.

33. " 'Grand St. Follies' Coming Uptown," *New York Times,* 24 May 1927, 23.

34. Clippings, Billy Rose Theatre Collection, mwez x n.c. 16,895.

35. Clippings, *New York Times,* 15 January 1928, Billy Rose Theatre Collection, mwez + n.c. 10,292, 1 of 2.

36. Postcard, Alice and Irene Lewisohn to Lillian Wald, 18 January 1928, Wald Papers, box 62, reel 75.

37. Helen Ingersoll, "Orchestral Drama," *Theatre Arts Monthly,* 12 (June 1928), 591, 594.

38. Irene Lewisohn to Lillian Wald, 13 June 1928, Wald Papers, box 62, reel 75.

39. Brooks Atkinson, review of *Bitter Oleander, New York Times,* 12 February 1935, 24.

40. Rita Morgenthau obituary, *New York Times,* 9 April 1964, 31.

41. Benardete, "The Neighborhood Playhouse in Grand Street," 608–9.

42. Ibid., 610.

43. "400 at Rites Here for Irene Lewisohn," *New York Times,* 8 April 1944, 13.

44. Crowley, *The Neighborhood Playhouse,* xxiv.

45. Benardete, "The Neighborhood Playhouse in Grand Street," 611–12.

46. Crowley obituary, *New York Times,* 7 January 1972, 34.

47. See, for example, Russell Lynes, *The Lively Audience: A Social History of the Visual and Performing Arts in America 1890–1950* (New York: Harper and Row, 1985), 206–8.

48. "Meeting of the Production Groups and Staff, March 30, 1924," Wald Papers, box 61, reel 74.

49. Macgowan, *Footlights Across America,* 50, 48.

50. Blood, "The Neighborhood Playhouse 1915–1927," 223.

Bibliography

Archives

Two archives were essential to the completion of this book. The most important of all was the very large archive left by the directors of the Neighborhood Playhouse to the New York Public Library in the form of "The Neighborhood Playhouse Gift." The archive exists in the Billy Rose Theatre Collection, and use of it is documented in endnotes to the library system of call numbers for dossiers and scrapbooks. The Lillian Wald Papers, which are housed in the Rare Book and Manuscript Room of the Columbia University Butler Library, were also helpful.

Printed Sources

Ansky, S. *The Dybbuk: A Play in Four Acts.* Trans. Henry G. Alsberg and Winifred Katzin. New York: Liveright, 1926.

Barker, Harley Granville. *The Madras House: A Comedy in Four Acts.* Boston: Little, Brown, 1920.

Baumol, William J., and William G. Bowen. *Performing Arts: The Economic Dilemma.* New York: Twentieth Century Fund, 1966.

Benardete, Doris Fox. "The Neighborhood Playhouse in Grand Street." Ph.D. diss., New York University, 1949.

Bernstein, Aline. "In Production." *Atlantic Monthly* 166, no. 3 (1940): 324.

Birmingham, Stephen. *"Our Crowd": The Great Jewish Families of New York.* 1967; rpt. Syracuse: Syracuse University Press, 1996.

Blaug, Mark, ed. *The Economics of the Arts.* London: Martin Robinson, 1976.

Blood, Melanie Nelda. "The Neighborhood Playhouse 1915–1927: A History and Analysis." Diss., Northwestern University, 1994.

———. "Theatre in Settlement Houses: Hull-House Players, Neighborhood Playhouse, and Karamu Theatre." *Theatre Studies* 16 (June 1996): 45–69.

Bordman, Gerald. *American Theatre: A Chronicle of Comedy and Drama 1914–1930.* New York: Oxford University Press, 1995.

Bryant, Louise. "The Poets' Revolution." *The Masses* (July 1916): 29.

Chambers, Clarke A. *Paul U. Kellogg and the Survey: Voices for Social Welfare and Social Justice.* Minneapolis: University of Minnesota Press, 1971.

———. *Seedtime of Reform: American Social Service and Social Action 1918–1933.* Minneapolis: University of Minnesota Press, 1963.

Cheney, Sheldon. *The Art Theater.* New York: Knopf, 1925.

Coss, Clare, ed. *Lillian D. Wald: Progressive Activist.* New York: Feminist Press, 1989.

Crowley, Alice Lewisohn. *The Neighborhood Playhouse: Leaves from a Theatre Scrapbook.* New York: Theatre Arts Books, 1959.

Darnton, Maida Castelhun. "A Playhouse of Wide Interests." *Survey Graphic* 51 (1 March 1924): 561.

Dickinson, Thomas H. *The Insurgent Theatre.* 1919; rpt. New York: B. W. Huebsch, 1927.

———. "Ten Years of the Neighborhood Playhouse." *American Review* 2 (March–April 1924): 134–38.

———. "Theatre Arts Chronicle." *Theatre Arts Magazine* 4 (October 1920): 344–45.

Duffus, R. L. *Lillian Wald: Neighbor and Crusader.* New York: Macmillan, 1938.

Dunsany, Lord (Edward John Moreton Drax Plunkett). *Plays of Gods and Men.* Boston: John W. Luce, 1917.

Eaton, Walter Prichard. *The Theatre Guild: The First Ten Years.* 1929; rpt. Freeport, NY: Books for Library Press, 1970.

Ellmann, Richard. *James Joyce.* New York: Oxford University Press, 1954.

Faragoh, Francis Edward. *Pinwheel.* New York: John Day, 1927.

Foster, R. F. *W. B. Yeats: A Life.* Vol. 1. New York: Oxford University Press, 1997.

Fovitzky, A. L. *Moscow Art Theatre and Its Distinguishing Characteristics.* New York: A. Chernoff, 1922.

Galsworthy, John. *The Mob: A Play in Four Acts.* New York: Charles Scribner's Sons, 1914.

———. *Plays: The Silver Box, Joy, Strife.* New York: G. P. Putnam's Sons, 1909.

Gelb, Arthur and Barbara. *O'Neill.* New York: Harper and Brothers, 1962.

———. *O'Neill: Life with Monte Cristo.* New York: Applause Books, 2000.

Glaspell, Susan. *The Road to the Temple.* 1927; rpt. New York: Frederick Stokes, 1941.

Guibour: A Miracle Play of Our Lady. Neighbourhood Playhouse Plays No. 11. New York: Sunwise Turn, 1919.

Hamilton, Clayton. "The Plays of Lord Dunsany." *The Bookman* (January 1917): 478.

Hapgood, Norman. "The Barker Season," *Harper's Weekly* (30 January 1915): 99.

Harrington, John P. *The Irish Play on the New York Stage*. Lexington: University Press of Kentucky, 1997.

Heilbrun, James, and Charles M. Gray. *The Economics of Art and Culture*. Cambridge: Cambridge University Press, 1993.

Holden, Arthur C. *The Settlement Idea: A Vision of Social Justice*. New York: Macmillian, 1922.

Holroyd, Michael. *Bernard Shaw*. Vol. 2. New York: Random House, 1989.

Howe, Irving. *World of Our Fathers: The Journey of the East European Jews to America and the Life They Found and Made*. New York: Harcourt Brace Jovanovich, 1976.

Ignatiev, Noel. *How the Irish Became White*. New York: Routledge, 1995.

Ingersoll, Helen. "Orchestral Drama." *Theatre Arts Monthly* 12 (June 1928): 591–94.

"Jephtha's Daughter." *Settlement Journal* 10, no. 4 (March–April 1915): 5–6.

Jones, Robert Edmond. *The Dramatic Imagination: Reflections and Speculations on the Art of the Theatre*. New York: Theatre Arts Books, 1969.

Kane, Whitford. *Are We All Met?* London: Elkin Mathews and Marrot, 1931.

Katz, Michael B. *In the Shadow of the Poorhouse: A Social History of Welfare in America*. New York: Basic Books, 1986.

Klein, Carole. *Aline*. New York: Harper and Row, 1979.

Knapp, Margaret M. "Theatrical Parody in the Twentieth-Century American Theatre: *The Grand Street Follies*." *Educational Theatre Journal* 27, no. 3 (1975): 359.

Krutch, Joseph Wood. "Figures of the Dawn." *Nation*, 11 March 1925, 272.

———. "Fireworks." *Nation*, 23 February 1927, 216.

———. "The Lion Tamer." *Nation*, 20 October 1926, 408–9.

———. "The Neighborhood Playhouse." *Nation*, 18 May 1927, 548.

———. Review of *The Grand Street Follies. Nation*, 15 May 1929, 594.

———. "Señorita Nora." *Nation*, 19 May 1926, 561.

———. "Summary." *Nation*, 22 June 1927, 702.

———. "Vale." *Neighborhood Playbill* 6 (1926–27): 2–4.

Kushner, Tony. *A Dybbuk*. Trans. Joachim Neugroschel. New York: Theatre Communications Group, 1998.

Langer, Laurence. *GBS and the Lunatic: Reminiscences*. New York: Atheneum, 1963.

———. *The Magic Curtain*. New York: E. P. Dutton, 1951.

Lasch, Christopher, ed. *The Social Thought of Jane Addams*. Indianapolis, IN: Bobbs-Merrill, 1965.

"Lectures at the Neighborhood Playhouse." *Theatre Arts Magazine* (April 1919): 135–36.

Lewis, Sinclair. *Ann Vickers.* New York: P. F. Collier, 1933.

Lewisohn, Alice and Irene. "The Little Theatre in Egypt." *Atlantic Monthly* (July 1924): 93–100.

Lynes, Russell. *The Lively Audience: A Social History of the Visual and Performing Arts in America 1890–1950.* New York: Harper and Row, 1985.

Macgowan, Kenneth. *Footlights Across America: Toward a National Theater.* New York: Harcourt Brace, 1929.

MacKaye, Percy. *The Playhouse and the Play: And Other Addresses Concerning the Theatre and Democracy in America.* 1909; rpt. New York: Greenwood Press, 1968.

Maisel, Edward. *Charles T. Griffes: The Life of an American Composer.* New York: Knopf, 1984.

Malleson, Miles. *Black 'Ell.* New York: J. S. Cram, 1917.

Marquis, Alice Goldfarb. *Art Lessons.* New York: Basic Books, 1995.

McAfee, Helen. "Lord Dunsany and Modern Theatre." *The Drama: A Quarterly Review of Dramatic Literature* 7 (October 1917): 474–84.

McCarthy, Kathleen D. *Noblesse Oblige: Charity and Cultural Philanthropy in Chicago, 1849–1929.* Chicago: University of Chicago Press, 1982.

"Miss Lillian D. Wald Speaks at the Neighborhood Playhouse." *Settlement Journal* 10, no. 4 (March–April 1915): 3.

"Mr. Belasco's Quarrel with the Experimental Theaters." *Current Opinion,* March 1917, 184.

Nathan, George Jean. "The Theatre." *American Mercury,* April 1925, 501.

Negra, Diane. "Consuming Ireland: Lucky Charms Cereal, Irish Spring Soap, and 1-800-Shamrock." *Cultural Studies* 15, no. 1 (2001): 76–97.

The Neighborhood Playhouse. New York: Neighborhood Playhouse, 1915.

"The Neighborhood Playhouse." *Nation,* 18 May 1927, 548.

"Neighborhood Playhouse." *The Theatre* (January 1917): 21.

Neugroschel, Joachim, ed. *The Dybbuk and the Yiddish Imagination.* Syracuse: Syracuse University Press, 2000.

"The New Season." *Theatre Arts Magazine* 5 (1921): 9.

Oliver, Revilo Pendleton. *The Little Clay Cart: A Drama in Ten Acts Attributed to King Śūdraka.* Urbana: University of Illinois Press, 1938.

Poggi, Jack. *Theater in America: The Impact of Economic Forces 1870–1967.* Ithaca, NY: Cornell University Press, 1968.

"Portmanteau Theatre." *The Theatre* (January 1917): 21.

The Repertory Idea. New York: Neighborhood Playhouse, 1927.

Review of *Dark Rosaleen. Theatre Magazine* (June 1919): 341.

Review of *Harliquinade. Theatre Magazine* (August 1921): 98.

The Rodgers and Hart Songbook. New York: Simon and Schuster, 1951.

Sayler, Oliver M. "The Neighborhood Playhouse." *Theatre Arts Magazine* January 1922: 15–16.

———. *Our American Theatre.* New York: Brentano's, 1923.

Sharma, Arvind, ed. *The Little Clay Cart.* Albany: State University of New York Press, 1994.

Stutman, Suzanne. *My Other Loveliness: Letters of Thomas Wolfe and Aline Bernstein.* Chapel Hill: University of North Carolina Press, 1983.

Throsby, C. David. *Economics and Culture.* Cambridge: Cambridge University Press, 2001.

Tomko, Linda J. *Dancing Class: Gender, Ethnicity, and Social Divides in American Dance 1890–1920.* Bloomington: Indiana University Press, 1999.

Van Doren, Carl. "Mountain Comedy." *Nation,* 16 January 1924, 69.

Veblen, Thorstein. *The Theory of the Leisure Class.* 1899; rpt. Harmondsworth: Penguin Books, 1979.

Wald, Lillian. *The House on Henry Street.* New York: Henry Holt, 1915.

———. *Windows on Henry Street.* Boston: Little, Brown, 1939.

Weber, Nicholas Fox. *Patron Saints: Five Rebels Who Opened America to New Art, 1928–1943.* New Haven: Yale University Press, 1992.

Welch, Robert. *The Abbey Theatre 1899–1999: Form and Pressure.* Oxford: Oxford University Press, 1999.

Whitman, Walt. "Salut au Monde!" *Leaves of Grass.* New York: Modern Library, n.d. 108–16.

Wolfe, Thomas. *The Web and the Rock.* New York: Sun Dial Press, 1940.

Woods, Robert A., and Albert J. Kennedy. *Handbook of Settlements.* 1911; rpt. New York: Arno Press, 1970.

———. *The Settlement Horizon.* 1922; rpt. New Brunswick, NJ: Transaction Publishers, 1990.

Wyszomiaski, M. J., and P. Clubb. *The Cost of Culture: Patterns and Prospects of Private Arts Patronage.* Washington, DC: American Council for the Arts, 1989.

Yeats, W. B. "Certain Noble Plays of Japan." *Essays and Introductions.* New York: Collier Books, 1961.

Young, Stark. Review of "The Little Clay Cart." *New York Times* 6 December 1924; rpt. in *Immortal Shadows: A Book of Dramatic Criticism.* New York: Scribner's, 1948.

Index

Italic page numbers denote illustrations.

JOHN P. HARRINGTON is dean of the School of Humanities and Social Sciences and professor of humanities at Rensselaer Polytechnic Institute. He was educated at Columbia University and University College, Dublin, and he earned his Ph.D. in literature from Rutgers University. He has written extensively on Irish literature and culture, including books *The English Traveller in Ireland, The Irish Beckett* (Syracuse University Press), and *The Irish Play on the New York Stage*. He edited W. W. Norton's anthology *Modern Irish Drama* and coedited with others *Politics and Performance in Comtemporary Northern Ireland* and *The Future of Irish Studies: Report of the Irish Forum*.